CONDUCTING CHILD CUSTODY EVALUATIONS

To Ruth, my wife, who found me on the eastern coast,
and to my wonderful children, Jason and Rebecca,
who have inspired me for years.

CONDUCTING CHILD CUSTODY EVALUATIONS

A Comprehensive Guide

Philip Michael Stahl

SAGE Publications
International Educational and Professional Publisher
Thousand Oaks London New Delhi

For information address:

SAGE Publications, Inc.
2455 Teller Road
Thousand Oaks, California 91320

SAGE Publications Ltd.
6 Bonhill Street
London EC2A 4PU
United Kingdom

SAGE Publications India Pvt. Ltd.
M-32 Market
Greater Kailash I
New Delhi 110048 India

Printed in the United States of America

Library of Congress Cataloging-in-Publication Data

Stahl, Philip Michael.
Conducting child custody evaluations: a comprehensive guide/
Philip Michael Stahl.
p. cm.
Includes bibliographical references and index.
ISBN 0-8039-4820-4 (cloth).—ISBN 0-8039-4821-2 (pbk.)
1. Custody of children—United States—Evaluation. I. Title.
KF547.S73 1994
346.7301'7—dc20
[347.30617] 94-18898

94 95 96 97 98 10 9 8 7 6 5 4 3 2 1

Sage Production Editor: Diana E. Axelsen

Contents

Preface

In 1981 I was thinking about a topic for my doctoral dissertation. I had worked as a therapist with many children of divorce, and Michigan was completing a new custody law, with a presumption for joint legal custody. Although joint custody was new to Michigan, Californians had been implementing it for a number of years. My research was on the attitudes and beliefs about joint custody among judges, attorneys, mental health professionals, and families who were practicing joint custody arrangements. I learned that little had been written and little was known about custody and shared parenting at that time.

In order to expand my own knowledge, I joined a group of other professionals known as the Michigan Inter-Professional Association on Marriage, Divorce, and the Family (MIPA). I later became active in an international group, the Association of Family and Conciliation Courts (AFCC). Both of these groups were formed to promote healthy resolutions for divorcing families to improve the consequences for the children. Through my early experiences with these groups I recognized the need to learn more about child custody and the need to network with attorneys and judges who have such an impact on divorcing families.

In 1984 I took training in divorce mediation. In the fall of 1985 I began to work for the Macomb County Psychodiagnostic Clinic to assist them with their growing need for custody evaluations. My interest in the task of custody evaluations and the need for reducing the destruction on children kept growing. By the time I moved to California in the spring of 1987, my goal was to continue learning more about divorce and custody and to continue working with others to promote healthier resolutions to divorce.

Over the years I have completed more than 800 custody evaluations. I have worked in both the public and private sectors in two divergent communities. Although I am no longer a member of MIPA, I currently serve with the Association of Family and Conciliation Courts as a member of the custody evaluation committee, a cochair of the private practice committee, and a member of the national Board of Directors. My need to learn from and network with other mental health professionals, attorneys, and judges remains as strong as ever.

I am concerned that despite the increase in custody evaluations, there is still little written on this subject. Attorneys and judges need help in learning more about child development and the psychological effects of custody battles on the children. New evaluators have limited understanding of the ethical dilemmas in working with families of divorce and little awareness of the many professional issues involved in doing custody evaluations. The material for this book is based on the sum of my experience gained from networking meetings, conferences, workshops, readings, participation on task forces related to custody work, and my own custody evaluations.

Readers may note that I have frequently changed gender throughout the text of this manuscript. I have attempted to be gender neutral, and there is no attempt to imply anything gender specific by the use of pronouns at any point of the text.

The families with whom I have worked have taught me a great deal. I have learned that there are certain principles and standards that must be maintained when doing custody evaluations. I have learned that children cannot be viewed as property and that divorcing parents often need to be taught to share their children. I look forward to the day when the courts and the laws get away from the legal concepts of custody and visitation and focus instead on helping parents learn to share parenting. Above all, we must view the family divorce through the eyes of the children. We must understand how the children feel, what they fear and wish, and what makes conflict resolution difficult to achieve. We need to stay focused on the needs of the children, who are vulnerable to the actions of their parents and who have the most to gain from a healthy resolution of the divorce conflict. It is my hope that from this book evaluators and other mental health professionals, attorneys, and judges can learn more about the many issues in child custody evaluations, so we all can reduce the pain for the children—the real pawns in the game of their parents' divorce.

Acknowledgments

I thank initially Karol Ross, friend and early mentor, from whom I learned my beginning skills as a custody evaluator. She told me about MIPA and AFCC and sparked my interest in networking and conferencing with these two organizations. I want to thank Marquita Flemming of Sage Publications for encouraging me to write this book and various colleagues from AFCC, especially Hugh McIsaac, Dorothy Howard, and Ann Milne, for supporting me. I particularly want to thank my many friends and colleagues who read early drafts of this book and whose editorial comments and words of wisdom helped me to clarify my own thinking and encouraged me to complete this task, including Judges Susan Snow and Josanna Berkow; evaluators Milton Schaefer, Phil Bushard, Andrea Jeremey, and Melisse Eidman; my friend and attorney colleague, Stuart Goldware; my cousin Eryn Kalish, an excellent editor; and my wife, Ruth, whose love inspired me to get back to work on this manuscript, after contributing to an 8-month hiatus when we met.

I also want to thank Terry Czapinski for her typing of the first drafts of this manuscript, Eileen Abels and my brother Stan for helping me with computer and technical assistance, and the many children of divorce who have taught me about their feelings and shown me how divorce affects them.

Finally, I thank my own children, Jason and Rebecca. Jason has a singular way of helping me see important and special aspects of life, and Rebecca maintains a sense of humor that keeps me enjoying all that I can, even when I work too hard. Their love and inspiration have helped me stay focused on the needs of children in all of my endeavors.

Philip Michael Stahl

1

Introduction

You get a call from Mr. Smith, a prominent local family law attorney. He is concerned because his client, Ms. Jones, has two children who returned from visits with their father sick and in need of medical attention. You were told he did not give the children their medication. Mr. Smith wants you to see the children so that you can ask the court to discontinue visits with their father until he becomes more responsible. You have worked with Mr. Smith before and found him to be a credible attorney who presents facts very clearly. What do you do?

You receive a call from Ms. Green, who has been told by her attorney to find a psychologist to see her children, ages 7 and 11, within the week because they are about to return to their father, who lives in another state. They are with Ms. Green on a 2-week visit during the summer. The children reported to their mother that they are abused at their father's home. Ms. Green and her attorney wish to have the children seen to verify the complaints of abuse, in order that the attorney might get a restraining order preventing the return of the children to their father. What do you do?

You receive a call from Mr. King, a family court mediator, who has reached an impasse with the family with whom he has been working. The couple are in the middle of divorce proceedings and are in dispute about custody and visitation of their children. Mr. King reports that he has serious concerns about the psychological fitness of both parents and is requesting psychological testing to help him with his mediation. He has very specific questions about parental fitness because he has to make a recommendation to the court if the couple cannot agree through mediation for a parenting plan for the children. Both attorneys are somewhat opposed to the question of psychological testing of their clients, but Mr. King is asking if you would accept the evaluation, if ordered by the court. What do you do?

Mrs. García has been married to her second husband for 9 years. He has just been transferred to another state across the country. Mrs. García's first husband, Mr. Clark, the father of their 13-year-old-son, is objecting to the move, claiming that his relationship with his son will deteriorate if his son moves. Mr. Clark's attorney calls and asks if you will see this family to help decide whether it is a good idea for the boy to move to the new state.

Johnny, age 11, is your client in psychotherapy. You have seen him for a year for school problems and difficulties in his family relationships. During the course of the therapy, you have had frequent contact with Johnny's mother, but little contact with his father. His parents have had a tumultuous marriage and have finally decided to get a divorce. Johnny's mother and her attorney ask you to make a statement to the court about Johnny's poor relationship with his father and to recommend rather limited visitation with him. What do you do?

These are but five of the hundreds of ways in which evaluators are asked to get involved in a family's legal dispute and the custody and visitation of the family's minor children. Although evaluations may take many forms and evaluators may have different training and background, there is one major reason that evaluations are requested or ordered by the courts. It boils down to helping the family and/or the courts understand the family dynamics in a way that will allow for the development of an appropriate plan for custody and visitation of minor children, when such custody and visitation is in dispute between the parents. An evaluation is used to gather necessary information about a family to help families who are stuck in their negotiations over custody get unstuck. Regardless of the actual referral question or questions, all evaluations ultimately focus on that broad issue. Individual and family dynamics are varied enough to cause considerable diversity in referral questions. Although the outcome of every evaluation will be to address the needs of the children in relation to their parents' divorce, there can be a variety of other desired outcomes from an evaluation. The purpose of this book is to address the many issues that come before the evaluator, to provide guidelines for conducting an evaluation, and to examine the many professional issues that surface when evaluations related to custody and visitation are requested.

The most important step in doing a custody evaluation is to understand the real question before you. Frequently there is a dispute over custody that centers around the question of time-sharing between the parents. Parents argue over who is the better parent, raising many allegations about the other and usually externalizing blame in the process. There are frequent charges of drug or alcohol abuse made by one parent against the other, as well as accusations of parental alienation, ignoring children, and so forth. Unfortunately, however, although these are important issues that need to be evaluated, they often have little to do with the real concerns of the parents. Parents have no place to battle one another except over custody of their children, and they use the custody battle as a backdrop for their ongoing couple's dispute. A custody evaluation may be over issues such as control, power, ideology, and lack of compromise, which are the same ones that caused conflicts during the marriage and were never resolved before separation.

Prior to the advent of no-fault divorce, couples battled in court over issues of property, who was to blame for the breakup of the marriage, and other issues that did not relate to children. By battling in court over these issues, the children were left alone as part of the divorce process. First with the advent of no-fault divorce and then followed by increasingly powerful men's groups and women's groups, issues of custody and parenting came to the forefront. Having no other place to battle, no other issues to battle over, and no real avenue for continuing the marital dispute, custody has become a major source and place for the new battleground.

Thus, as the parents discuss their beliefs about parenting issues and their needs, as well as their perceptions of their children and their children's needs, it is very important for the evaluator to maintain a diligent third ear that listens to the real problems between the parents. Even when the issues are obvious, such as when one parent wants to move away or when a child is stating that he wants to live with a particular parent, it is always important to try to understand the additional factors that lead to the custody evaluation, rather than just surface problems as stated by the parents. If evaluators understand all these issues, there is a greater likelihood of assisting the family in resolving the custody issues and finding a solution that is truly in the children's best interests.

HOW THE COURT BENEFITS FROM AN EVALUATION

In most jurisdictions, in any legal action in which there is a dispute over custody a judge will look at the best interests of the child and make a ruling regarding custody and visitation. Judges, although well trained in the intricacies of the law, often feel poorly trained to understand the dynamics of family relationships. Frequently judges will have two parents in the courtroom who both appear to be good enough at parenting and therefore have a difficult time making a ruling that might be best for children. Judges have the dilemma of making decisions based on both legal and psychological principles. Increasingly, judges look to the mental health expert to assist in understanding the complex psychological questions of parental fitness, psychological attachment, sibling relationships, and the developmental needs of the child, and balance this with the legal facts and principles by which they are to rule.

In addition, questions of parental relocation, drug and alcohol abuse, domestic violence, child abuse, and religious and moral values are often in dispute. The mental health expert is often viewed as the individual who can integrate these issues into a comprehensive understanding of the family and its needs. Ultimately, the judge has a need for very specific recommendations to formulate a legal ruling based on all of the facts in the case.

Finally, in a more subtle way, the mental health expert ultimately serves as a consultant to the court. By evaluating the family and its dynamics, the evaluator can open the eyes of the judge to the many complexities involved. Unlike property issues, in which the judge can hear from different appraisers regarding the value of the property and then make a determination of its real value, there are no formulas for which to determine how to divide the children. Instead, the evaluator presents the many complexities of family dynamics to the judge in an understandable way to assist the judge in making a rational decision regarding the children and their needs. Often evaluators see issues that the judge did not even know existed. Evaluations can help in identifying the appropriate issues, as well as in defining the complex family dynamics. From this the court can reach appropriate recommendations for postdivorce resolution of the conflicts.

HOW THE FAMILY BENEFITS FROM AN EVALUATION

By the time a family is referred or ordered for an evaluation, there is usually a tremendous amount of conflict and disagreement between the parents. When parents agree on the custody and parenting needs of their children, an evaluation is often unnecessary. When an impasse has been reached in mediation efforts or when chaotic family conditions exist, an evaluation is necessary to help sort out the many issues facing the family.

A number of benefits are available to a family. First and most important, the evaluation provides an opportunity for parents to voice their concerns to an expert in child development and mental health so that they are truly heard by someone. Many people going though the divorce process feel that no one, not even their attorney, hears them and that no one really cares about their children. Many parents view attorneys as legal advocates who do not have the time or ability to fully understand the family issues. In court they may be given little, if any time to speak to the judge, who has a very busy calendar with many cases to be heard. An evaluator will spend considerable time with each parent trying to understand his or her concerns and perceptions of the children's needs. This can be comforting to parents, who have a need to be heard about their many concerns.

Although evaluators are not therapists with their evaluation clients, they often provide therapeutic value to the parents. Certainly, in listening to children, evaluators may provide the first therapeutic contact for a child, helping the child to look at his or her feelings about the parents and their divorce. By listening to the parents and their children, encouraging the participants to talk about their feelings, and focusing on parenting and the children's needs, evaluators can provide therapeutic benefit to all members of the family.

By listening to the children, evaluators can also help children identify that they are in the middle of a loyalty conflict and begin to help the children learn ways out of this conflict. After listening to the children tell me how they are afraid to tell each of their parents how they feel, I have encouraged many children to find ways to understand their feelings and communicate those feelings accurately and honestly to each of their parents. Although the evaluator is clearly not the child's therapist, by being an advocate for the child and by being therapeutic in efforts, the evaluator can begin to help children understand and express themselves in clearer and more direct ways.

A third benefit for families comes from the fact that the same mental health person is observing all family members in the evaluation process. Often, especially in the midst of a bitter divorce, people have different therapists. Each parent have his or her own attorney/advocate and all of the family's information gets very fragmented. Attorneys have different agendas for their clients. Certainly, as someone's therapist it is important to truly understand that individual and to help with his or her own psychological issues for the purpose of therapeutic growth. When the same evaluator talks with all family members, a more comprehensive view of the family and its needs can be gained. The evaluation, therefore, has a single purpose, that is, to address the needs and best interests of the children, without the fragmentation of information or purpose so common in divorces. The family benefits from this because the parents can get a more complete understanding and end the fragmentation that would otherwise exist. At the time of evaluation, and through the evaluation process, it is very helpful for the family to focus on the family's needs and to have a single expert who is addressing these needs in a comprehensive manner for all concerned.

A fourth benefit is educational. The typical family knows very little about the psychological effects of divorce on themselves or their children. Although the primary purpose of an evaluation is to evaluate and provide information to the court, it is clear that evaluators have a special opportunity to help parents understand the complex issues facing their children. Many times an evaluator is asked by parents about the psychological effects of divorce on children. A good evaluator who is up to date on current research can help parents understand issues around custody and visitation, shared parenting, reduction in conflict, child development, and so forth. This enables the parents to be more effective parents after the divorce. This educational component, although not a primary purpose of the evaluation, is nonetheless valuable in giving parents assistance in understanding their relationships with each other and their children.

This leads to the fifth benefit to parents. Most people come to an evaluation because they are in conflict with one another in how to best address the parenting of the children in a postdivorce environment. Mediation efforts have usually failed because parents cannot learn to see eye-to-eye on the children's needs. This may be caused by parents viewing the needs of their children through their own eyes. They cannot reach agreement because they are looking at different pictures of their children and their needs. A well-done evaluation that comprehensively addresses all the issues leads to a single set of recommendations that can often direct the parents toward an opportunity for solution and compromise. Parents who have been looking at fragmented pieces of the puzzle can now take a more comprehensive view of their children's needs and have a broad foundation from which to reach an agreement. Mediation can now succeed when the parents and mediator are looking at the same picture. There can be a reduction of conflict, a lowering of anxiety, and a renewed commitment to the children and their needs. Thus, it is hoped that the evaluation can be used as a settlement tool, thereby saving the family money and emotional turmoil by avoiding a protracted court battle.

WHEN EVALUATIONS ARE NOT HELPFUL OR COULD BE HARMFUL

There may be times when an evaluation should not be done. Sometimes parents may still be ambivalent about the divorce. If that is the case, marriage counseling should be attempted before engaging in a lengthy, costly evaluation that may not be necessary in the first place. Similarly, it is often helpful if parents have attempted mediation before embarking on an evaluation. It is usually best if families can make their own decisions about their postdivorce parenting plans. There is likely to be a greater sense of mutual satisfaction if parents have reached their own solution through the use of mediation. Typically, after an evaluation, at least one of the parents is frustrated with the recommended outcome so a mediated solution may lead to a greater commitment to make the plan succeed. When mediation services are available, I often recommend that a family try mediation first.

Finally, there may be times when a custody evaluation cannot be done because there is no cooperation from one of the parents or because the proposed evaluator has had some prior contact with the family. Several of the examples at the beginning of this chapter alluded to situations in which the proposed evaluator might be cautious in doing the evaluation, or in the case of the child's therapist, would refuse to do one outright. Although an evaluation might be beneficial for each of these families, this book will address many of the ethical issues that will guide evaluators in making sound decisions on other times when an evaluation should not be done.

WHO IS THE CLIENT/CONSUMER?

When I do evaluations, I am often asked, "Who are they for?" Sometimes evaluations are done by stipulation or court order. In many states evaluators are appointed the court expert with quasi-judicial status and immunity. This means that they cannot be sued because their role in the public sector is like that of a judge. Many evaluations are done by family court service personnel who work directly for the courts. Because of limited public resources and overburdened family court systems, private evaluators are hired, either by court order or by agreement and stipulation between the attorneys and their clients.

When evaluations are done in the public sector, there is often little or no cost to the family for the evaluation. Some jurisdictions charge an hourly fee for evaluations, but it is often on a sliding scale to ensure that all families in need have an available evaluation. In the private sector, the costs for an evaluation may be paid for completely by one parent or shared in some fashion between both parties. On rare occasion, a parent's health insurance may cover some of the costs of a custody evaluation, though most health insurance plans reject claims resulting from a legal referral. In situations where only one parent pays for the cost of a private evaluation, the other parent is often concerned that the evaluator may show a bias toward the parent who pays. Obviously, it is important to allay those fears immediately. Finally, parents who do not trust the judicial system tend to fear that the evaluator will be looking more closely at the court's needs than their children's needs. It is important to help the parents recognize that the two are actually the same, that is, the court by law is looking out for the best interests of the child.

Regardless of who appoints the evaluator or who is paying the fee, the client must be the entire family. Although the evaluator hopes that an evaluation can assist the court and the attorneys in meeting the family's needs, it is clear that the family, especially the children, are the clients to be served. In an overburdened legal system with pressures from judges and attorneys, evaluators sometimes lose sight of the fact that the families are the clients and that helping the family understand and meet their children's needs is the job. Certainly evaluators can try to help judges make sound decisions and can try to assist attorneys in directing their clients toward settlement, but in all instances, the primary goal must be to help the parents understand the needs of their children.

I believe that the ethical duty of evaluators is to meet the needs of the family first and foremost, even if that leads to possible conflict with the needs or wishes of the court that has ordered the evaluation. Although this is unlikely because the court is looking for help to understand the best interests of the child, the family's needs—in particular the children's needs—must always be the paramount issue for the evaluator. The family is the consumer and the evaluator's ethical responsibility is to the family and its individual members. The children must be the main concern, as they are the most vulnerable and the ones in need of an advocate to safeguard their emotional and developmental needs. Thus, no matter who is paying for the evaluation, or in what context it is ordered, the children of divorce are the primary clients and their needs must be served first.

EVALUATOR BIASES

Before people agree to an evaluation, they are often curious about the beliefs of the evaluator. Parents themselves often come into an evaluation with biases: Fathers may be concerned about women evaluators; mothers may be concerned that women can be charmed by their husbands; parents may be concerned that both male and female evaluators will always side with the mother or that society is focused only on father's rights, and so forth. There are often religious, education, and economic questions, and parents fear that evaluator biases will be the major element in the outcome of an evaluation.

In reality most evaluators do have some biases that affect how we analyze the information and process it in an evaluation. For the most part, biases come from our understanding of the research on child development and divorce, and, therefore, we assume that our biases are justified. Nonetheless, some evaluators are under the belief that young children need a stable home environment, preferably with one parent at home with the young child.

Many evaluators have a bias that both parents need to maintain an active role in children's lives and that access to both parents should be relatively equal. Some evaluators have a bias that good schools or religious values or family stability are important to children in postdivorce parenting plans; other evaluators believe that economics play a role in determining how parents can best meet their children's needs. Many evaluators believe that adolescents, in particular, should get to choose where they live, although most evaluators believe that asking children to choose between their parents can be harmful to children. Many times the evaluation question will raise issues of evaluator bias, such as separating siblings, moving across county or state lines, and so forth.

Finally, when there are questions of child abuse, spousal abuse, sexual preference, drug and alcohol use by parents, parental alienation, parental dating and sexual practices, and so on, evaluator biases are often tested to their extremes. In many ways, biases contribute to the ultimate recommendations evaluators make.

I believe that as evaluators we need to make such initial biases clear to parents, attorneys, and judges, before starting the evaluation. To imply that we have no biases is inaccurate, and it conveys to the family a misunderstanding. As evaluators, we use our biases as well as the facts we learn in an evaluation to reach conclusions. In relation to specific complex questions that are often at issue, we need to inform parents of our biases around religious issues, homosexual rights issues, parental contact in connection with abuse issues, and so forth, so that they can have a framework from which to understand our recommendations when we make them.

For example, if we tell parents at the start of an evaluation that we believe access to both parents is important to a child's emotional growth and development and then we give primary physical custody to a mother, the father cannot assume that we were biased in favor of the mother when such a recommendation is made. Similarly, when one of the evaluation questions is whether or not to separate the children, I believe it is imperative that evaluators express their bias about this issue to both parents prior to the start of the evaluation so that there can be no question regarding the issues involved when the recommendation is made.

Finally, as evaluators, we must be cognizant of our own biases, whatever their nature, so that we can incorporate our understanding of the issues with our biases when we make our recommendations. It is critical that our biases have some theoretical basis, are not unfounded, and relate to the issues of divorce and child development as we know it. Evaluators must remain up to date in knowledge of the literature as well as experiences in order to continually confront biases to understand if they are valid. By understanding biases and values and by communicating these biases at the beginning, evaluators can be certain of evaluating each family uniquely on the basis of its needs and complexities.

CHAPTER SUMMARIES

This chapter has presented an overview of the many issues related to custody evaluations. In focusing on the purpose of evaluations, both to the court and to the families, and in developing a view of how to assist the family in this work, I have outlined many of the basic issues with which evaluators are confronted. In the following chapters I address many of the specifics that are critical in an evaluator's job.

Chapter 2 focuses on the many roles that mental health experts often take in working with families of divorce. Often we assist each other in this work and, at times, we can be confronted with a possibility of a dual role. I address my beliefs about the integration of these roles and the pitfalls we sometimes experience when we try to do too much. Chapter 3 provides an overview of the fundamental issues that are often addressed in custody evaluations. These large issues often include capacity to parent, bonding and attachment of children to their parents, forming custody/parental access plans, and understanding the theoretical best interests of the children. Chapter 4 addresses the specific developmental needs of children in relation to parents and divorce. I focus on the developmental issues that play significant roles in a child's adjustment to divorce and how to translate those developmental needs into parental access plans.

The middle chapters, 5, 6, and 7, focus on performing the evaluation and completing the report. Chapter 5 covers the specifics related to the evaluation of parents. Chapter 6 explores in depth the issues related to the evaluation of the children. In Chapter 7 I discuss issues related to report writing and recommendations.

Chapter 8 addresses many of the more complex issues often facing custody evaluators, such as domestic violence, drug and alcohol abuse, supervised contact, mental illness, parental alienation syndrome, relocation of one or both parents, and the need for ongoing updated evaluations. Over the years I have found that it is these more complex issues that often lead a family to require an outside custody evaluation.

Chapter 9 discusses issues of professional interest, focusing largely on the impact of these evaluations on the evaluator. I focus on issues such as working with attorneys and the courts; completing reports and their access; guaranteeing payment; bias, release of information, and other ethical issues; testifying; burnout; training and competency; and balancing ethics and all of the needs of courts, attorneys, families, and children within the context of an adversarial system. In many ways the professional issues are the most critical ones facing evaluators. We must learn to work with attorneys and the courts in a productive way for clients. We must learn about the legal system while teaching attorneys and the courts about the psychological and developmental needs of children and their families. Providing expert testimony in court while maintaining ethical integrity is critical. The need for trained evaluators who are expert in the fields of divorce and child development is equally critical.

At the end of this book are six appendixes, including sample forms, letters, and court orders, and other information useful to those doing custody evaluations. I provide sample questions to ask parents and children during the evaluation along with sample reports and a listing of psychological tests and games used with adults and children. The last appendix includes a review of the rules and guidelines formulated by organizations around the country. I hope that this will encourage other groups to formulate guidelines, as well. Finally, I have included at the end a glossary of legal terms and suggested readings on the numerous topics raised in the book.

2

The Mental Health Expert's Many Possible Roles

The mental health expert is brought in under many different circumstances when working with families of divorce. Each possible role is unique and requires a mental health expert to provide a very different type of response to the individual or family in need. Often the family asks the mental health person to engage in more than one role, and, in my experience, there may be times when this is helpful. On the other hand, there are many times when the complications and risks of blending or changing roles far outweigh any possible benefit to the family. In this chapter I outline the various roles that mental health practitioners may experience, suggesting styles of practice that work for each role. The chapter ends with a discussion of the risks associated with dual relationships, especially to those doing custody evaluations.

THERAPIST

Traditionally, a therapist for an individual will see her role as being that of an advocate for the mental health needs of that individual. The therapist gets to know the inner thoughts and feelings of her client, comprehends her client's many conflicts, and understands her client's strengths and weaknesses as an individual. The therapist often hears about other family members through the eyes of her client and will learn about her client's perceptions about the relationships he has with his spouse and children. The therapist gathers this information to help understand the perceptions of the client to help him with the problems he experiences in his life. She recognizes that the things he tells her are a function of his perceptions and not always the truth. In her role as therapist, truth does not matter as much as perception, because the client's perceptions are of paramount importance in helping him with his internal and relationship conflicts throughout his life.

As a child's therapist, she may be trying to help the child with specific behavioral problems, or, during a particularly messy divorce, she may be trying to provide a refuge from the tensions in the child's life. A child's therapist needs to be very careful if the parents are divorced or in the midst of an ongoing divorce battle. It is important to ascertain that she has the permission of *both* parents, and she needs to be clear that she will be providing treatment to the child, not providing information to be used in a custody dispute. A child going through the divorce of her parents often needs the assistance of a therapist to sort out her feelings, not a therapist who is caught in the advocacy of her parents. She may need the therapist to be an advocate in communicating with her parents about her fears, feelings, and so forth, but not in the acrimonious battle between the parents. When she works with her client's parents, the child's therapist is an advocate for the child and assists the parents in issues of parenting and improving the communication and relationship between the child and her parents. Again, the child's therapist is an advocate for a single member of the family. She recognizes that her information is the result of the child's perceptions, not always a complete measure of the truth. In fact, many children, when they perceive the therapist to be in the middle of their parents' custody disputes, are unwilling to trust in the therapeutic alliance any longer.

A family therapist, although aware of more of the family's truths because she sees the entire family together, also has a primary focus. That focus is clearly to assist the family system improve its functioning, with more open communication and often less overdependence between family members. The goals of the family therapist are usually to bring about change within the family dynamics and to help members function more autonomously, while simultaneously improving unity and communication and encouraging more functional dynamics for the family. Often the family therapist is trying to help the family to stay together, and, as such, is unprepared to tackle the complex issues of the divorce and recommendations for the best interests of the child.

Finally, a couple's therapist usually focuses on the marital relationship, trying to help spouses learn to communicate better and assisting them to work toward an improved marital relationship. Although the therapist may have talked about the children, she usually does not know too much about the children and their individual needs. Clearly, she knows a lot about the marital partners—how they communicate and what their issues are. Yet, she, too, is not in a position to make recommendations about custody/visitation because there are too many gaps in her knowledge.

PSYCHOLOGIST EVALUATOR

For a variety of reasons, an individual may have undergone a psychological evaluation. A child may be evaluated because of school or behavioral problems or as part of an overall diagnostic assessment prior to beginning therapy. An adolescent or adult with drug or alcohol problems may have participated in a psychological assessment as part of the initial determination of appropriate treatment planning for her substance abuse. An adult who has been hospitalized for an acute depressive reaction may have completed a psychological evaluation in order to assess his psychological condition. A woman with a chronic mental illness may have had several psychological evaluations over time in order to assess any change in her functioning as part of ongoing treatment plans. The goal of these psychological evaluations is clear, that is, to assess the individual's cognitive and/or emotional functioning, usually for the purpose of assisting in the development of appropriate therapeutic intervention. Although the client is usually part of a family, the individual psychological evaluation is not related to family functioning in any comprehensive way. The evaluation is an analysis of the individual, not within the context of the family. As such, the psychologist evaluator is not in a position to make an assessment of the complex issues of custody and/or visitation.

MEDIATOR

A mediator is directly involved in the divorce process, either appointed by the court or seen in private practice to help the divorcing couple settle their disputes and reach solutions that assist in conflict reduction during the divorce process. In some situations the mediation process is confidential, which prevents the mediator from participating in the adversarial court process. This confidentiality enables the mediator and the couple to work more effectively in trying to resolve conflict, without fear that things said in mediation can be used against the other person in litigation. Many mediators view such confidentiality to be essential for mediation to result in a successful outcome.

Even in the absence of such confidentiality, a mediator's primary objectives are to help the couple reduce conflict while reaching solutions about the issues on which they disagree. More often than not, mediation focuses on the custody disputes, and the mediator will try to use her knowledge and negotiation skills to assist a couple in coming up with their own parenting plan. Whether such mediation takes place in a private mediator's office or in a court-connected setting, the goal of mediation is to assist the couple in developing their own plans for the children, without actual recommendations from the mediator. Especially when there is no confidentiality, a mediator can assist a judge in understanding the family dynamics, so that a judicial order regarding custody can be made. Either way, a mediator will have had prior contact with the family that automatically interferes with being a neutral evaluator of the family, should the case be referred for a custody evaluation.

CONSULTANT TO ATTORNEYS

A family law attorney and a mental health practitioner may develop a working relationship in which they will periodically consult with one another on more complex cases. I have been asked by attorneys to review psychological evaluations or other privileged information (with appropriate consent) in order to help the attorney understand some of the dynamics involved in a particular family matter. I have also been asked for my perception of the risk to children based on limited information, to see if a custody evaluation might be in order. Mental health experts may also be asked by an attorney to review a custody evaluation or psychological evaluation, to assess its thoroughness, and to see if the recommendations made by the evaluator followed the material obtained.

Although many mental health experts will not engage in unilateral assistance of one attorney, there are occasions where it may be very appropriate, as long as the consultant does not make specific recommendations regarding custody or visitation. The goals for such consultation are to assist the attorney in understanding the aspects of family dynamics while providing suggestions to the attorney about how to proceed in the case. Though many observers see a certain degree of risk in such consultation, I have found that, as long as the psychologist adheres to her ethical principles, she can provide consultation to the attorney that is ultimately useful for all members of the family, not just the attorney and the client.

EXPERT WITNESS

During litigation the court may require the expert testimony of a psychologist or other mental health professional to assist in understanding certain factual information in the case. In this situation I am referring to testimony not derived from the completion of a custody evaluation, but connected simply to one's knowledge of problems of divorce, general psychological principles, or child development. I have seen psychologists provide testimony to the court to assist in determining whether or not a custody evaluation is necessary. On other occasions I have known psychologists to provide expert testimony associated with some aspect of child development that is quite complicated and therefore a significant issue for the court's understanding. In such instances, the mental health expert is providing a specific function to the court in the absence of direct knowledge of a particular case. Although less common than some of the other roles, a forensic psychologist will often find herself being asked to testify in court to assist the judge in understanding the dynamics of a particular matter. Again, once she has done this, she will have rendered an opinion on the facts of the case and therefore cannot provide the complete neutrality that is necessary in custody evaluations, should the case be referred for one.

SPECIAL MASTER (MEDIATOR/ARBITRATOR)

In growing numbers, mental health professionals are being asked to take on the role of Special Master or Mediator/Arbitrator. The tasks of these are generally the same, though different jurisdictions identify them in different ways. For purposes of this section, my reference to Special Master will include either of these roles, which may have even different titles in other jurisdictions.

Usually the Special Master is appointed following the completion of a custody evaluation when the evaluator recognizes that the parents will need someone outside of the court to continue in an ongoing way to monitor or settle issues between them. In California the role of Special Master is defined by statute and refers to the quasi-judicial task of hearing all sides to a dispute and making binding decisions on the parties. In many instances the task of the Special Master is narrowly defined, for example, to address issues of transportation and to monitor the drop-off and pickup of the children. In other situations the task of the Special Master is broadly defined, such as to address all outstanding disputes between the parents, to help them settle, and, if they can not, to order binding decisions on them. California does not allow a judge to order a Special Master to assume judicial authority in the absence of the parents' stipulation. In practice, the best method may be to stipulate that the Special Master's order will become binding unless appealed by either party within a defined reasonable period of time (e.g., 20 days).

In my experience, the Special Master's actual task is complex and involves skills of the detective, evaluator, therapist, educator, teacher, parent, mediator, and judge, depending on the issues that need settlement. Because the Special Master's authority extends only as far as the parents are willing to agree, the Special Master needs to use all of her skills to keep the family out of the court and focused on the needs of their children. The stipulation and appointment of a Special Master, especially when the role is carefully defined, is a useful way for encouraging some of the more litigious clients to learn less litigious and more cooperative ways of coparenting, to stay out of court, and to lower the economic and emotional costs of their divorce. Finally, although the Special Master cannot become an evaluator because of the need for complete neutrality, when a subsequent evaluation is needed the Special Master's input would be valuable.

CUSTODY EVALUATOR

When a mental health professional is given the task of completing a custody evaluation, that evaluator must come into the process completely neutral, without hidden bias, and with no prior contact with any member of the family. Such an ethical statement would preclude anyone who has been a therapist, mediator, consultant, expert witness, psychologist evaluator, or Special Master to anyone in the family from being the neutral, court-appointed evaluator. Unlike the other professional roles outlined, it is the task of the custody evaluator to neutrally assess the entire family, focusing on the dynamics of the family, the strengths and weaknesses of each parent, and the functioning of the children, while making recommendations to the court regarding the children's best interests. It is a unique role, and must be, in my opinion, kept separate from the other roles outlined.

DUAL RELATIONSHIPS

Many professional associations are beginning to develop ethical rules regarding custody evaluations. In addition, most of these same associations have ethical prohibitions against dual relationships in professional work. For many evaluators, the simple rule is "never conduct a custody evaluation when the evaluator has had a prior relationship of any kind with any member of the family." Thus, if the evaluator has given expert testimony to the judge related to a particular family's dynamics or if he has been a therapist to any member of the family, or a mediator, or a consultant to one of the attorneys in this family, it is inappropriate for him to conduct a custody evaluation. A custody evaluation must be completed by a neutral, impartial mental health expert who gathers facts about the family and its individual members in order to make a recommendation for the custody and visitation plans of the family. Prior knowledge of any family member would make such neutrality impossible.

In many situations, it may be perfectly helpful for the other mental health expert, usually a therapist or mediator, to talk with the evaluator and provide input to the evaluation process. In such circumstances, the evaluator will need to gather such information as an adjunct to the rest of the facts of the case.

There may also be times when the other mental health professional may not want to talk with the evaluator. In those circumstances, he may compromise himself and could possibly violate his client's rights if he is not careful. At least two such situations come to mind. One is the mediator who has ensured the confidentiality of the mediation process from the litigation. Even if both parents sign a release of information authorizing the evaluator to speak with the mediator, it may be beneficial for the mediator to claim confidentiality, as her knowledge was gained with that in mind. Providing information to the evaluator knowing that the evaluation could ultimately end up in litigation could therefore be a mistake. In addition, if, following the evaluation, the couple were to go back to mediation, it would be difficult to trust the mediator in the future if confidential material had been disclosed.

A second circumstance in which confidentiality is critical concerns the child's therapist. When I have worked with children as a therapist when their parents are in the midst of the most heated custody disputes, my primary task during this time was to provide a safe haven for the child to express herself. A therapist ensures the client's confidentiality, even when the client is a child, unless authorized to share information with another professional. Even though parents may authorize the release of information, there are times when maintaining silence is critical in order to assist the child in staying out of the middle of the parental dispute. If the child fears that her communications could end up being divulged to the evaluator or to her parents, this child is likely to hold back from sharing necessary feelings and thoughts with her therapist. By ensuring confidentiality and maintaining it even when an evaluation is in progress, the therapist provides a place of safety for the child. Obviously, there may be times when it is critical for the therapist to talk with the evaluator, such as when she feels that there is a degree of risk for the child in relation to one of his parents. Clearly, the therapist must balance the child's right to privacy and need to stay out of the middle with the need for the evaluator to have crucial information about the child and his relationships.

To safeguard the need for confidentiality of the child's therapy, in many jurisdictions the court will become the holder of the child's psychotherapeutic privilege. Then when a dispute arises regarding this question, the judge will make a decision about confidentiality and the extent to which the child's therapist should provide information to the evaluator and whether this information should be safeguarded and kept out of the report and the legal proceedings.

Similarly, the therapist of an adult client may wish to maintain confidentiality from the evaluator. A therapist may feel that he cannot divulge confidential information, even when a release was signed, as it will interfere with his ability to be a therapeutic advocate for his client. At all times, the evaluator needs to be sensitive to the ongoing goals and needs of the other mental health experts when consulting with or seeking information about the family or an individual member of the family.

Another possible source of controversy among evaluators is the blending of the role of evaluator and mediator. In many occasions, when an evaluator begins working with a family for evaluation, an evaluator who also does mediation may find that a particular couple may not be that far apart and could benefit from mediation rather than going through the evaluation process. Many attorneys and court personnel might suggest that the evaluator could easily shift roles and try to mediate the issues between the parents.

After all, a working alliance is being established, and some may argue that the evaluator would be the best person to attempt such mediation.

Although I agree that the timing may make sense, I believe that if an evaluator senses that mediation would be more appropriate, he should suspend his evaluation and refer the couple to a willing mediator and assist that mediator in understanding the dynamics that suggested that such mediation could be successful. The primary reason that I am opposed to changing roles in the middle is that should mediation efforts fail, it would be difficult for the evaluator to reestablish the necessary impartiality to complete the evaluation. It is my belief that once an evaluator blends roles, he loses effectiveness in whatever role he ends up taking. By maintaining the integrity of a single role from beginning to end, the evaluator can ensure the family that he is undertaking that role to the best of his ability, with no other agenda in mind. When complete neutral impartiality is required, it is easy for the evaluator to always maintain it, as long as he never changes roles during the evaluation process.

Finally, as an evaluator, I have often been asked to continue as a mediator, therapist, or Special Master after the completion of an evaluation. Though I recognize that a certain degree of flexibility is in order once the evaluation has been completed, I have come to the conclusion that it is best for me not to mix roles even after the completion of an evaluation. Often I am asked to complete an updated evaluation at a later date, and if I have shifted roles after the completion of an evaluation, I can no longer maintain the necessary neutral impartiality. Similarly, I have seen many cases go to trial as long as a year to 18 months after the completion of an evaluation. If I have taken on another role in that time and my testimony related to the evaluation is necessary, it is likely that this testimony will be compromised by my new role in the case.

The more evaluations I complete and the more I see the possible complications of blending roles, the more I am convinced that it is safest to maintain rigid boundaries when I have done an evaluation. The only time that I recommend that an evaluator shift roles after an evaluation has been completed is in those geographic areas where there are few experts and where the shifting of roles may be required in order to provide the necessary therapeutic or mediation assistance after an evaluation has been completed. Even in such circumstances, it would be wise to caution the family and to seek the advice of the court prior to undertaking such a shift in roles.

Thus, I believe that mental health professionals must keep separate the many possible roles when working with divorcing families. This is why I would never do a custody evaluation, or even make statements related to custody, when I have been the child's therapist (as questioned in the first chapter). During the course of an evaluation, the evaluator may seek information from other professionals who have worked with various family members, and confidentiality may be more important than assisting an evaluator with an assessment. Once an evaluator has begun an evaluation, the evaluator must not change roles, though a suspension of the evaluation might be in order if efforts toward mediation could become successful. Finally, except in rare circumstances, it is best not to change roles even after the evaluation in order to maintain evaluator integrity in case there is a need for updated evaluations or testimony associated with the evaluation in the future.

3

Fundamental Questions in Most Custody Evaluations

Custody evaluations are most often requested by the courts or the attorneys in order to address some specific question or questions related to the divorce of the parents—often the custody and visitation of children. These questions can often be rather narrow and may relate to a complex issue. Chapter 8 will deal with many of the specific issues that frequently lead to conflict and competition between the parents. In this chapter I focus on the fundamental questions involved in nearly all custody evaluations. Essentially, there are five main topics: (a) "the best interests of the child"; (b) the bond between the child and his parents or siblings; (c) psychological dysfunction, the capacity to parent, and the strengths and weaknesses associated with each parent's ability to parent, nurture, and understand the children and their needs; (d) the nature of the coparental relationship; and (e) recommendations for how the parents can share the time with their children. This is often called the custody and visitation plan. Although more complex evaluations will often necessitate additional recommendations, almost all evaluations, by their very nature, will end with some type of recommendation related to the parenting plan.

THE BEST INTERESTS OF THE CHILD

Just what are the best interests of the child? In a legalistic way, state laws define the best interests of the child around parameters such as nurturing, guidance, religious and economic issues, emotional attachments, stability, the maintenance of a healthy relationship with both parents, and so on. Many state laws, in an effort to guarantee access to both parents, recognize that the best interests of the child also encompass a supportive effort by both parents to provide a healthy attachment to the other parent.

In most laws there is vagueness about the issues that are at the core of the question of the best interests of the child. Some argue that the laws are purposely vague to allow the courts broad discretion given the unique facts of each family. Mental health professionals and parents relate to psychological constructs in understanding the best interests of the child. Parents, especially, are less concerned about the law than they are about their children. Custody evaluators are often faced with specific questions in the midst of complex family issues. Rarely is it a simple process to evaluate both parents and the child and develop a parenting plan that is clearly in the best interests of the child. Instead evaluators are often faced with many complex and competing needs of children and their parents. Although the needs of the children must come first, it is often necessary to set up these needs in a hierarchical pattern from which to reach a solution.

For example, if an adolescent child wishes to leave her primary residence with her mother to live primarily with her father and she has two younger siblings who are going to remain with the mother, evaluators must look at the best interests of this adolescent child and at those of her siblings, as well. Focus must be not only on the needs of the older child vis-à-vis her relationships with each of her parents, but also on the needs of both her and her siblings and their relationships with one another.

This can get quite complex. For example, in one of my recent evaluations, the family had a preexisting custody arrangement in which the older adolescent boy lived primarily with his father and the younger preadolescent boy lived primarily with his mother. The boys saw each other during the week and visited each other's home every other weekend. This provided regular contact with the brothers and fairly regular contact with the noncustodial parent. The evaluation centered around whether or not the younger brother should move to a different state with the mother and stepfather, who was transferred because of his job. Because his mother and stepfather were definitely moving (they had been married approximately 7 years and the stepfather had known the younger boy most of his life), the issues were clear. Does the younger boy stay with his mother as primary custodial parent and continue a visiting relationship with his father, but risk a significant change in his relationship with his father and brother because he would see them only at holidays and for extended periods of time over the summer? Or should he stay with his brother and father, have a significant change in his day-to-day lifestyle, miss his mother and stepfather a great deal, and visit them along with his brother during holidays and vacations? As the evaluation progressed, it was clear that there was no perfect solution for *his* best interests, short of the stepfather having good employment in his original community. Given economic circumstances at the time, that was an impossibility. Although many different solutions could be in the best interests of this child, it appeared in this particular family that it would be best for the boy to move with his mother and stepfather to a different state.

Similarly, I recently completed an evaluation 2 years after the divorce in which it was clear that both parents and both children (ages 4 and 6) still missed the family unit. The children were clearly wishing that their parents would get back together, and both parents were still in mourning over the loss of the marriage. They shared custody of the children on an equal basis, but again, one of the parents wished to move in order to grow in her life. In many ways, it may have been in the children's best interest for this couple to have resolved their relationship and marital disputes, which were mild in comparison to many of the conflicts we often see, and remain married. Because they did not choose that course several years before, they were facing a need to review the custody and parenting plan of their children because one of them needed to move. No good solutions could be found in this case because the needs of the children were to maintain the equal time with both parents, and, in order to help one of the parents with her mourning, that parent needed to move forward psychologically and felt that a geographic move was necessary. In many ways, to truly meet the best interests of their children, parents would rarely divorce in the first place, but instead look for ways to rekindle their love and maintain a healthy family environment for their children.

During the 10 years that I have done evaluations, based on research and my own personal experience, I have reached the conclusion that a few fundamental needs are required to meet the best interests of the child. First, the best parenting is achieved with two parents. With relatively healthy parents, it is important for the child to maintain healthy relationships with each parent, knowing that he is important to them both, with each parent remaining actively involved in as much of his daily life as possible. Both parents need to take an active interest and participation in the child's school life, social life, and activities.

Second, it is important for children to see that their parents can develop a postdivorce relationship that is relatively free of hostility and in which the relationship with the other parent is promoted to the child. A third need for children is that they share time with each parent in a way that has fewer rather than more transitions over a short period of time and that the transitions flow naturally in the *child's* life. At the very least, these transitions must make sense to the child and the way she lives her life, such as around school times or days, parents' work schedules, and so on.

Fourth, it is important that the parenting plan makes sense developmentally, according to the age and abilities of the child (see Chapter 4). Fifth, it is important that when there is serious conflict between the parents or between a particular child and his parents, there be a mechanism by which the conflicts can be managed and reduced. Sixth, if one of the parents is dysfunctional or abusive or is engaged in a relationship that is physically destructive or emotionally toxic to a child, the child's needs for safety must always come first. Ultimately, to the extent possible, if a postdivorce relationship between a child and her parents can stay either similar to or become healthier and more positive than the predivorce relationship, we are succeeding in developing an arrangement that will truly be in the best interests of the child.

THE FAMILY'S BONDS

There is a great deal in the psychological literature about attachment and bonding between parent and child. One of the most important aspects to evaluate is this attachment between the child and his parents and whether or not there is a difference in the bond between the child and his mother or his father. In previous years there was a great deal written about the child and her psychological parents and the belief that mothers, as a whole, were more nurturing and important to the children than were the fathers. In more recent years, there has been considerably growing evidence that the child has a bond with both of her parents and a need to maintain and grow in her relationship with them both. As such, we need to assess the current state of that bond to promote growth in the attachment over time.

Many parents are not much different in how they parent after their divorce relationship, but other parents are. Once free of the emotional constraints of a tension-filled marriage, some parents become healthier and more nurturing in their parental role. By attempting to understand the nature of the bond and attachment between a child and her parents and the psychological functioning of the parents, evaluators will be able to provide recommendations that can lead to an enhancement and growth of that attachment with both parents.

When assessing this bond and attachment, evaluators are looking not only at the relationship between the parents and the child, but also at the ability of each parent to promote and encourage the growing attachment and bond of the child to the other parent. Evaluators need to understand the conscious and unconscious behaviors that promote such a bond and that can lead to a sense of security for the child. Because this security comes from the formation and development of a healthy bond with nurturing parents, it is very important during the evaluation to assess each parent's ability to promote the bond between the child and the other parent. In order to allow for that, evaluators must understand how each parent is able to let go of the couple's issues and shift to a coparenting role for the benefit of the child.

PARENTING STRENGTHS AND WEAKNESSES

The third global issue that is a part of every custody evaluation relates to gaining an understanding of each parent's relative strengths and weaknesses and his or her relative ability to understand and meet the needs of the child. While listening to parents during the evaluation process, evaluators often hear of the many ways that each parent believes that he is better than the other parent. Parental strengths include the ability to focus on the children's emotional needs; understand issues of psychological growth and development; provide stability, nurturance, and guidance to the children; and promote a positive relationship with the other parent and a well-rounded, stimulating life for the children.

Some parents are extremely vague and seem able to concentrate only on their perceptions of the shortcomings of the other parent. These parents, many of whom have significant psychological dysfunctions, have a very difficult time talking about what they have to offer in the way of parenting one's child. As in a nastily run political campaign, many parents can focus only on the negative things about the other parent.

In order to fully understand all of this, we need to use several ways to develop an understanding of each parent's capacity to parent and psychological fitness. Through the use of thorough clinical interviews, with direct observation of parents and children together, and with structured questions that are designed to understand this issue, we hope to come to an understanding of each parent's capacity to parent over a broad spectrum. Frequently, we are trying to assess drug and/or alcohol use, severe psychological dysfunction or personality disorders, or other features that may significantly impact a person's ability to meet his or her child's needs. We might need to use psychological tests and/or drug testing to better understand these issues.

Above all, it is critical in every evaluation to understand each parent's personality as it relates to the issues of parenting and reducing the post-divorce parental conflicts. In order to do an evaluation that is clearly helpful to the child and his parents, we need to recognize that parents are not all good or all bad and focus on each parent's specific strengths and weaknesses and the issues of the coparental relationship.

Specific skills that parents of divorce need to develop include, but are not limited to (a) keeping the children out of the middle and not asking children to carry messages between the parents; (b) not saying derogatory things about the other parent; (c) not talking with the children about the issues of the divorce; (d) not asking the children about the other parent's activities; (e) not inducing guilt over loneliness when the child is with the other parent; and (f) not arguing with the other parent at the time of drop-off and pickup of the children. By asking questions about these issues and understanding how the parents deal with them, evaluators can better understand strengths and weaknesses of each parent regarding the divorce.

THE COPARENTAL RELATIONSHIP

Because most custody evaluations result in a recommendation for sharing the job of parenting, even when recommending one primary custodial parent and one visiting parent, evaluators need to understand the nature of the coparenting relationship. The primary task of coparenting is to cooperate with the other parent in raising the children regardless of how one feels about the other parent. In order to coparent, one must be able to separate the couple's issues from the children's needs. A good coparent is able to keep the children out of the middle of the divorce issues and avoid the pitfalls noted in the previous section. Parents need to communicate with each other, not through the children, about school, religion, activities, health, and other areas of importance to the children. The best coparents can do this in a businesslike, neutral way, without emotional entanglement.

Research suggests that children of divorce do best when their parents cooperate in parenting and they do worst when their parents remain in conflict. Children function reasonably well when their parents are disengaged. One task of the recommendations is to encourage conflicted parents to become disengaged and then to help disengaged parents to cooperate and communicate with one another. By understanding the coparental relationship—whether it is cooperative, hostile, or disengaged—evaluators can recommend ways to help the parents improve the situation for their children.

TIME-SHARING RECOMMENDATIONS

As evaluators, it is our job to take these broad issues—that is, the best interests of the child, attachment and bond between the child and her parents, each parent's strengths and weaknesses and relative capacity to parent—and put them together to formulate a plan for sharing the time between the parents. Some time-sharing plans are quite specific, such as every other week with each parent, or primary custody with one parent, every other weekend with the other, and specific plans for sharing holidays. Other time-sharing plans are quite vague and may state simply that primary custody is with one parent and there is reasonable visitation with the other. In my experience, there is less room for ongoing conflict between the parents when the schedule is specifically defined, and there is benefit to the children (especially older ones) if there is some flexibility in the structure (especially at the child's request). Balancing these needs is one of the evaluator's tasks.

Even in relatively dysfunctional situations, it is likely that each parent will spend some time with the child, even if the visit is supervised. Evaluators must be as creative as possible in the development of a time-sharing plan that maximizes the strengths of each parent, provides for the stability necessary for the child, and, when possible, meets the parents' needs as well. It is important to understand each parent's needs in doing an evaluation, because, to the extent that they complement the needs of the child, it is an added plus when they are reflected in the time-sharing plan.

Finally, it is critical to help each parent understand the reasons for the recommendations so that each parent can accept, promote, and implement the plan. During the years I've been doing evaluations, I have found that the best recommendations take into account the attachment and bond between the child, siblings, and both parents, as well as the ability of each parent to understand and meet the child's many needs. Once we do that, we can formulate a plan that hierarchically addresses the competing and varying needs of the child and try to enlist the parents' mutual support in following the recommended parenting plan. Usually, we need to help each parent feel that he has won something. This can best be accomplished if each parent knows that the solution is a winning one for the child. If either parent feels that she has significantly lost and cannot understand how the recommendations are beneficial to the child, it will be very difficult for that parent to support and work to make that parenting plan succeed.

In essence, this chapter has focused on the broad issues related to typical custody evaluations. As described, each of these issues is fundamentally connected to the other special issues frequently addressed in most custody evaluations. When looking at narrower issues of sexual, physical, or emotional abuse, spouse abuse and domestic violence, unusual medical needs, drug and/or alcohol addictions, severe mental illness, criminality, parental alienation, relocation issues, or others, we need to understand them in relation to each of these broad questions.

Even drug-abusing and alienating parents have certain strengths, and although we may recommend limited or supervised visitation until the parent gets off drugs or stops the alienation, we still need to understand how to enhance relationships between the child and *both* parents. We do this by delineating both the strengths and weaknesses of each parent, as well as by describing the nature of the bond between each parent and the child.

4

The Children and Their Needs: A Developmental Perspective

One of the most crucial aspects of a custody evaluation is addressing the developmental needs of children when recommending custody and parenting plans. Some evaluators seem to focus more on parents' rights than on child developmental needs. It is my opinion that this is a mistake. Some evaluators take a very conservative approach and believe in rigidly adhering to a fairly traditional understanding that a child needs a primary parent or one home more than anything else when her parents divorce. I believe this is equally a mistake.

In general, children of different ages have different developmental needs vis-à-vis their relationships with their divorcing parents. There are individual differences in children regarding temperament that will affect how they react to their parents' divorce and their parents' particular parenting plan. Some children are more sensitive and reactive to their environment; others are more invulnerable to the stressors of divorce, their parents' conflicts, and transition and change in their lives.

The evaluator needs to understand and address the competing and complex needs of the child and recommend a parenting plan that takes into account the hierarchy of these needs. In this chapter I focus primarily on developmental needs and suggest some broad guidelines to help ensure that the parenting plan can continue to promote the basic developmental needs and attachment goals necessary for the child. Within the context of these broad guidelines, it is important for the evaluator to understand the particular nature of the child's temperament when recommending a parenting plan.

Many parents speak of stability when talking about children's needs—stability both in terms of place (often referred to as the child's home) and also in terms of relationships with parents and peers. There is also a degree of stability and security that is achieved by meeting the developmental needs of the child and using these needs to formulate a parenting plan that is truly in a child's best interest. This chapter focuses on the developmental needs of four major stages of a child's life as they apply to issues of divorce and parenting plans: infancy and toddlerhood (birth to age 3), the preschool years (ages 3 to 6), grade school years (ages 6 to 12), and adolescence (ages 13 through 17).

INFANCY AND TODDLERHOOD

In the first 6 months of life, the child is beginning to learn in a very concrete way whether or not the world is a safe and nurturing place or a place of anxiety, fear, and insecurity. Basic trust is being established, and that basic trust becomes established with the formation of a primary relationship, usually between child and mother. Surrogates can take on some aspects of the primary mother's role, but it is clear that a primary attachment relationship must develop within the first few months of a child's life for the child to be able to develop and form secondary and tertiary relationships as he grows. Essentially, during these first few months of life, the child is developing a bond, primarily to one parent and secondarily to another parent. This initial attachment is critical for all future stages of development. This bonding in the first year is so essential for the development of the child's basic trust and security that I believe it is the most important factor to consider for children under the age of one when there is a custody dispute between parents.

Contact with both parents needs to be maintained on a frequent basis in order to provide an opportunity for growth of the relationships with both parents. If parents separate during that first year of life, I recommend that each parent have an opportunity for frequent contact with the child, and, when possible, no separation from either parent should last more than 2 or

3 days. However, the primary attachment object must be available to the child for the largest blocks of time for the child's sense of safety and trust to develop. It is important for a very young child to have predictable routines in his life. In a fairly traditional setup, a young child will often live mostly with his mother. The father will visit three or four times per week, a few hours at a time, and take on the parenting role during his contact with his child. If the parents are not competitive with one another and can allow such a plan to work, it is expected that, by the end of the first year of life, the child will have established both the primary attachment that is critical for future development (usually with mom), and the beginning secondary attachment that is also critical for formation of a bond with his other parent (usually with dad).

Between 6 and 18 months of age these attachments grow, and predictability becomes very important for the young child. With the needs of the child being paramount, overnight visitation is not recommended at this time as the anxiety of the child is usually too great. If both parents wish to have an opportunity for overnight responsibilities, it is recommended that the child remain in his home, and the parents move in and out on occasion, so that each parent can be available at different times during the child's day. Again, for that first year, I believe that the primary attachment parent needs to be there most of the time, but during the next 6 months, to age 1½, there can be some expansion of time with both parents. It is important to keep in mind that very young children have no time concept whatsoever, and out of sight can be quickly out of mind. This can lead to a high degree of insecurity for the child, which may result in regression in areas of feeding, sleeping, and toileting, and in developmental delays, irritability, and other symptoms. Care must be taken to reduce the sense of loss and abandonment that the child feels by maintaining predictability and relationships during this time of life. In order to reduce such insecurity and to minimize the risk of such symptoms, one parent must sacrifice some time with the child in order for the child to develop psychologically healthy.

Following the healthy development of basic trust and attachment comes the process of separation and individuation that develops from approximately 18 months to 3 years of age. This is a process in which the child begins to develop her own autonomy and her beginning sense of self, while separating herself from the primary attachment object(s). Separation and individuation is now the primary task, with the goal being the development of the child's autonomy. It is critical that a parenting plan be established that allows for this. Usually such a plan has an increased amount of time with the other parent, but primary time still with one parent. Sometimes there will be overnight contact with each parent. It is usually best for the child if this is introduced gradually in order to reduce any significant anxiety on the child. Many parents have a difficult time during these years with a child's temper tantrums, demanding behavior, and stubbornness. Parents refer to this period of time as "the terrible twos," because the nature of this developing autonomy can be so troubling for both child and parent. Yet this behavior is necessary for the adequate development of the child's autonomy. It is critical that if both parents are going to share the parenting during this period of the child's development, they agree on issues of structure and discipline. During this time, security to the primary attachment parent is necessary for proper development. In addition, the very young child needs consistency and positive nurturing during these difficult years. It is often a relief to have the assistance of the other parent in spending some quality time with one's child during these years because this period can be so demanding for both parent and child. If a healthy primary and secondary attachment has been established and if the parents can be relatively consistent with one another in how they treat the child during these years, the establishment of the child's separate self will be enhanced.

Frequently seen in older children of divorce is a sense of psychological "splitting" between the parents, which starts during these years. In normal child development such splitting occurs during the age of 12 to 24 months, as the child views both himself and his parents in largely good and bad terms. I often see children of divorce split their parents into good and bad, seeing one parent as good and the other as bad. I believe that this is caused by the natural developmental process gone awry as a result of the complexities of the divorce process. It is this type of splitting, that is, regarding one parent as being primarily good and the other parent as being primarily bad, to which I refer in this book. Given all of these issues, it appears that the primary tasks for the very young child of divorce are the development of a separate, secure, autonomous self and the growing attachment to each of her parents. This ensures that by age 3, neither parent will be all good and neither will be all bad. Otherwise, future relationships with both parents will be impaired, and the child might have ongoing difficulties with splitting in her future relationships.

Finally, children are learning improved language skills during their first 3 years of life. In order to learn and understand language, the child needs to feel secure and be relatively free of anxiety. Early language problems that develop during the 2nd and 3rd year of life are frequently the result of tension that the child experiences. Thus, children raised in a high-conflict environment may have language disturbances, such as delayed expressive language, stuttering, articulation difficulties, and other speech and language problems. It is critical for the child's natural development to encourage parents to minimize this tension and anxiety so that the child's development and language abilities grow unimpeded. Evaluators must pay attention to all aspects of the child's development and recognize that developing language skills often are an indicator of the amount of stress being experienced by the child during her parents' divorce.

By age 3, if a child has gone through the process of separation and individuation with minimal difficulties, has developed fairly adequate language skills and an autonomous self relatively free of anxiety and the splitting of his parents, and has a healthy bond and attachment to each parent, he will have reached the developmental milestones expected by this time. For his parents to help him accomplish this, they must work together and be cooperative and supportive with one another while minimizing their conflicts and their competition for the child's time and love. If the evaluator can help the parents learn to view their job as a cooperative venture for the establishment of a healthy 3-year-old child, she will have done an effective job of helping the parents meet their child's needs.

Evaluators must concentrate solely on the developmental needs of this very young child and continually encourage parents to focus not on their rights, their selfish motives, their competing interests, and their blame of one another, but on the child. Evaluators must encourage them to promote for their child a world that is nurturing and secure and in which both parents grow in their healthy bonds with the child. In essence, when conducting an evaluation for an infant or toddler, a major task will be educating and helping the parents understand the child's needs and how they must work cooperatively toward meeting those needs.

THE PRESCHOOL YEARS

During the next 3 years of life children have tremendous growth and development. Children who are free of stress and conflict grow in their socialization, begin their sex role identification, begin and gain a fairly healthy understanding of their feelings and emotions, and grow in their conceptual understanding of ideas, time, relationships, language, and so forth. Attachments and bonds with other significant adults grow dramatically, and the

3- to-6-year-old child has a zest for life and learning that is often unsurpassed at any other time in her life. As with the toddler, there is a strong need for predictability, consistency, and structure, but there is also a growing tolerance for separation from primary attachment objects and a growing ability to tolerate beginning differences in the way their parents do the job of parenting. Preschool children continue to view the world in a fairly concrete way and need concrete structure from their parents to help them understand their place in the world.

If parents begin their divorce when their children are preschoolers, the children often have nightmares, whining, separation anxiety, confusion, aggression, and severe regression to earlier functioning, primarily because the emotional and developmental milestones that were achieved by age 3 are still relatively fragile. Children of this age are quite sensitive to their parents' moods and look to their parents to see how they should understand and feel about the world and others in their environment. They need their parents to be relatively free of conflict, or else their anxiety quickly surfaces and their ability to attain developmental goals is reduced. They need to understand what is occurring in their life, and they need two healthy parents to support them.

The primary goal of an evaluator is to encourage an environment and a parenting plan in which the child's developmental needs can flourish. Parents can place their children in a preschool, and both parents can participate in the preschool activities. The preschool child can more easily move between two homes, so long as there is predictability and structure to this movement. A structure can be developed for overnight contact with both parents, which will be more free of anxiety for the child. A preschool child is cognitively concrete, and parents need to use calendars to mark the days that she is at mom's house or dad's house. This will reduce her anxiety and insecurity about her place in the world. Both parents can get actively involved in the child's developing friendships, assist her in going to her first birthday parties, and begin participation in some of the activities in which she starts to show an interest. In this way, the child begins to view both her parents as being actively involved in her life, and she feels important to both of them. Similarly, she views her parents as cooperating on her behalf. Again, these are the issues that are paramount to this young child as she moves through her developmental needs.

At age 3 and 4, many mediators and evaluators begin to recommend joint physical custody and equal sharing of time for the child with each of her parents. Children of this age have a growing ability to develop separate and overnight contact with each parent. This is healthy in the formation of the primary and secondary attachments. However, it is often difficult for a 3-year-old to spend a week away from the primary attachment parent. Such dividing of the time can lead to regression in the normal psychological development of the child. In such circumstances, the child may blame the parent with whom he has the secondary attachment when he misses his primary parent. He then views the secondary parent as bad because he feels insecure in this arrangement.

For the young preschooler, I recommend instead short blocks of time for the child to be with this other parent and increased overnights (such as one or two nights during the week and every other weekend) as a way of establishing increased contact with both parents for greater lengths of time. Again, this balances the developmental needs of the child with the growing attachment with both parents. Children can then begin to tolerate more equal time with each parent, especially if there is phone contact and a midweek visit with the other parent to aid in the overall adjustment. It is likely that this will be done most easily if the child gets used to spending significant time in two homes. By age 5 or 6, when a child enters kindergarten or first grade, she can begin to tolerate and often flourish with a week-week sharing of time with her parents. Overall, however, for the young child, evaluators should encourage conflicting parents to share in the activities and daily lives of the child to the extent that their time and geography permits, rather than compete over time.

If evaluators have assisted the parents in meeting the developmental needs of this child, by the time she is 6 she will have a healthy attachment and strong bond with each of her parents, continue to be relatively free of anxiety and free of the psychological splitting of her parents into good and bad, have a good understanding of her emotions and a healthy ability to express these emotions in an age-appropriate way, and continue the zest for life that she had when she was 3. Her cognitive skills will have matured so that she will have a fairly good understanding of time, place, and relationships. Her socialization skills with peers will be relatively free of the conflicts and tensions that are often the result of highly conflicted divorces. In general, the healthy 6-year-old child of divorce will be ready to start grade school and expand her activities and social relationships in an environment in which she is free to love both of her parents and grow in her attachment and bond with each of them. Having completed these tasks, she will be free to move to the next large stage of development.

THE GRADE SCHOOL YEARS

The school-age years are filled with a variety of tasks for the developing child. School itself is very important, as is the continued growth and development of cognitive skills. With this continued growth in cognitive understanding comes a need for things to make sense to the developing child. The school-age child becomes much more involved in his world and begins to make more active decisions that make sense to him. Structure, rules, and activities play a very important part in the child's life at this age. The growing socialization skills are very important, and the child at this age either develops continued improvement in his self-confidence or begins to develop feelings of inadequacy, insecurity, and inferiority in comparison to others. At this age, intense loyalty conflicts can grow out of proportion as a child often wishes to please his parents, while simultaneously beginning to please himself. Expected symptoms at this age can include sadness, crying, depression, temper tantrums, dependency, school problems, and hostility toward one or both parents. To reduce these symptoms, the school-age child needs his parents to shield him from parental hostility and blame, and he needs to understand and be free of guilt about his parents' divorce.

Routine and structure is also critical to a child of this age. Structure minimizes anxiety and allows the child to feel secure while making sense of the world around him. The school day, games, and activities are structured and have rules, and it is important that the child of divorce has a structure to the time that he spends with his parents. In the early school-age years, putting this schedule on a calendar readily accessible to the child eases the transition between parents' homes. As a child becomes older and more used to the schedule, this may not be necessary any more.

It is very important that the grade school-age child understand the structure of when he is going to be with his mother and his father. He can handle almost any structure that is clear and makes sense and that has few transitions over a span of time. Regardless of the structure itself, the child needs to have a time and a place to do his schoolwork, a time and a place to see his friends, and an opportunity to be involved in his chosen activities. If the parents live close enough to one another, have similar daily routines and rules, and are both willing to be actively involved in their child's life, a relatively equal time-share may be of benefit to most children of this age. If they do not live close enough, or if the child cannot tolerate such a time-share, the recommended custody plan should enable both parents to actively participate in each part of their child's life to the extent feasible.

It is very easy for the school-age child to develop loyalty conflicts between his parents. A child of this age wants to please both parents and does not yet understand his own needs vis-à-vis his relationship with both parents. In trying to please, he will often feel conflicts in which pleasing his mother will automatically lead to feelings of rejection from his father and vice versa. In doing an evaluation for the grade school-age child, it is very important to understand these loyalty conflicts and the ways in which the child experiences them.

Such conflicts are usually blind to both the child and his parents, especially when both parents believe they are doing what is best for their child. Later in this book, as I focus on interviewing techniques with children, I show how to find clues to such loyalty conflicts through children's drawings, through their affect as they talk about their parents, through their play, and through their anxiety as they focus on their experiences. Children who are afraid to get involved in their own activities because of such loyalty conflicts are beginning to internalize their parents' battle to their detriment.

For example, I recently had an evaluation in which a child chose not to play soccer because his father was angry at his mother and believed that the soccer coach was too close a friend of the mother's. This conflict was unhealthy for the child because he allowed it to interfere with his activities. In contrast, a child who is free to engage in his activities (e.g., music, sports, etc.) and makes friends easily is unlikely to be experiencing as much loyalty conflict. Such a child might tell his father that he wants to play soccer anyway, pushing his father to understand his needs, pulling himself out of the parental conflict. It is hoped that he can do this relatively free of guilt, as well. Thus, the child has a sphere of interests and activities that is outside of the parents and their conflict, and it is important for the child to be able to engage in such activities without guilt.

Children tend to replay with their peers many of the conflicts they experience from their primary attachment objects (parents). With most children, we often witness the way in which a child experiences such loyalty conflicts by the way he relates with his friends. This is especially true in unstructured activities, as in school-yard playgrounds. By understanding how a child relates to his peers in such settings, we can develop a better understanding of how the child deals with his loyalty conflicts with his parents. For the school-age child, it seems that we must understand the child's need for structure and the child's sense of loyalty to his parents more than anything else.

It is also at this age that the child begins to assert his autonomy again. Children will begin to need to be involved in their activities, to the exclusion of contact with one or another parent. Birthday parties and peer activities take on an importance larger than seeing the other parent. Problems in the home or feelings of insecurity may cause children to become angry at one of their parents as well. It is hoped that both parents can understand the child's feelings and actively participate in all of the child's activities, but if one parent is unable to do so, that parent may begin to feel a sense of isolation from the child.

Evaluators are often faced with trying to understand the source of the child's displeasure with one of his parents. Certainly, a parent may be struggling in her parent-child relationship and may have a hard time seeing her own role in the problems. A child might want to have more autonomy or participation in his own activities with peers than spending time with his parent. One parent may attempt to encourage alienation against the other parent. Additionally, school-age children generally have predictable, unavoidable reactions to divorce, such as sadness, anger, and confusion. Any of these things might cause problems in child-parent relationships. Typically, one parent blames the other for the child's feelings, but it is common for the grade school-age child to have his own feelings separate from the desires and feelings of the parents. If both parents have stayed involved in all phases of the child's life and both parents are adequately integrated into the child's life and activities, the child is less likely to be forced to choose between his activities and one of his parents.

The school-age child also becomes increasingly abstract in the way he understands the world around him. Things begin to make sense across a broader spectrum of dimensions, and he is less likely to view things solely in terms of black and white. There is a growing understanding of ambivalence and mixed feelings and a growing awareness that different people can have different beliefs, objectives, and feelings associated with their experiences. The older school-age child tries to make sense of things, which is a sign of growth when compared with the younger child, who often does not understand what he experiences. When his parents are in conflict, the school-age child tries to develop his own sense of this conflict and its meaning. Although he may feel insecure and experience feelings of sadness and anger, the school-age child also tries to understand his parents' behavior and, especially at times of higher stress, the source of his feelings. Unless he is internalizing too much, the school-age child will begin to tell his parents what he thinks and what makes sense to him.

During an evaluation, the school-age child is a strong ally in understanding the family's particular issues. As the evaluator tries to understand what makes sense to the child, she has a better chance of understanding the parental conflict. She gets clues by the child's words, level of stress, understanding, and also by the level of emotional response that the school-age child might be experiencing during the evaluation process. If the evaluator can get a picture of the child's experiences with his parents through the child's eyes and if the evaluator can recognize the child's understanding of the conflicts, she can more easily understand the parenting plan that will be in the child's best interest.

A child of this age understands that it does not make sense when a parent is seeking sole custody, yet does not come to school events or athletic activities. He understands when a parent is attempting to buy love rather than be there for him. Finally, he understands when both parents truly love and nurture him, participate in his daily life, and encourage and support his need for a growing, healthy relationship with the other parent. As an evaluator seeks to assess the child's understanding of his relationship with both parents and what makes sense to the child, she can use his help in developing the parenting plan that will make sense to him.

Because children need continuity in their lives, the parenting schedule must be structured. It is quite useful if the rules and structures in both homes are relatively similar. If the values of the parents are significantly different and if the rules in the two homes are not even close, it is difficult for the school-age child to manage if the time is shared relatively equally. This child will likely need his parents to come closer together in the rules, structures, and values, or else he will need to spend a larger portion of time at one parent's home, with less time at the other parent's home.

If, by age 12, the child is successful in school, has gained self-confidence with peers and his activities, and has a minimal level of loyalty conflict between his parents, we can feel good about his overall development. If, on top of that, the 12-year-old child is now asserting himself and his needs and wishes to both parents, beginning to grasp the complexity and meanings of his relationships, feeling more secure about his sense of self, and understanding how to please himself while doing well in school and in the community, he will be ready for his next level of development. As evaluators, it is our job to assess this child's needs vis-à-vis these developmental tasks and to promote a parenting plan that can assist both parents' active participation sufficient to meeting those goals.

ADOLESCENCE

On the assumption that most prior developmental tasks have been established by the time the child reaches age 13, the adolescent begins to address tasks of importance for her developing young adulthood. Primary tasks include the development of independence and an increasing sense of autonomy, the need to make decisions and to learn from one's mistakes, and the need to try to resolve conflicts still remaining from earlier childhood. At this age, peers are extremely important. Especially in today's society, adolescents are subjected to tremendous peer pressure along a variety of dimensions. These include, but are not limited to, school, athletics, music and artistic activities, politics, drug and alcohol use, and sexuality. Adolescents strive to be independent from their parents, yet they are simultaneously dependent on the approval of their peers in order to feel successful and self-confident. Adolescents struggle with a resurgence of feelings of all kinds. This usually includes feelings of sexuality and aggressiveness and leads to behaviors that are controlling, demanding, and rebellious. Adolescents begin to demand more control of their own lives and often rebel against parental rules, values, and beliefs as they grow in their concern about their own future. As adolescents continue to make their own sense of their world, they develop and formulate their own ideas, often rejecting parental values and beliefs, at least for the short term. They may experiment with drugs and alcohol, may start to take more risks in their world, and may question authority to a larger degree.

It is likely that adolescents of divorce may develop immature behavior and some increased confusion over sex role identification. Symptoms may also include academic disturbance, depression, early or late development of their independence, and worry about their loss of family life. Adolescents of divorce have a strong desire for a single place to call home. Because their friends take on a greater importance than their parents at this age, they begin to reject the shared parenting structure that was so helpful during the school-age years. It is usually quite important to adolescents that their friends know where and when to find them. They want a home in which they can feel comfortable to invite their friends and where they believe their friends will feel welcome. Adolescents tend toward the mercenary to some degree in that they want to be with the parent who lets them do what they want, gives them the things that they want, and essentially allows them their own life. However, they continue to have a need for parental guidance, structure, and consistent discipline, and not to be left to the dangers of their adolescent world. Adolescents become very self-centered and usually develop more interest in money, cars, and their sexuality. They worry about their education and their future. There is a strong tendency on the part of adolescents to gravitate toward the parent who will allow them to feel better about more of these things.

In doing an evaluation in which adolescents are involved, we must recognize that most judges understand that adolescents are going to do what adolescents want vis-à-vis their living arrangements with their parents. It is best if the evaluator tries to assess parental effectiveness at understanding and meeting the adolescent's emerging needs. At the same time, the evaluator needs to listen to the adolescent describe the nature of the relationship that she would like to have with both of her parents. In so doing, the evaluator can help the parents understand the adolescent child and her needs and the importance for each parent to find a way to have an ongoing role with the child. Just as the very young child may have a lesser relationship with one parent while developing a primary attachment to the other, the same situation may exist in adolescence, as the adolescent child may spend most of her time with one parent and go back to a visiting role with the other. Both parents need to recognize that this may have nothing to do with them, but is part of the natural separation that the adolescent child achieves from both parents. It is difficult for the adolescent to maintain two households and achieve these developmental tasks at the same time.

Unfortunately, there are growing numbers of children who appear to be in serious conflict with one or both of their parents. As with the preschool child, the adolescent often has a reemergence of the psychological splitting, seeing one parent as all good and the other parent as all bad. Given the nature of the adolescent, the adolescent will often reject one of her parents because of the feelings that she has toward the way she is treated by that parent. This is very difficult, and it is important for the "good" parent to try the dual task of honoring the adolescent's feelings while simultaneously promoting the relationship with the other parent. As an evaluator, it is useful to find a way to understand how to best help the child under these circumstances. It is then the task to help both parents recognize their roles in assisting their child to complete her developmental tasks through this stage.

Sometimes it is best for an adolescent to have only minimal contact with one parent through this stage if she views that relationship as toxic. Adolescents struggle enough with their anxiety and self-esteem. They need to have some say in how and when they are going to deal with this parent whom they find offensive. Societal pressures and adolescent demands take a significant toll on the adolescent child of divorce, and there are tremendously complex issues that lend themselves to the splitting of feelings that often occur. An evaluator can only hope to understand it to the best of his ability and make recommendations that reduce the child's anxiety and help the adolescent grow in her self-control, self-determination, and ultimately in her self-confidence and self-acceptance. If the adolescent can emerge at age 18 feeling successful within her world and feeling little insecurity about normal developmental issues such as career, education, and her young adulthood, she might then be able to reestablish a relationship with the parent she viewed as bad on her own terms and in a way that feels less offensive to her.

When an adolescent has this type of relationship with one of her parents, evaluators should assist the adolescent in feeling empowered, while helping the adolescent to understand and accept the individual differences between her parents. We must also encourage the parent to be understanding of the child and her needs, including a need for respite from that parent, when necessary. We might recommend therapy to help everyone with these difficult issues and to work on the rebuilding of damaged relationships. Although the goals should always be the long-term resolution of such conflicts, during the adolescent years it is often difficult to establish resolution in a meaningful way.

I have focused this chapter on the developmental needs of children. Simultaneously, I have focused on the ways in which both evaluators and parents can help children grow and mature through these developmental tasks. The more we, as evaluators, promote these goals for families, the more we can help children minimize the negative effects of their parents' divorce. By keeping these needs and tasks in mind during the evaluation process, we will be able to develop a plan that is more clearly in the best interests of the child.

5

Conducting the Evaluation, Part I: Observations and Techniques With Adults

In the previous chapters I set the stage for understanding many of the dynamics of child development, the major issues of most evaluations, and the various roles that a mental health professional may play in doing evaluations. In this and the next two chapters I outline the actual steps of performing the custody evaluation. By understanding the evaluation process and ensuring that we follow a similar process under most evaluation circumstances, we can conduct custody evaluations that are more valid and consistent with expected protocol. As evaluators, we are obligated to maintain multiple avenues of data gathering, which include interviews, observations of family members, gathering of collateral information, and possibly psychological testing.

This chapter focuses on the issues related to the start of the evaluation and the evaluation process with the adults. Chapter 6 addresses the issues involved in understanding and evaluating the children and the various techniques in working with them. Chapter 7 addresses the product of the evaluation and summarizes the process I use to synthesize and integrate all of the findings into a comprehensive written report.

THE INITIAL STEPS

There are several steps that are best to take before actually beginning the custody evaluation. The first steps include the initial phone call and a review of the court order. It is very important to talk to both parents before scheduling appointments in order to determine whether they both agree to do the evaluation. Ideally, both parents have agreed with their attorneys to participate in a custody evaluation, but even if such an agreement is not possible, there should be a court order that authorizes the evaluation to take place. An evaluation must include both parents and the children, and it is best if the parents have agreed rather than been ordered to participate.

During that initial phone call, it is important for the evaluator to explain the process he will use in conducting the evaluation and answer any questions about credentials, experience, inherent biases, and other professionally related questions that a parent might have. By answering such questions, the evaluator can assure the parents that he will be doing an evaluation that focuses on the children's needs and that he will work toward understanding and resolving issues between the parents. He can assure the parents that he will recommend a complete parenting plan that is in their child's best interest. Even with a reluctant parent, the evaluator can use the initial phone call to answer questions and concerns and ease that parent's resistance about participation in the evaluation.

By explaining the evaluation procedure, the evaluator can reduce the parents' initial anxiety about the evaluation. Such anxiety is quite common for people who are involved in court proceedings. It is important for the evaluator to remember that most people involved in a custody dispute have been in constant warfare and often receive little information about what they can expect through the court process. If the evaluator thoroughly explains the evaluation process and answers all of the parents' questions, he can assist the parents in reducing such anxiety and encourage them to feel better about the process.

In addition, it is important for the evaluator to understand what the parents are expecting from the evaluation. Frequently, there are stepparents, stepsiblings, grandparents, and significant others whom parents wish to be seen as part of the evaluation. There may be many people whom the parents want the evaluator to talk with in order to get historical or other information. It is very important in this initial phone call to elicit from the parents their understanding of the components of a complete custody evaluation and what they want the evaluator to do. Often parents are worried about the effect of the evaluation process on their children and have questions about how the evaluator intends to see the kids. If there are siblings, they may want to know if their children will be seen together or separately and may have a preference about this. By answering their questions and eliciting their assistance in their evaluation, the evaluator can ensure that the parents become participants who are actively involved in the decision making regarding their child.

THE INITIAL CONTRACT

It is best if the local court develops a standard order for evaluation that will be used with every family. Such an order will provide for (a) quasi-judicial immunity for the evaluator (in California that comes with appointment under Section 730 of the Evidence Code); (b) direction to the parents to participate in testing and interviews for themselves and their children; (c) direction regarding the allocation of costs; (d) direction regarding contact between attorneys and the evaluator, as well as the judge and the evaluator; (e) clarification of confidentiality, especially with the children; (f) direction regarding the gathering of collateral information; and (g) direction regarding the report and its dissemination. Finally, it is often helpful to families if the court includes in its order a statement about whether anyone can take the child to therapy during the evaluation. This prevents parents from trying to gain an edge and putting a therapist in the middle during the evaluation process. I have included a sample copy of a standard order from my local court in Appendix 1.

It is critical to have a copy of such an order signed by the judge prior to commencing with the evaluation. This prevents an attorney from later questioning the neutrality of the court appointment. It is also important for the evaluator to assure himself that both parents understand the order, especially the issues being evaluated, their duty to cooperate, and their need to encourage their children to be willing to participate, as well.

THE FIRST APPOINTMENT

Over the years I have found that the easiest way to begin an evaluation is to meet face to face with both parents for the start of the first session. Because I include psychological testing in nearly all evaluations that I do, the logistics of this first appointment are very easy. I meet with the parents together for

20 to 30 minutes. During that time I am able to answer their questions, allay their anxiety, provide more information about the direction of the evaluation, establish my neutrality, and focus on the primary issues of the evaluation. This is the time to ensure that the parents understand their court order. I encourage parents to ask me any questions about myself, my experience, and my biases. I talk openly with parents about my general bias that it is best for children when both parents share in the postdivorce parenting and that it is best for children when their parents can agree on a custody plan rather than remain in conflict with one another. I tell parents that I hope that the evaluation will help them find a solution to their conflicts over custody and that research shows that children can tolerate most any solution that settles the conflict better than the ongoing conflicts that some parents continue. I try to answer any questions parents may have about such issues when both of them are together as a way to explain the importance of their cooperation when the evaluation process is complete.

The first interview is also the time to talk with them about how to talk to their children about the evaluation, taking into account the ages of the children. For preschool children, I encourage parents to explain that I am someone who wants to meet them and see them with each parent so that I can help each be a better parent. For older children, if the evaluation is at the beginning of the divorce, I encourage parents to explain to their children that they are in disagreement about how they are going to share the job of parenting now that they are getting divorced and that I will be talking with them to understand their thoughts, fears, wishes, and feelings about their parents and their parents' divorce. If the evaluation is significantly postdivorce, I encourage parents to talk openly, but without emotion, about the realities of the conflict and to tell the children that I am there to help the parents settle the conflict. At all times, I tell parents to encourage their children to express any feelings they may want and that I am there to listen to them and help them understand and express feelings about the divorce—both good and bad feelings about both parents.

This appointment is also my best opportunity to see firsthand the nature of the interaction between the parents. During that time, I can see which parent acts more compliant, angry, controlled, feels more powerless, and so on, and begin to get an idea of the interaction that leads to this. I can begin the process of understanding the ways in which the couple's conflict is contributing to the custody dispute and the way that the parents can (or cannot) communicate about their child. This is very important information as I begin thinking about the kind of parenting plan that will be most useful for the parents and their children.

Because I use psychological tests with most custody evaluations, it is then quite natural to separate the parents. I have one parent take some psychological tests while I interview the other parent in another room. In the individual clinical interviews (usually two or three with each parent) there are several things to look for. My first question to parents is always, "Why are we here?" This gives each parent an opportunity to tell his or her story. Rarely, until the couple gets to a custody evaluation, has either parent been truly able to tell the story to someone who will listen. Attorneys are advocates for their clients and, although they often provide a quasi-counseling role when they listen to their clients, their primary task is to focus on the legal issues involved in the divorce. In the courtroom, there is little time and almost no opportunity for the parents to talk to the judge about their children or the marital problems. If the couple has been to mediation, they are so focused on solving the problems that there is little opportunity for talking about the history or the pain the parents have experienced. Sometimes this one question takes up the entire first interview as I get to hear the information that the parent needs to tell.

It is my belief that in an effective custody evaluation we will spend a considerable part of the interviewing time listening to the parents talking about their story. If we understand their pain, the sources of the conflict through their eyes, and the nature of their fears and beliefs about the other parent, it will assist us in the overall evaluation of the family. Through these interviews we can hope to get a snapshot of the family and the family dynamics that will enable us to see how we can best intervene and solve the custody issues. This is very important psychologically because if parents feel heard, they may be more likely to go along with the evaluator's recommendations even if they do not agree with them.

In addition to listening to the story of the parents, there is a great deal of other information that we want to focus on during the evaluation. We want to ask questions that allow us to understand each parent's views of his strengths and weaknesses as a parent, as well as each parent's perception of the other parent's strengths and weaknesses as a parent. We need to talk about discipline, structure, guidance, and the other factors that are often related to the question of the best interests of the child. We need to understand what each parent's childhood was like and the extent to which each parent's own childhood experiences is affecting the current custody dispute. We want to look for clues that parents are idealizing their own histories, as it is a sign that they might be idealizing their own parenting abilities. Obviously, we need to understand each parent's view of the child's functioning and needs and the child's need for a relationship with the other parent. Appendix 2 has a list of the kinds of questions that I typically ask parents in a custody evaluation.

Finally, as clinicians, evaluators focus on the affect of the client and the client's psychological functioning. We are looking to understand whether or not the parent can stay focused on the issues at hand or whether the parent rambles a great deal. Of significant importance is how much the parent can look at himself and try to understand his role in the nature of the problems. Most parents come to evaluations blaming each other and may have considerable difficulty seeing any way in which they contribute to the problems. It is very important for the evaluator to understand the extent of projection, externalization of blame, denial, and so forth that each parent brings to the evaluation. Although these psychological traits might not preclude a parent from having reasonable time or custody of their children, understanding them helps the evaluator develop the rationale for all of the recommendations at the end of the evaluation. All of these factors are the essential ingredients of the clinical interviews with the parents.

One final important area of focus is on why the parents can't agree. Evaluators look at the interactive dynamics between the parents, in addition to the individual dynamics of each parent. Issues of power and control, anger and hostility, couple conflicts, as well as the individual issues noted above of blaming, projection, and denial contribute in some way toward the inability of parents to reach a mutually acceptable solution for their children. In all evaluations we recognize that the parents cannot agree on parenting their children; therefore, it is critical to understand through these interviews why this breakdown has occurred. Frequently, parents don't even talk to one another, and an agreement can't be reached because of that. They may continue to harbor tremendous bitterness and resentment for the failed marriage, which also leads to an inability to cooperate for the benefit of their children. In understanding these problems, evaluators can use this information in the recommendations and parenting plan.

WHAT TO BELIEVE?

One of the important issues confronting evaluators is to determine what to believe. We do not get the truth by reading court affidavits; they simply measure the temperature of the case. Evaluators need to know that the task is to gather all of the family's truths and that there is never a single truth for the family. Quite frequently parents tell completely different stories. Each believes that he or she is telling the truth and is insistent about the events described. Certainly, in situations where abuse/neglect or substance abuse is an alleged issue, we hear quite conflicting sides. But even in evaluations in which parents are generally positive about each other's parenting, we hear different stories. In such families, we might hear the mother talk about the lack of involvement by the father in the child's day-to-day life—then hear the father talk about how he is the baseball coach and is home helping with the homework several evenings a week. Determining truth can be very difficult and yet is one of the most necessary tasks in the evaluation.

I have learned that truth is clearly in the eye of the beholder. Sometimes one or both parents are clearly lying or trying to deceive the evaluator. Sometimes both parents are telling the truth, but simply looking at different pictures. There is a continuum that ranges from parents who are lying or actively deceiving the evaluator to parents who simply perceive the same situation differently. Deceptive parents may lie about the amount of time that each parent helped with homework, whereas the misperceiving parents respond to their feelings. The mother remembers that the father was only limitedly involved in the child's life, having missed birthday parties and school events, and she remembers the number of evenings home alone with the children while the father was at work or with other activities. Her picture is one of having been left with the responsibilities of single parenting even when married, as she remembers the many times that the father failed to participate and expected her to do it all.

In contrast, his picture does not include those events, but focuses largely on the times that he helped with big homework projects, coached Little League, and helped with Cub Scout projects for his child. Because he wants to view himself as a capable and involved father, he is looking at the picture that tells that side of the story. In reality, neither one is lying, but rather they are both looking at a different piece of the whole picture through the eyes of their feelings and concerns. The task of the evaluator is to understand the extent to which a parent may be deceptive and lying, defensive, or narrowly focused on this small picture. The more disparate the perceptions of each parent, the more critical this determination is.

There are three techniques that I believe are extremely useful in understanding the truth of the family. The first technique is through confrontation and observation. By confronting the story that is presented by each of the parents, we can see whether or not the stories make sense or change. By observing the affect of the parents through this process, we can identify defensiveness and projection as opposed to openness and looking at one's self and one's real strengths and weaknesses. If, for example, every time we confront the father about the question of his minimal involvement, he blames the mother rather than answers the question, we can suspect that at the very least the father is defensive, evasive, and possibly lying. However, if the confrontation leads the father to acknowledge that he wished he had done more and was pleased to be involved in some activities and if the affect was warm as he talked about the activities with this child, we can assume that at least he is telling the truth. Similarly, when we ask the mother about activities the father did participate in and she continues to focus on "what a jerk he is" and how he was never around when she or the children needed him, we can assume that her anger at him is coloring her view of the whole picture. Thus, with confrontation and observation, we can begin to get some clues to the real picture and the extent to which each parent is distorting or minimizing the issues.

The second technique that I find quite useful in determining truth is for the evaluator to play the wise fool. Just as TV detective Columbo kept asking his suspects innocent questions that enabled him to finally get the truth, the skilled evaluator can also ask many innocent questions to try to understand the picture that the parent is trying to present. In a way, we lull parents into telling us things we need to hear, so that we can learn the larger picture. Over the years, I have found that parents will frequently tell us what we need even when it goes against their main story. By playing dumb, we can often illicit from parents the information necessary to get a truer picture of each parent's real involvement with their children and with the problems at hand.

A good way to draw parents into this is by repeating to parents what they have been telling us, continually clarifying and supporting their statements. When they talk of helping with the homework, coaching, putting their kids to bed, and other such things, listen attentively and supportively to this. Then, just when the parents think we completely understand and agree with them, use a form of confrontation to elicit specific examples of their parenting or to question them about something that the other parent or the children have been saying. For example, in a recent evaluation, a father was telling me how much his son wanted to come over more than he was allowed by the mother. I kept listening to him, trying to understand him more. Then, just when he thought I understood, I queried him about his son's statements that he was angry at his father for leaving his mother. I suggested that although his son did miss him, that did not mean that he wanted to visit more.

Rather, it may have meant that he missed the family unit. Through the confrontation, the father was able to see how he misinterpreted his son's statements to validate his own wish to see his son more often.

The third technique that I find most useful is to talk with the children. Certainly, children see and hear a tremendous amount from their parents, and through their eyes and ears we can see more of the truth, as well. In several recent evaluations, adult children told of a long history of physical and emotional abuse from their father that had been denied by him. Younger children will frequently talk about the feelings they have when a parent says derogatory things in front of them about the other parent, even when the parents swear that they never talk about the other parent in front of the children. Although I do not advocate acting like a detective with children or giving them "the third degree," by skillful questioning, evaluators can use the information from the child interviews to develop a better sense of the parents' truth. It is these interview techniques that enable a skilled evaluator to understand the truth and the whole picture, which is necessary in assessing a family of divorce.

It is important to point out that, no matter how hard we try, we may not be able to discern the truths in the family. Some parents are good at deception, some children are very reluctant to share significant information, and psychological tests do not always reveal whether either parent is more defensive or deceptive than the other. In such circumstances, it is important for the evaluator to explicitly state in the report that there are not enough clues to determine the truth and that the recommendations are based on the best interpretation of available information.

COLLATERAL INFORMATION

These techniques alone, although useful, are not sufficient. In order to understand the complete truth, the evaluator must also integrate information gathered from psychological tests (described later) and from various collateral sources who have experience in working with the family in order to completely understand the real truth. I try to avoid talking with family friends and relatives, many of whom either feel in the middle of the divorce and do not like to choose sides between the parents or are clearly interested in choosing sides and are just as caught up as the parents in the battle. Although I do not like to exclude anyone from giving me information, I do not call people who may have limited useful information to provide. Instead, I tell parents at the beginning of the evaluation that they can have family members or friends send me letters that I will gladly review, and follow up on, if necessary. In this way, clients have control in guaranteeing they can provide me with any information they want me to have, while I simultaneously reduce the number of phone calls that I need to make in an evaluation.

I find the most reliable collateral sources to be other professionals who have worked with the family such as teachers, school principals, physicians, therapists, attorneys, day-care personnel, and others who have a professional relationship with one or more family member. Mediators who are not obligated to maintain confidentiality are also good sources of information. From these other professionals, evaluators can get an objective view of the family struggle and the ways in which each parent participates in it. We might learn from teachers which parent has been active in parent-teacher meetings, or, if the parents are temporarily sharing the custody, we might hear that a child is consistently unprepared and/or late to school when she is with her father. We can learn from therapists which parent is more receptive to understanding the child's feelings, and we can hear from day-care personnel about the battles that they have personally witnessed at the drop-off/pickup site. In this way, the information we gather from the collateral sources becomes a useful adjunct to rounding out the overall information that we receive in the evaluation.

Through the years I have found that it works best to delay the gathering of collateral information until I have formulated my initial opinions and have sufficient questions to ask these other people. If we try to talk to them too soon, it is much more difficult to integrate their information with our questions, and, if we are not careful, their perceptions may preempt our formulation of the complex issues. It is very important that the end result of an evaluation be the opinion of the evaluator, and not the restating of the opinion of one or more of the collateral sources. Should the parents not be able to agree even after an evaluation, and a trial becomes necessary, an evaluator will need to show that her opinion was derived from all of the material, and not from collateral sources alone. By waiting until we have specific questions and have begun to formulate our own opinion, we can safeguard against this concern.

THE USE OF PSYCHOLOGICAL TESTS AND THEIR LIMITATIONS

There is a great deal of question about the use of psychological tests in custody evaluations. Certainly, many evaluators are not psychologists and do an effective job in their evaluations. On occasion, evaluators who are not psychologists may feel that very specific questions need to be answered by psychological testing and will refer to a psychologist, seeking answers to very specific questions which they think testing can answer. In practice, they will make a referral to a colleague who is used to doing psychological testing as part of a custody evaluation, and will integrate the findings from the testing into their custody evaluation report. Many psychologists, like myself, use psychological tests routinely in their work, although others use them only when there are specific questions that can be more easily addressed by psychological testing. In this section I focus on some of the advantages and disadvantages of using psychological tests as part of a custody evaluation, the kinds of tests that are often used, and their limitations. Along with this, I discuss the kinds of questions that can be addressed by the use of psychological testing and how to integrate the knowledge derived from the tests into a comprehensive evaluation report.

The easiest way to talk about psychological tests is to focus on their limitations. As of now, there is no psychological test known to me that adequately measures parental fitness. In a world in which people look for diagnostic tests to determine just about everything, it would be nice if there were a simple test that we could administer to both parents to help understand their abilities as parents. However, given the complex nature of relationships and parenting, as well as the complexity of the issues associated with custody and shared parenting, no such test is available. At best, we hope that the psychological tests can provide some insight into psychological dynamics and other issues that are peripherally associated with parenting or the custody dispute itself.

One of the very important issues associated with psychological testing is that most of the psychological tests used for purposes of custody evaluations were designed for a different purpose. One of the most widely used tests in custody evaluations, the Minnesota Multiphasic Personality Inventory (MMPI), was designed for hospital use in diagnosing severe psychiatric disturbances. The recently updated MMPI-2, although it has been normed over a broader population, has been described by many psychologists as significantly flawed outside the hospital population. Other psychological tests that are frequently used include those such as Depression Rating Scales, the Rorschach, and drawings, which are projective in nature and tend to yield clinical results that have nothing to do with parenting. The Rorschach can provide a good understanding of the adult's affect, organization skills, and reality testing, but, except for the most dysfunctional parent, it will not do much to answer questions about day-to-day parenting.

On the other hand, parenting inventories such as the Parenting Stress Index or the Parent-Child Relationship Inventory provide a better measure and comparison of each parent's understanding of his or her child. In addition, there are some projective techniques that can be used with children (described in more detail in the next chapter) that might also be more relevant to the nature of a custody evaluation.

Given this information, namely the strong limitations of the use of psychological testing in this context and the lack of an adequate test for truly measuring one's parenting ability, it is safe to ask, why do testing at all? I have found that developing a standard procedure for custody evaluations helps ensure that I do not miss something important and relevant in my evaluations. Because it is quite common to have to address issues of hostility, impulsivity, reality testing, defensiveness, sociopathic tendencies, and so on, the use of the same procedure for all custody evaluations allows me to do a more thorough and more valid job along the way. If I chose to do psychological testing only some of the time, I might miss something that would have shown up in the psychological testing of a particular parent. By giving the psychological testing early in the evaluation process and scoring the tests before the last interview with the parents, I have additional information that can be used in the last interview to help me in knowing what to look for.

The MMPI and similar computer-scored objective tests are useful for providing a rough assessment of personality dynamics, defensiveness, affect, ability to deal with hostility, and aggression, which is important in a complete understanding of the person's psychological functioning. The Rorschach, Thematic Apperception Test (TAT), projective drawings, and other more subjective tests, which have a variety of scoring systems depending on the training of the psychologist, are also useful in providing similar information into the psychological functioning of the parents. At times, intelligence testing may be useful if an evaluator is unsure about the parent's cognitive skill level, in case that might have a bearing on parenting ability. Finally, as indicated, a test such as the Personality Inventory for Children (PIC), Parenting Stress Index, or Parent-Child Relationship Inventory that can be filled out by the parents about the child or the parent's perceived relationship with the child may also provide useful information, not only about the child involved, but about the parent's feelings and perceptions, especially compared with one another. Appendix 5 contains a listing of the more commonly used tests and information about the use of each within the context of a custody evaluation.

Thus, with adults, evaluators have a wide variety of resources from which to understand the issues they present, their hidden agendas and real questions, and their understanding of the children and their needs. Through the use of individual interviews, we can determine a history and understand each parent's story. Through the use of conjoint interviews, we can observe the interaction between the parents and help gain some understanding about why they are unable to resolve these conflicts on their own. In all of the interviews we can learn a great deal from confrontation and observation and by playing innocent and eliciting more information from the parents, almost in a detectivelike manner. At times, when we are trying to determine the truth, to understand each parent's ability to understand and meet the children's needs, and to determine the appropriate parenting plan for the families in front of us, evaluators feel more like detectives than psychologists. By integrating the skills of the psychologist with the diligence of the detective, however, it is hoped that we can gather this sufficient information. With collateral contacts, we can get some additional information that we might not be able to observe, but which is useful in terms of the overall dynamics of the case. Finally, with the careful use of psychological testing, we can gain insight into some of the psychological dynamics of each individual and the role that these dynamics play in the overall assessment.

6

Conducting the Evaluation, Part II: Observations and Techniques With Children

The interviews with the children are a crucial part of understanding both the family dynamics and the relationship between the child and his parents. Many evaluators are used to conducting interviews with adults, yet have little or no experience in working with children. This is because a large percentage of mental health professionals never gain much experience in working with children during their training or professional careers. This chapter begins by focusing on the kinds of information evaluators need from interviews with the children and then examines the ways to get such information from children of various ages. Issues such as seeing children and parents together, siblings together, the role of children's preference, home visits, and other techniques will be discussed.

At the outset, we must recognize two important things. First, it is very easy for an evaluator to inadvertently add to the distress that a child feels. A major goal when working with children during a custody evaluation is to help ease the child's anxiety and assist the child in feeling more secure about his relationship with *both* of his parents. To help with this, I talk with children about their pain and my recognition that they do not like to choose between their parents. I encourage children to talk openly about their feelings about both parents, and I make it clear that I am there to listen to them and their feelings more than the thoughts and feelings of their parents.

Second, we must also recognize that children's language skills are not the same as those of adults. We must develop a good feel for the language of children when we do our evaluations. This is hard to come by without practice, but it is important to know that children often do not understand the things that we may ask, yet they may respond as if they understand. As such, I will ask children to repeat or to explain what I have said so that I can be more sure that they understand me and that I understand them. If we pay attention to children's words, and ask them questions that they understand, we are more likely to be clear about their feelings, fears, and wishes.

SIGNIFICANT ISSUES IN THE ASSESSMENT OF CHILDREN

In evaluating children, there are a few things to pay attention to even before they come to the office. First, we want to understand their thoughts and feelings and learn how the children comprehend their parents' behavior and the issues of the divorce. Many young children do not even know what a divorce is; all they know is that their parents fight all of the time and dad recently moved out. Often they are reluctant to share their feelings with a total stranger, and other times, they have been primed by one or both parents to tell the examiner everything. In the best of worlds, the children have been told that they are coming to the evaluation so that the evaluator can help the parents understand them and their feelings and can work with the parents to improve the relationships and reduce the fighting. If children know that we are *their* allies and our purpose is to understand the parents' divorce through the children's eyes, they can be more relaxed and reassured at the beginning of the evaluation.

Second, we must help the children understand the issue of confidentiality. Children usually do not know what confidentiality means, but they know they are sometimes scared to say things that will be told to their parents. Some children are afraid of having us talk to their parents about what they have said; other children do not care how much of what they say gets shared with their parents. I specifically tell children that I will be writing a report and it may include things that they have said, unless they tell me they do not want me to put something in the report. This allows me to understand the child's feelings about this early in the assessment process, because it will affect how I deal with the information I receive from the children. Children need to know that we can make an effort to protect their words (and will do so in the report), but they must also know that there will be times when we will need to discuss with a parent something that the child tells us during our interviews. By explaining all of this at the early stage of the interviews with the children, we can help the child feel safe, reduce the child's anxiety, and get a clearer understanding of the child's conceptualization of the issues, the child's feelings, and the child's true wishes regarding his future relationships with his parents.

The third important issue centers around finding a way to get the necessary information from the children without acting like an interrogator and adding to the children's anxiety, tension, and loyalty conflicts. On first meeting children, for example, we might reduce their anxiety by trying to understand who they are, just as we did with the parents. We can talk openly about such anxiety, empathizing with how they might be feeling. We can then talk with them about their friends, their hobbies and interests, their school, their likes and dislikes, and so forth as a way of building trust and interest in the evaluation process. We can use this information to then begin talking about their parents and their feelings about each parent. For example, finding that the girl we are evaluating loves music and that her father discourages her musical talent because he wants her to be an A student tells us something about the father-daughter bond. When we learn that she loves sports and that her father encourages and coaches her in a positive way, while also supporting her in school, it indicates something different about the father-daughter relationship.

Finally, most evaluators discourage asking children where they want to live because most children do not want their parents to divorce or they want to live with both of their parents. Asking such a question increases the loyalty conflicts that most children feel in the divorce. In fact, I tell children early on that I do not plan to ask that question because I assume they love both parents and want to spend some of their time with each parent. This gives me an opportunity to hear the child's response, which may include a statement about his preferences. I also like to talk with children about their likes and dislikes regarding each parent just as we did when talking about their friends. In this way, we can try and gather the necessary information without putting the child at risk for higher anxiety. We must be alert to the possibility that some children clearly have a preference about how they spend time with each of their parents and about how much they want to move back and forth between two homes. This is a tough balancing act that requires the evaluator to avoid directly asking children where they want to live, while listening to what children say about where they want to live.

DIRECTLY ASSESSING THE PARENT-CHILD BOND

A fundamental purpose for observing children is to understand the attachment and bond between a child and parents. In young children, we must see children and parents together, observing the way they relate with one another. Do they play together, smile and laugh with one another, or stay relatively distant and isolated from one another? Does the child seem pleased when the parent enters the playroom with the child, or does the child seem uninterested? When the parent is in the room, it is important to listen to the words of the parent. Parents may want to talk about things that are very inappropriate to talk about in front of the child because they have a felt need to provide more information to the evaluator. This helps to understand the parent's ability to utilize adequate boundaries and keep the child freer from anxiety. In addition, when the parent does this, we can try to understand how the child feels about it, responds to it, and interacts with the parent about it. We may see children get into arguments with their parents about things that parents say, which provides valuable information about the interaction between parent and child.

During a recent evaluation, a father was telling me that the son's mother always said bad things about him in front of his son. The boy got into an argument with his father about this, defending his mother. In this way, I could understand and directly see the child's psychological splitting of his parents into good and bad. In another assessment, a girl who was afraid to see her father and was critical, controlling, and omnipotent in the interview with her father simultaneously drew a picture with rainbows and gave it to him, with the signature *love* attached. Thus, we could directly see the ambivalence that the girl felt toward him and her fear that giving up her control would provoke anxiety for her. Obviously, therefore, such direct observation is useful for understanding not only the individual functioning of both the parent and child, but their interaction with each other, as well.

We can provide structured and unstructured tasks for parent and child together. Encouraging a father and his daughter to draw a picture together, for example, will help show how they can work together to complete a task. Are they cooperative, are they playful, do they use each other's assistance, or do they become quite competitive with one another? As we observe these behaviors, we have a clue to the bond and the nature of the attachment and whether or not it is relatively free of stress. Unstructured play, in which the child initiates an activity of her choosing, is also quite useful because it gives an opportunity to see how responsive the parent is to the child in *her* space. Many parents can interact quite well with a child when the parent chooses the activity, but they may feel awkward and insecure when the child chooses the activity. Through this observation, we can see how well the parent can go to the level of the child, and at the very least, attempt to interact in a neutral or positive way with the child and her activity. As we observe all of this, we are also observing whether the parent and child are having fun, whether they are relaxed, or whether the time is as tension filled as the relationship between the parents.

I may not include conjoint sessions between children over age 10 and their parents. Certainly, for younger children who are less verbal, the observational interaction is important in understanding the nature of the relationship and the bond between each parent and the child. With older children, we can talk about the relationship and the child's perception of the parental attachment. Through such discussions, we hear of the child's wishes, feelings, and fears. Children usually feel most free to express themselves verbally without the parents present. In such a nonthreatening setting, we can provide a therapeutically safe environment for the child to express herself, though we must let the child know about the limits of our confidentiality during the evaluation (as described previously). Regardless of the issue of confidentiality, however, most children are pleased to have an opportunity to talk individually with the evaluator about their life, their relationships, their desires, and their feelings, separate from their parents.

It is sometimes necessary to see an older child and her parents together. Often this is when there is a very clear and obvious conflict between the child and her parents. In such a situation, the observations of child and parent together will assist in determining how far we can push either the parent or child to understand each other's position. This is especially true for adolescents who are resistant, rebellious, and struggling with issues of autonomy and independence. By directly observing the interaction between the child and parent we can better understand the hostility, the empathy, the willingness to compromise, or the resistance of both parent and adolescent, and thus understand their relationship more completely. Often an adolescent wants less time with one parent than that parent wants with him. If we are going to support his desire to have only limited contact with one of his parents, it is necessary to see them together and watch the interaction and the ways in which the adolescent and parents function as we discuss these issues.

Another reason for seeing a parent and older child together might be because of the wish of the parent. Sometimes a parent wishes to talk to her son with the assistance of the evaluator to better understand for herself some of the son's thinking. Sometimes during the course of an evaluation a child will reveal some information in a way that is markedly different from the story the parent told. Seeing the two of them together may assist the evaluator in better understanding the truth of the experience. Any time we see an older child and her parents together, however, it is important to minimize the anxiety that the child feels as we try to see how the parent can understand the child from the child's perspective. Just as a conjoint interview between parents helps to better understand their conflict and the nature of it, the conjoint interview between a child and parent in a conflicting situation will assist in evaluating and understanding the source of that conflict, as well.

SIBLINGS TOGETHER, OR NOT?

Evaluators often face the question of whether to see siblings together or separately. Some parents have a preference about how this should be done, as do some evaluators. I have found there are no rules for determining what makes the most sense except to keep an open mind about the process. I find that advantages of seeing siblings together can include a reduction of anxiety for the children, an opportunity to learn more about the family and the family dynamics, and an opportunity to observe the nature of the relationship between the siblings. With younger children, observing their play together can be quite beneficial. Two children, especially opposite-sex children, sometimes display a mirroring of the parent conflict. Observing siblings' affect and level of cooperation during play and hearing their words provides a tremendous amount of information about the family dynamics when seen together.

In contrast, however, there are some risks assumed if siblings are seen only together and not individually. If one child speaks for the sibling group, we have a difficult time knowing whether or not that child's opinion is shared by others or is being imposed on the other siblings. In a family it is typical that one child will be stronger than another. If there are some family secrets or significant problems that this powerful child does not wish to have divulged, it is often difficult for another child to speak in front of the more powerful sibling. Siblings run the risk of less confidentiality when seen with a sibling, as the child may fear, accurately or inaccurately, that a sibling will tell the parents what was said. Thus, there could be a tendency for greater silence, with a strong reluctance to talk about the parents and the structures within the home. Some children demand to be seen individually; other children refuse to be seen unless with a sibling. Because it is the goal to understand the family dynamics and interactions as much as possible, it is generally recommended that children be seen both individually and conjointly, especially in more complicated evaluations.

CHILDREN AND THEIR LANGUAGE

For people with only limited experience with children, it is important to point out that one of the major differences in interviewing children is to use language the children can understand. As evaluators seek to elicit information from children and to understand the relationships with their parents, it is critical that questions and statements be at an age-appropriate level. As I noted in the chapter on developmental issues, language skills improve significantly between ages 3 and 6, with much further language growth occurring from the ages of 6 to 12. During the preschool and early grade school years, children's ability to understand abstract reasoning and time is more limited, and discussions with these children need to be at a more concrete and very specific level. Similarly, children during that age range have a greater difficulty verbalizing feelings or talking about things that they like and do not like about each of their parents. We cannot talk about custody with children in general because it is a legal concept they generally do not understand. However, children do understand that they spend some of their time with mom and some of their time with dad, and they can begin to think about how they enjoy their time with each of their parents.

I find that one way to begin talking with children and to understand their language skills is to ask them what divorce is. Once we have met, the child is at ease in the interview situation, and we have explained that we are there to help their mom and dad, questioning their understanding of divorce helps to understand both the language skills of the child and the extent of the child's awareness of the evaluation process itself.

Some children, as if primed by their parents, come in and start talking about the divorce and custody in words that are clearly not child oriented. I have had 5-year-old children come into my office and say, "I want to have custody with my mommy." It was clear that they had no idea what they were talking about. In such situations it is quite likely that someone has suggested to the child that he tell the evaluator that. When a child uses adult words, especially when not prompted by the evaluator and when the words are totally out of context at the given point in the evaluation, it is quite likely that the child's statements were rehearsed by one or both parents. On the other hand, if we are talking about divorce with the child and the child spontaneously states that he feels scared at daddy's because he does not let him sleep with a night-light, we can assume that the emotion is more accurate to what the child is truly experiencing.

Talking in the child's language is even more critical when attempting to understand issues of possible abuse, drug and alcohol abuse, and mental illness from the child's perspective. For example, in issues of possible sexual abuse, the evaluator should listen for child words, not adult words, from the child when exploring the child's experiences. Children are highly suggestible, so it is important to use nonleading questions to elicit information. As with the adult, if the evaluator acts somewhat perplexed and conveys he does not understand, a child is usually willing to provide additional information that helps the evaluator understand what the child is trying to explain. By being sensitive to the child's language, as well as anxiety and emotions during the discussion, an evaluator can do a more thorough job of understanding the child and gathering the necessary information.

GATHERING INFORMATION ABOUT THE CHILD'S EXPERIENCES

It is important to elicit information about the child's likes and dislikes about each parent. It is also important to assess whether or not the child can talk about both good and bad traits for each parent. If a child is afraid to talk about any of these traits or can talk only about good traits for one parent, there may be a sense of anxiety associated with the evaluation process, the divorce, or the quality of the relationship with one of the parents. If, in particular, a child can focus on only the good traits of one parent and the bad traits of the other parent, it is quite likely that a certain degree of psychological splitting is in operation, which will need further examination. Just as with adults from whom we are trying to elicit the truth, we can use a combination of surprised inquisitiveness and confrontation to elicit more complete information about each parent when we are interviewing children.

When we have two or more sessions with a child and when we see siblings in various combinations (individually and conjointly), we can compare and contrast their words and get a truer understanding of the child's real feelings. In addition, by using a combination of verbal and play techniques, we can get a broader sense of the child's view of his relationships and, in particular, his likes and dislikes about each parent.

Another issue that is important to understand through the eyes of the child is the issue of limits and discipline within each household and with each parent. We can monitor some of this through dollhouse play. We can set up structured play situations for even very young children. For example, with generally nonverbal children, we might structure dollhouse play in which a child is angry and elicit from the child the parent's response. Over the course of several interviews, we might see how the child portrays the father's response and the mother's response to this situation. We can talk with the child about whether or not her parents spank her, send her to her room, yell at or berate her, and so forth, again using play or appreciating the child's language skills in gaining this understanding.

With somewhat older children we can talk about not only what makes the child angry, but what her parents do when she gets angry. With multiple siblings, we can understand what each parent does when the siblings argue with one another and see if there is a difference in the amount of fighting between siblings in each household. We hope we will learn that the parents try to talk with the children, negotiate, and work out problems between them, rather than use corporal punishment or verbal abuse. The more we utilize both play and verbal techniques to understand the limits and discipline in each household, the more we can understand the child's perception of her relationship with each parent.

A similar issue is one of structure and routine in each household. Often some parents are fairly rigid in their routine and structure, with a set schedule of activities. Mealtimes and bedtimes are generally consistent, and a child tends to gain a sense of security and confidence as her family life is relatively structured. In contrast, some families have a different routine nearly every day, and it appears that there is almost no structure to their lives. We can look for differences in the routines of each parent and try to understand the extent to which they are similar to one another and the extent to which they are a potential problem for the child.

Certainly, if a young child spends a portion of her time in each household and the routines are quite disparate, she may have more difficulty. This may lead evaluators in their recommendations to encourage the parents to develop similar routines and structures. As a child gets older, this may be less problematic, as long as she is able to do her schoolwork and get to school and activities on time from both houses. In general, as children get older and become involved in a variety of activities, their daily routine becomes a bit less structured anyway. However, it is important to understand whether or not each parent is structuring regular mealtimes, bedtimes, and schoolwork times, probably the three most important routines for school-age and adolescent children.

By understanding all of these issues, evaluators can get a more complete picture of the relationship between the child and each of her parents. As we understand the child's behavior in each home, the child's likes and dislikes about each parent, the nature of each parent's limits and discipline, as well as the structure in each home, we gain a fairly good idea about the child's experiences and the nature to which she feels secure and insecure with each of her parents. If the parents are already separated and each parent is living separately, this understanding will also provide a good opportunity for recognizing the ability of each parent to adequately meet the child's needs independent of each other. As evaluators, we hope that through the play and interviews with each child we can develop a broader perspective of the child's relationship with each parent and use this to complement the understanding derived from the interviews and testing with each parent.

In addition to these critical areas, there are several other issues to examine. It is important to understand how children express their feelings to their parents. Again, this is somewhat easier when assessing older children who express themselves verbally. With younger children it is difficult to get this sense through their play, and evaluators will probably need to rely on the descriptions of the parents for this information. With older children, however, we can often determine through direct and indirect observations and questions how children express themselves to their parents. Many children are afraid to tell their parents how they feel about things. This may be especially true for adolescents. Other children find a time and place to talk about most everything with each of their parents. In all families, but even more so with families in divorce, individual children often express their feelings differently to each of their parents. By understanding these issues of emotional closeness and security, evaluators can relate them to recommendations of custody and parenting.

Another important issue to understand is the extent to which the child feels caught in the middle of a loyalty conflict between her parents. In my playroom, I have two dollhouses. This provides a wonderful opportunity for observing children's interaction as it relates to living in two households. In their play, children can relate their experiences and anxiety about the conflicts between their parents. I have seen children characterize dollhouse play in an extremely anxious way. I have seen children portray the transition between two homes in my office, looking quite anxious in their play. In contrast, a young child who does not feel such loyalty conflicts might portray play in which she spends some time in one dollhouse being nurtured by one parent and then moves to the other dollhouse being nurtured by the other parent. Affect in that regard looks more positive and suggests that there is less of a loyalty conflict between the parents.

With older children, I often ask direct questions about loyalty issues as we start talking about their experiences. It is easy to ask children how they feel when one parent talks badly about the other, and sometimes we can directly ask whether or not children are worried about upsetting one parent while pleasing the other. Children who experience tremendous loyalty conflicts will often feel anxious when talking about their efforts at pleasing one of their parents, usually because of the insecurity they feel about displeasing the other parent. It is often difficult to ascribe a sense of blame to this because the conflicted child does not wish to hurt or say anything bad about either parent. Instead, the best we might understand is the existence of the conflicts within the child, related to his inability to express any dislikes about either parent.

The final area to understand about the child and her life is her various support systems. These support systems are useful in helping her deal with her anxiety and conflicts and in allowing her to have a normal everyday life. A child's support systems include her friends, teachers, relatives, family friends, activities, and often a therapist. Some children feel very isolated, afraid to talk with anyone about their experiences and their fears. At the other extreme, some children seem to talk to everyone and are very needy, struggling with the emotions they experience. For both types of children, it is likely that their support systems are failing them and that the anxiety they are experiencing through their parents is overwhelming to them. It is hoped that a child can have an opportunity to maintain the same support systems following separation and divorce that they experienced before the separation, as this allows the child to ease into a more simplified postdivorce adjustment. Such a transition is made more difficult when there is a significant disruption for the child in terms of her activities, peers, and so forth. Evaluating this issue is critical in understanding not only the extent of the distress that the child experiences, but also how she deals with the distress and the extent to which the parents understand this as a problem for the child and work to solve it.

Some parents are so locked in their own issues, especially in the midst of the custody battle, that they forget about the child's support systems and how beneficial they can be. This is critical to understand, as a result of the child's experiences and needs and also as it relates to the parents' ability to meet those needs. For example, I recently completed an evaluation in which a mother who was feeling very lonely because her child spent the majority of her time with the father was seeking full custody, even though it would mean a significant change in the support systems for the child. This mother even had a difficult time encouraging the child's participation in Scouts because the mother felt lonely when the child was away from her. In evaluating the child, it became clear that his support systems, in particular peers and Scouts, were very important to him. Although the child wished to have more time with his mother, it was not that critical for him in comparison to some of these support systems. In formulating the appropriate parenting plan for this child, it was important to find a way to maintain the child's support systems while increasing the amount of time spent with his mother. Ignoring the support systems could have easily resulted in missing an important element in this child's life.

USING PLAY AND OTHER TECHNIQUES IN UNDERSTANDING CHILDREN

In addition to talking with children, we often use the child's symbolic play as a means of understanding issues related to the parents and the parents' divorce. Evaluators look for all opportunities to understand the child's conception of what the divorce is all about and the relationships with each parent. In attempting to gather this information, we can observe dollhouse play and see whether or not there is a difference between the child's affect or characterization of the mother or father doll. Sometimes a child has the father doll leave the house and not return, while the mother doll is very nurturing. On the other hand, I have also seen a child have the father doll leave the house and then the mother doll becomes very angry and hostile toward the child. These and other play experiences give some clues as to the quality of the relationship between a child and parent. I find the use of two dollhouses often stimulates play that is connected with the sharing of two households for the child.

Nonsymbolic play, such as with cars, sand trays, Legos, and other such toys, provide an opportunity to help the child relax while talking about a variety of issues in the child's life. It is quite rare that a child will simply come into my office and talk about the issues in his life without engaging in an activity at the same time. These activities can be symbolic, such as with the dollhouse play, or nonsymbolic, such as with Legos, but in each instance they allow the child to feel more comfortable with the evaluator and express himself in some way.

In addition, evaluators can often engage in other activities with children that help to understand some of their experiences. Most children like to draw, and we can ask children to draw a family doing something, which may represent their family experiences. This provides an understanding not only of the child's place within the family, but also of the way that he perceives the relationship between each of his parents. Similarly, other projective techniques, such as the TAT, Children's Apperception Test (CAT), or Family Apperception Test (FAT), allow the child to portray relationships in a nonthreatening way. Various games, including the "Talking, Feeling, and Doing Game," "The Ungame," and so forth also allow a child to express feelings in a somewhat less threatening way. It is beyond the scope of this work to fully discuss the many ways in which tests, games, and family drawings can be used projectively with children, but they can be quite useful in understanding a child's perception of himself within the family. A more comprehensive listing of such tools is included in Appendix 5.

HOME VISITS

Some evaluators find great benefit in doing home visits. I find them quite helpful when seeing children under age 5, but less so as they get older. Although home visits are logistically difficult, they allow an opportunity to observe children in their natural environment. This may significantly reduce the anxiety that the child might experience as a result of the evaluation itself. In the child's own home, we can observe firsthand the place a parent has provided for the child and get a qualitative feel for the differences between the parents in this regard. During an interview with a child, we might ask questions about their bedroom and the family sleeping arrangements, which is quite important in understanding the child's sense of space and privacy within the home. However, asking about it and seeing it firsthand are two different things. Home visits allow us to view the child interacting with his own toys, in his own room, and often in a more natural environment with his own siblings. Because home visits are always scheduled ahead of time, it is extremely rare to find any real level of disorganization or serious problems when conducting a home visit, though on occasion, a home visit will provide information that shows a serious problem in the ability of one parent to make space for the child at his home. However, this is usually discussed during the interviews with the adults, and they can usually provide sufficient information to address this issue without actually seeing the home environment.

Evaluators who routinely use home visits indicate that they provide a natural understanding of the children in their home environment and may ease the anxiety for the child through the evaluation process. Evaluators who use home visits on a more limited basis tend to look for specific reasons why a home visit will be beneficial in a given evaluation and then try to gather as much information as possible related to that specific question. It is important for evaluators to know that a home visit can be a technique for discovering additional information that can be useful in formulating the appropriate parenting plan for children.

In doing the home visits, it is useful to spend time with the child touring the house, often with other family members, and also to spend time alone in the child's room. The time in the child's room is a good opportunity to talk with the child about his relationships with his parents. We can use the time to talk about the routines in the home and learn more about the child's friends and activities from that home. It is also useful to talk about the other parent so that the child feels safe; he does not have to worry about this parent listening in to what he has to say. Ultimately, when we do a home visit, we do our best to keep the child feeling safe and to find out how the child views his relationships and his time in that home.

THE PREFERENCE OF THE CHILD

Many evaluators dispute whether or not children should be included in the decision-making process for where they should live. As I previously mentioned, we typically do not ask children with whom they would like to live because it raises their anxiety and continues to put them in the middle of the parental dispute. Nonetheless, even relatively young children (ages 7, 8, and 9), spontaneously mention a preference about where they want to live and how they would like to spend their time with their parents. Adolescents, in particular, have a very strong preference on this issue.

Regarding this issue, the task is twofold. First, we need to understand the child's rationale for this request. Sometimes, the request is being made at the suggestion of one parent or the other. In this case, it may not relate to the child's preference at all, but to the child's feeling stuck in expressing her mother's or father's wishes. Thus, we need to understand whether it is truly the *child's* preference or the child's words mirroring the preference of one of her parents. Clues to this can be discerned by listening to the timing of the child's request, the exact words from the child, and the way in which it matches the parents' words regarding this subject. Obviously, the closer the words, and/or the quicker the child states her preference without any prompting by the evaluator, the more suspect is the preference.

The second task, however, is even more complicated. If we discover the child is truly expressing her own preference, we need to understand all the issues that are associated with the child making such a preferential statement. We need to understand the nature of the conflict between the child and the parent with whom she does not wish to live (if there is one) and the way the child's preference may fit into developmental issues noted in Chapter 4. If an adolescent expresses a strong wish to be primarily in one parent's home and for a relationship with the other parent that is on her terms in relation to school, job, and peer activities, we are likely to give a tremendous amount of weight to this child's preference. This would be expected developmentally given all of the issues with which adolescents must deal. On the other hand, an 8-year-old child's expressed desire to move into her father's home and away from her mother and siblings may reflect a desire for preferential treatment from her father, conflicts with siblings, or a need for privacy that needs to be understood more completely. Regardless of the age of the child, we need to fully understand the child's desires and the ways in which they relate to her conflicts, the parents' conflicts, and/or her normal developmental issues. We must give more weight to the wishes of an older child, but all children need to have their feelings and wishes heard and understood.

I believe that although it is best for an evaluator not to ask the child her preference, when a child has stated her preference and it does not appear to be a mimic of a parent, it must be given weight in defining the parenting plan. If we do not do so, we risk alienating the child and leaving the child to feel as if adults do not listen to her. Although we may have very valid reasons for not recommending the parenting plan requested by the child, we must give the child an opportunity to feel heard and understood. In some cases it may be necessary to explain directly to that child why we are recommending something different than the child requested. In many jurisdictions, the adolescent's wishes are often granted, unless there is a significantly overriding factor that might interfere. On the other hand, young children who express their preferences are all too often ignored, which I believe could be a mistake.

Finally, there is one other issue in which a child's preference is very important, even for younger children. This is in the relocation of parents and the possible move to another community. A move can have such a profound impact on children that we need to ask children to think about this impact on them, especially if they are of at least school age. In relocation evaluations the preference of the child might be given added weight because of the child's specific wishes and the rationale behind these wishes. I have found that when confronted with this issue, many 8-, 9-, and 10-year-olds can provide a great deal of insight about what they expect this to feel like. Most of these children have very strong preferences about whether or not they wish to move with one of their parents and change the relationship with the other to become more of a visiting one. Although this subject will be discussed in greater detail in Chapter 8, it is important at this point to emphasize that children's preferences in relocation issues provide crucial knowledge for the evaluator. Thus, although most evaluators do not like to ask children where they want to live, we must listen carefully when children do express preferences.

CAUTIONS IN INTERVIEWING CHILDREN

I have discussed the need to shield children from too much interrogation during the evaluation process. In spite of this, I do advocate a certain confrontation of children, especially when trying to understand the complex issues connected to the child's feelings, fears, wishes, and needs. I try to keep such confrontation relatively mild, but I always ask for clarification from them, rarely taking at face value what they initially tell me. Children generally feel a certain degree of stress when they come into the evaluation. I suggest that we balance the amount we push them versus the amount we hold back. If we push too hard, we run the risk of adding to the child's alienation and anxiety related to the divorce. If we do not push hard enough, we run the risk of not getting enough information about the child's real feelings and not having enough information to fully understand all of the complex issues through the child's eyes. Again, because the task of the evaluation is to understand the child's needs vis-à-vis the issues of the parents' divorce, we should push hard enough to complete the task, while simultaneously minimizing the risk of increasing the child's emotional distress. This is a tough balance, one that gets easier as we gain experience and learn from our mistakes.

By the time the evaluator has completed the interviews with the children and parents, reviewed the written materials supplied by the parents and/or their attorneys, and spoken with the collateral sources, it is time to prepare the report. The next chapter addresses the process in which the evaluator takes all of the information, synthesizes it, and integrates it into a comprehensive report that will educate the parents and help the attorneys and the courts reach a mutually acceptable solution to the conflict.

7

Sharing the Results of the Evaluation: The Evaluation Report

In many ways the evaluation report is the culmination of all of the evaluator's psychological and detective work. In a sense, knowing how to organize reports helps in knowing how to organize the entire evaluation process. Formulating a plan for doing reports before seeing clients assists in guaranteeing that the evaluation report accurately flows from the evaluation process itself. Although there are many different ways to write the evaluation report, certain principles should be followed and certain information must be included so that the report is useful for the family, the attorneys, and the court.

The evaluation report is used by attorneys and court to understand the family dynamics and to help determine the ultimate custody and visitation plan for the family. The report is the vehicle through which the evaluator educates the judge and attorneys about the family. It becomes a document of the court. Judges require that the report (a) focus on the issues and problems of the family; (b) be credible, well reasoned, clear, and thoughtful; (c) be fair, balanced, and neutral, avoiding advocacy of one parent and accentuating positives when possible; (d) avoid jargon and diagnosis, yet remain behaviorally focused; and (e) contain recommendations that are child focused and that clearly flow from the material in the report.

In this chapter I describe the necessary information and discuss many of the issues surrounding the writing of recommendations and their specificity. For purposes of clarity, I give examples of various sections of a typical report. These examples are from many different reports and highlight the specific concept I am describing. Finally, two complete sample reports are included in Appendix 4.

INFORMATION THAT MUST BE IN EVERY REPORT

Background Information

The report should describe the reasons for the referral. It is helpful if background information is provided to enable the reader to understand the family's difficulties and the evaluation questions. Obviously, if the questions and problems of the family are complicated, this initial section of the evaluation needs to be more comprehensive. Rather than simply indicating that the evaluation is to assess custody and visitation planning, the background information should contain a reasonable description of the problems between the parents, the difficulties they have in resolving differences, and some statement of how each parent believes that the custody and visitation issue needs to be settled. Once that is outlined, the specific reasons for the evaluation are more clear and can then be delineated.

For example, in a recent evaluation I completed, the father felt that the mother was attempting to alienate the children against him and to disrupt, both covertly and overtly, the father's visitation with the children. This was the primary motivation for the father to seek custody of the children. In contrast, the mother felt that the father was extremely hostile and degrading to both her and the children and was not at all sensitive to the younger child's insecurity about the transfer of his care to his father. In addition, each parent described the other as distorting the truth and lying, and each felt that the other was doing a poor job of taking care of the children when in the other's care. They could not speak to one another without arguing and becoming totally enraged. They rarely could allow a transfer to take place without some type of outside assistance. This was the backdrop for the evaluation, which had several questions around parental competency, distortions of reality, psychological diagnosis, and possible parental alienation. By being specific about the reasons for the evaluation at the beginning, the evaluator can then write a comprehensive report that answers those questions in detail, leading to the overall recommendations of the evaluator.

Example 1

According to information available to me, this couple has had considerable conflict for several years, both during the marriage and postseparation. They present very different stories about the experiences that they have had during these times. Ms. Smith portrays Mr. Smith as an uninvolved father who is very threatening, primarily to her, but also to others in the community. She states that the children have witnessed his violent behavior and outbursts, that they are afraid of him, and that they wish to have only limited contact with him. She indicates that Erica, in particular, is fed up with her father and wants nothing to do with him except for occasionally talking to him at the house or on the phone. She expressed many concerns (see below), all of which center around her perception of Mr. Smith's irresponsibility and violent tendencies. She says she would like nothing more than for the children to have a good relationship with their father but feels that this has to come from him as he learns to become more responsible and appropriate in his time with the children.

In contrast, Mr. Smith portrays himself as a devoted and involved father who has been actively involved in the children's lives. Although he acknowledges a tendency to be a hothead in the past, he says that over the past year he has settled down a great deal and is currently much less explosive than he used to be. In addition, he blames Ms. Smith for much of his explosiveness in the past, accusing her of denying visitation, alienating the children and neighbors against him, and overreacting. Even during the evaluation, he cited several examples in which he perceived that Ms. Smith was denying his visitation and lying about their behavior. He also believes that Ms. Smith sets the children up to be afraid of him and thus succeeds in alienating the children against him.

Over the past year or more, there have been numerous incidents in which the police have had to be called. On one occasion, when Mr. Smith did not know where Ms. Smith or the children were, Mr. Smith got very angry and went to Ms. Smith's attorney, enraged. He reportedly demanded to talk to Ms. Smith's attorney and created a sufficient scene at the attorney's office that the secretaries felt compelled to call the police. By the time the police arrived, Mr. Smith had already left. The attorney withdrew representation of Ms. Smith the following day, and Ms. Smith believed that it was a direct result of this incident. Both Mr.

Smith and Ms. Smith gave several examples of other incidents in which the police were called, either because, as Ms. Smith saw it, Mr. Smith was violent and overreactive and threatening, whereas Mr. Smith engaged the police when he felt Ms. Smith was withholding and denying his visitation. Apparently, the police in ________ are fed up with the Smiths. (I attempted to contact Detective Albert of the _______ Police several times, but we were unable to connect with one another.)

Even during the evaluation process, when people are often at their best, there have been numerous battles between Mr. and Ms. Smith. On several occasions, Mr. Smith has accused Ms. Smith of withholding the visitation, whereas Ms. Smith continues with her belief that Mr. Smith upsets the children, causing them to refuse to go with their father several times. Just as Ms. Smith denied that she was doing anything to alienate the children from their father, Mr. Smith denied that he has done anything to cause the children harm or to wish that they did not have to visit him. Erica is refusing to visit with her father, and the boys are often ambivalent about whether to go with him. Rarely will one of the boys go without the other. The Smiths have not discovered a mechanism to provide for secure and less troublesome exchanges.

Since I've been involved, Mr. Smith had a 6-day vacation with the boys (Erica refused to go with him), following a court hearing on May 14. After his vacation, Ms. Smith wanted to take the children for a vacation, stating that she had originally planned a vacation with the children during the time that Mr. Smith was awarded his vacation and that she had to make a change in her plans. However, Mr. Smith was upset that he would lose his weekend visitation with the children, indicating that she had all summer to take her vacation. He went to court to block her vacation. This caused tremendous stress between them.

Similarly, because of numerous complaints at drop-off and pickup, they had arranged to exchange the children at ________restaurant, but even this did not reduce the tension at the exchange. On several occasions, Jim continued to cry and cling to his mother, and Mr. Smith would pull Jim away from her. Erica was always with them, even though she's never going to go with her father, and Billy gets anxious and confused as he witnesses this battle between his parents over Jim.

Similar difficulties have existed whether the transfer took place at a neighbor's or with the police. We discussed the assistance of Safe Exchange, but they never worked it out. In essence, the tension continues to be quite high. This evaluation was requested in order to understand all the dynamics involved in this matter and to assist the family, attorneys, and the court in determining the parenting arrangements that are in the children's best interests.

Although this example is quite lengthy, it reflects the kinds of information that need to be in the background section of the evaluation report.

Procedure

After completing this initial background part of the report, it is necessary to describe the evaluation procedure. In the procedure section evaluators describe all interviews, whether conjoint or individual, in office or in the home, giving the dates that people were seen. Some evaluators also include the total time of each interview. Any written material, audiotapes, or videotapes brought in by clients (or sent by their attorneys) for the evaluator to review should be noted as well. It is very important to detail the collateral contacts who were called, explaining their role with the family (e.g., teacher or baby-sitter). Any psychological tests administered should be named. Sometimes evaluator teams work together, and if different people share in the process of the evaluation, it is important to describe who did what part of the evaluation. This is especially true if a nonpsychologist evaluator has a psychologist provide psychological testing to assist in the evaluation process. Similarly, if one evaluator sees the adults and another evaluator interviews the children, this information should be described as well. In other words, it must be clear from the written report what the evaluation procedure was and who participated in the completion of the evaluation.

Example 2

This evaluation consisted of the following:

Conjoint interview, Mr. and Ms. Smith, __/__/__.

Individual interviews, Ms. Smith, __/__, __/__, __/__/__.

Individual interviews, Mr. Smith, __/__, __/__, __/__/__.

Conjoint interview, Smith children, __/__/__.

Individual interviews, Billy Smith, __/__, __/__, __/__/__.

Individual interviews, Erica Smith, __/__, __/__, __/__/__.

Conjoint interview, Billy, Jim, Mr. Smith, and Ms. Smith, __/__/__.

Conjoint interview, Billy, Jim, Mr. Smith, and Susie (Mr. Smith's friend), __/__/__.

Review of much written material, audiotapes, and videotapes provided to me by Mr. and Ms. Smith.

Many phone calls with Mr. and Ms. Smith. Additional phone calls with: (give names/titles)

- mediator
- attorneys
- psychologists
- pediatricians
- police (attempted)
- family friend

> In addition to the above, I administered the following psychological tests to each parent:

- Bender Gestalt
- Projective drawings
- Rorschach
- MMPI

Such a complete description of the evaluation procedure is necessary for the attorneys and the judge to know that a complete, credible evaluation was done.

THE PARENTS

Once the background information is completed and the evaluation procedure is outlined, the evaluator should include a description of the people seen. It is important to devote a section of the report to the mother, another section to the father, and a third section to the children. Each parent should be described individually, usually in a narrative style that gives a complete sense of each parent's story of the problems. I find that it is best to break these sections down into five parts.

A. It is important to provide some idea of the parent's affect, how she related, how defensive or open she was, how much she blamed the other parent, and how focused she was. In this way, the evaluator is reporting some beginning sense of the way in which the parent was perceived.

Example 3

> Ms. Smith presented as an angry, somewhat rambling woman who related a bit distantly from me. As she talked, she focused extensively on her perception of Mr. Smith as a hostile and violent man, who had

emotionally abandoned herself and the children for many years. Although she acknowledged that he was never physically abusive to either her or the children, she still indicated that she was quite frightened of Mr. Smith and believes her children are, as well. This is because of the tremendous amount of emotional abuse that she feels they have all suffered, as well as her perception of the threats that he has made against herself, her family, her daughter's horse, neighbors, and so forth. As she talked about all of this, affect ranged from tears to anger and did not change significantly throughout the entire evaluation process. For the most part, she had difficulty focusing on herself and any role that she might play in any of the problems, projecting all of the blame onto Mr. Smith.

B. It is important to elaborate on the parent's concerns regarding the other parent and the issues for the evaluation. This is usually an elaboration of the issues outlined more briefly in the background section already completed. In this section, the evaluator provides more of the details of the concerns and describes the parent's evidence. The evaluator should be clear that this section describes the parent's perceptions and not yet any report of findings. This section may also focus on how the parent responded to some of the questioning, especially when the allegations do not seem clear. In all, this section of the report should provide a clear picture of who the parent is and how she portrays her concerns, complete with her evidence (or lack thereof).

Example 4

Ms. Smith presented many examples of the concerns that she has had through the years. She talked of the fact that Mr. Smith was rarely home and rarely involved in activities with the children during the time they were married. She described Mr. Smith as someone who worked a lot, was off at his baseball games, or took lengthy motorcycle trips for days or weeks at a time. She believes that he had numerous affairs throughout the marriage and, in the last few years, endangered her because of the risk of AIDS. She indicated that he rarely got involved with the children and their schoolwork or their activities and rarely spent any time with them at all. (It is important to note that Mr. Smith disputes this, saying that he was gone at times, but most times he was home and helped with homework, put the kids to bed, etc.)

She reports that this continued for many months after the separation, as there were many periods of time when he had no contact with them at all. She believes that he has gotten interested in the kids only when they started spending more time with her current boyfriend. She stated that Mr. Smith has left threatening and hostile messages on the answering machine, much of the time related to financial issues between them. She reports that he often calls her vulgar names in front of the children during exchanges. She feels that, when they were together, he blamed her for everything, even for the many affairs he had. She brought me tapes and transcripts of many answering machine tapes reflecting his vulgar statements and threatening behavior toward her.

It is this behavior on his part that Ms. Smith believes is at the root of the children's fear of Mr. Smith and Erica's specific desire to have nothing to do with him. She denies that she tries to alienate the children or "force them to listen to tapes" as he suggests, instead indicating that it is Mr. Smith who leaves such vulgar and threatening messages, knowing the children might listen to them. She feels that he should use better judgment because Erica, in particular, often listens to the answering tape on her own to see if there are any messages for her. She portrays Mr. Smith as hostile, emotionally abusive, verbally threatening, and vulgar toward her, all in clear view of the children. In addition, she views him as abandoning and rejecting both her and the children and is not surprised that the children do not want much to do with him because of this behavior.

C. It is important to give a sense of the parent's own childhood. Although a complete history of the parent's own childhood is not necessary, often a parent's behavior during divorce mirrors concerns about his own childhood. For example, a man whose own father abandoned his family when he was 10 might be seeking custody of his three latency-age children in order to prove that he is not irresponsible as his own father had been. He does not want his children to hurt as he did, and, therefore, he is driven by the need to make right the wrong that was done in his own childhood. It is important in this section of the report to provide such information and tie it together with the referral questions and parental concerns.

Example 5

Mr. Smith did acknowledge some of the issues raised by Ms. Smith regarding his childhood, describing his father as a "rage-a-holic" who would break into rage all the time. He explained that his father was often angry and pounded on things and that this included "pounding on us kids." He acknowledged that it was "devastating" growing up in that kind of environment.

He would like to do better for his children. He perceives himself as a devoted and caring father who has been actively involved in the children's lives. He was Billy's baseball coach last year and believes that he is doing much more with his children than his father ever did with him. He did acknowledge that there might be periods of time that he was away from the family, but he said that most of it was because of business. He often did construction business outside of the Bay Area. He acknowledged the affairs during the last couple years of the marriage, but said that it was connected to his relationship with Ms. Smith, and not the children. Certainly, in contrast to his father, he has been a caring and devoted father, but in relation to Ms. Smith's perception of what a father should be, he has been quite remiss in meeting the children's needs.

D. The parent's perceptions of his child and his needs should be described. In so doing, this section focuses more closely on the parenting issues in the evaluation and on the parent's ability to understand the child developmentally, respond to his child's emotional and structural needs, and understand issues of limit setting and discipline. For those parents who have a good understanding of their child and his needs, the evaluator might have mostly positive things to report. However, for those parents who are focused largely on issues that do not pertain directly to their children, this section might point out how each time the evaluator asked questions about the child, the father kept avoiding them and maintained his criticism of the mother. Or the evaluator might mention instances in which the mother had difficulty separating her own anger and needs from those of the children. Addressing more complex questions, such as parental alienation, is critical in this section of the report because too many parents forget about the kids when they continue their barrage against the other parent. I am always surprised when parents who want custody of their children cannot focus for even a few minutes on their children and their needs and instead either rigidly criticize the other parent or ramble to other issues that have nothing to do with their child. This section of the report is the best place to put this critical information.

Example 6

As he talked about some of the issues with the boys, however, he seemed to focus much more on his frustrations with Ms. Quincy and externalize blame to her rather than taking any responsibility for himself or his behavior. For example, when he talked about Ms. Quincy being upset that he doesn't give the children a bath, he was upset that she never gives him clean clothes. He connected the two by saying, "Why should I force the kids to take a bath if I have to put them back in their dirty clothes again?" He did not talk about the possibility that he could get his own clothes for the boys and simply return them in the clothes they came with. If the kids lose sweatshirts or other items of clothing, he talked about their irresponsibility rather than his own. He responds to her vigilance against him with attack and with little or no awareness of his own role in some of the problems that the boys may be experiencing when they are with him.

In talking about the boys, he *does* recognize that they have lots of problems. He clearly feels that Fred is overwhelmed by all the pressures, and he knows that Henry feels stuck in the middle. He feels that Fred can be temperamental and that Henry has a problem wetting the bed at times. He believes that there is way too much pressure on the boys. However, in contrast to Ms. Quincy, who feels the pressure is caused by him, he feels that all the pressure is caused by her by keeping the boys embroiled in the midst of their battle. He believes that the children have many friends at his house, and he feels they get along pretty well with the kids there. He's concerned that the boys don't play enough with other kids when they are at their mother's. He stated, "I guess the boys are acting as they should under the circumstances." He elaborated more on his frustration that Fred has said things like "We'd like to see you more, Dad, but Mom makes the rules." He's frustrated that he hasn't seen his children on Father's Day for the last 4 years and that Ms. Quincy does not adhere to agreements. By the second interview, he was quick to point out his perception that she is doing everything she can to divorce the children from him. He reports that "she wants her new husband to be called 'dad' to give everyone the illusion that everything is wonderful in their life." As he talked about this, his hostility increased, and it was clear that he is extremely angry by his perception of these behaviors.

When asked what the children need, he said, "a father and a mother who both act like adults." He said that they have got to stop the aggravation and the bickering, recognizing that the kids "will never be well adjusted if the battle goes on." Although this is similar to what Ms. Quincy said, he projected all of the blame onto her, saying, "As long as she thinks she can hound me, it will never stop. She can't have the power to divorce the kids from me." He elaborated that "I've done everything I can to be a good guy to the kids; she is just so jealous and spiteful."

> He feels that both of them love the boys very much and he reiterated that he is not jealous of Mr. Quincy (Ms. Quincy's new husband). He said, "Every day, I thank God everyday that they are not with someone bad." Ultimately, he believes that the two of them need to talk as parents and communicate on the issues regarding the children. He feels that the boys need for him to be a "real part of their life."

E. Finally, in the next portion of the report the evaluator addresses his clinical understanding of the parent, relying on all available information from psychological testing, clinical interviews, observations of the parent and child together, and other components of the evaluation. This section can provide a more complete sense of the parent's psychological functioning, defenses, and ability to meet the child's needs. This should be done without jargon and in relatively descriptive, not diagnostic, terms. At times, when the pathology is serious and the evaluator is concerned about a personality disorder, it is best to describe the behaviors that create concerns rather than just diagnosis the parent. For example, judges need to know that the father is volatile, externalizes blame, denies any wrongdoing on his part, gets delusional and paranoid at times, has made threats toward hurting the mother and the children, and so forth, rather than just be told that the father has a Borderline Personality Disorder. Descriptive writing makes it easier to understand why the evaluator recommends supervised and limited visitation with the children.

This section should also address the significant strengths (e.g., coaches the sports team, understands emotional needs, etc.) and weaknesses (e.g., drug abuse, temper outbursts, etc.) that relate to the initial evaluation questions and any other findings that the evaluator may have. For example, the evaluator may note that the father is psychologically healthy, has actively participated in the child's schooling, and is responsible in encouraging a healthy relationship with the mother. Such findings support a recommendation for primary physical custody with the father. Similarly, an evaluator may not be clear if the father is alienating the children against the mother but can descriptively explain the father's style of exploding rage and difficulty separating his own hurts and fears from his perception of his children's hurts and fears. In so doing, a recommendation for therapy for the father makes sense as it relates to the needs of the children. Ultimately, by the end of this section, the evaluator will have connected these clinical findings to the issues of parenting and the parent's ability to meet the needs of children. Remember to keep the referral questions and the needs of the children as the primary focus of reports so that the judge and attorneys will better understand the reasons for all of the recommendations.

Example 7

> Clinically, based on all available information, Mr. Miller presents somewhat of a mixed picture. On the surface, he is anxious, angry at his former wife, and overwhelmed with his emotions. He has a tendency to be defensive, deny common human frailties, and externalize responsibility for many of the problems in his life. He is easily overwhelmed by his emotions and works hard to control them as much as possible. There is evidence that he tends to be angry and impulsive at times, though he tries to manage this as much as possible.
>
> Underlying these issues, however, appears to be strong feelings of dependency, vulnerability, and a high degree of internal anxiety. His self-image is weak and he tends to guard against this poor self-esteem with attacks on others. He is inclined to be suspicious of others and oversensitive. His problem-solving skills are weak. He seems to feel threatened by the security and comfort of others, and in this particular situation, I suspect he feels frustrated by Ms. Post's success and self-confidence. He tends to view her growth and progress in a somewhat narcissistic way, assuming that she is doing well to alienate him and is trying to take away his esteem with the children. Unfortunately, because he has such little self-esteem within himself, it is difficult for him to combat this, adding to the problems. Ultimately, although he tends to externalize blame and assume that Ms. Post is needing status and power, I suspect that these are stronger needs of his, which he is projecting onto her.
>
> When he *is* able to absent himself from these feelings and focus solely on the boys, however, he does show some good insight and awareness into their needs. In his relationship with them, he is trying to understand them, and he appears to be trying to separate them and their functioning from his feelings toward their mother. This is difficult for him. He would like to be an autonomous father, and he recognizes many of the needs that the children have. I believe he is amenable to meeting the children's needs if he can be encouraged and supported as a father in their lives.

At the end of the section on one parent, the evaluator now goes back and does the same for the other, describing the other parent's affect, concerns, own childhood, and perceptions of the children and their needs, plus a clinical evaluation. Frequently, I decide which parent to describe first by the way in which they are accurate in their perception of the other parent or by the nature of the pathology. For example, if the mother is quite accurate in her perception of the father, I might report on the mother first. This allows for a natural transition to reporting on the father in such a way that flows from the mother's concerns. Similarly, if one parent is psychologically healthier than the other, I usually report on the healthier parent first and contrast this for the second parent. When possible, I try to have the report flow naturally from one parent to the other, tying in the issues between them. No matter how it is done, it is important to report on both parents in these sections of the report and to do so in a narrative way that describes both the issues that they present and the ultimate impact of these concerns on the children.

Example 8

> Unfortunately for the children, Ms. Long is just as Mr. Long described—extremely angry, spiteful, and derogatory toward him. She was clear that she did not want to participate in the evaluation and felt that it was totally unnecessary. When asked if an evaluation might be necessary for the children, she said that "they are happy and comfortable with the people they are with." She made it clear that Mr. Long never listened to her, and that "he doesn't listen to anyone." She expressed a tremendous amount of anger toward him for being forced to take care of "his child" (Tom), saying "it wasn't easy." She clearly feels that "he betrayed me." She is very angry that he left her for another woman and very angry that he was never around during the marriage. She thinks that he has no strengths as a parent whatsoever and that she has no weaknesses as a parent. She feels that "he has no relationship with his children because he was never around."
>
> When asked how she would recommend sharing the parenting with him, she said, "Keeping it the way it's always been, him not around, and them with me. He can continue paying the bills because that's all he did anyway!!!!!" At another point, she said, "I can't get over the anger at what he did," adding that she doesn't want him to come back. When asked if the kids had ever expressed feelings that they might want their father back, she said, "Only if I want him back. If it made me happy, they'd want him back." When asked if the children have any of their own feelings, she said, "They don't seem to have any feelings about him at all." She stated, "I'm involved in everything," elaborating that he's never been involved in anything. As she talked about all these issues, it was clear that she viewed things in a polarized way, believing

> that she is all good with the children and that he is all bad. She sees no purpose for him to ever get involved in their lives.

THE CHILDREN

The next major section of the report concerns the children. In this section the evaluator writes about observations and impressions of the children, especially the children's perceptions of their parents and the divorce. It is best if this section is written from a developmental perspective so that the reader has a clear understanding of the children's needs. Essentially, there are five primary issues that must be included in this section in each report.

A. First the evaluator describes how the children related in the evaluation—whether they were scared, open, defensive, prompted by parents, inhibited, and so forth—focusing on their general demeanor during the entire evaluation process. An evaluator might note if there is a difference in how they interacted with either parent, or, if a home visit was made, any differences in how they responded in the office compared with at the home. Observations on sibling interaction and any difference for a child when seen individually or conjointly with siblings should be noted. Essentially, the first part of this section focuses on the children's overall behavior during the sessions.

Example 9

> Fred and Henry both presented as their parents described. Both of the boys are highly anxious, overwhelmed with their emotions, and clearly caught in the middle of the parents' battles. As they talked, it appeared that Henry, in particular, is struggling with his feelings of being overwhelmed and stuck, while Fred is attempting to stay out of the middle as much as possible. Henry especially uses primitive defenses such as the psychological splitting of his parents, in which he must perceive Mom as all good and Dad as all bad, as a way of reducing his anxiety. At times he feels trapped by both of his parents, and at other times, he feels more relaxed and is able to express himself and understand his emotions better. Both parents are accurate in their perception that the boys are caught in the middle of a war and that being prisoners of the war is taking its toll on the boys. Fred has little ability to deal with conflict, has temper tantrums, and is easily overwhelmed as tensions increase.

B. Next the evaluator reports on the child's feelings and concerns. As I indicated in Chapter 6, verbal children usually have a lot to say about their parents, likes and dislikes about them, and feelings that they may have about their parent's divorce. Here the evaluator must be careful about confidentiality. I will often make quite general statements in this part about the child's reports. However, when the child has given permission and the issues are clear, I may use quotes as a way of adding emphasis to an understanding of the child's statements. It may also be useful to relate these concerns to statements made by either parent, again as a way of having the report flow smoothly.

For example, if the section on the parents discussed the mother's attempts at alienating the children against their father and the father's temper outbursts, the evaluator can connect that here when reporting on the child's concerns about both his parents saying mean things about the other parent to him and how this makes the child feel sad and scared. Similarly, the evaluator might also say that the child "hates it" when his mother does not "let" him see his father just because she is angry at the father. Thus, from understanding the child's concerns and feelings, we can better understand the behaviors described in the reports about the parents. As such, the purpose in this section is to make clear to the reader any significant feelings and concerns raised by the child during the evaluation process and to report them in a way that makes sense with the rest of the evaluation report.

Example 10

> Victor appears to be angry and depressed. He talked a great deal of many concerns regarding his mother, all of which sounded very much like his father's concerns. He talked about child support, money, allegations of abuse, and so forth, just as Mr. Smart did. In short, he appeared to be "a little Mr. Smart." He is so clearly identified with his father that it is hard to separate his own beliefs and feelings from those of his father, frequently preceding his statements with the words, "Well, my dad told me . . ." Victor believes that he is doing much better in school since he has been with his father, states that he is happier, and makes it clear that he expects to continue living with his father. He does feel sad when his father is too busy to do things with him, misses Sean quite a bit, and wishes he could have more time with his brothers. However, even if his brothers stay at their mother's, he wants to continue living with his father. He added that he would like his father to spend more time with him.

C. Next the evaluator reports on the child's perception of her relationship with her parents, siblings, friends, community, school, and other aspects of her life. Obviously, in the context of a custody evaluation, there are many complex issues that need to be understood, and this general view of the child's perception of her functioning provides a better idea of what to recommend for her. For example, suppose there is a question of relocation and the child tells the evaluator that she does not want to move away from her dad, friends, and activities because of what they all mean to her. The evaluator should report her statements in this section to help explain how her concerns are taken into account when making recommendations. Similarly, if a child says that she has no friends at her dad's house and is usually quite lonely there, even though she loves him, the evaluator needs to report this to explain why a fairly equal time-sharing between her parents is not recommended. In essence, this section of the report allows the evaluator to tie together the child's perceptions of herself in her family with her sense of herself in the larger world.

Example 11

> Regarding the move, Brenda made it clear that although she did not want to hurt her mother's feelings, she does not wish to move. She sees no redeeming quality to anything about moving and indicates that she has told her mother on numerous occasions that she simply does not wish to move. She does not want to leave her friends, her swim team, or her father. She does not accept her mother's arguments that she might make new friends, could join a different swim team, or could see her father on extended holidays and vacations, as that is not sufficient for her needs. She was clear that if her mother wished to move to _______, she would rather stay in __________ with her father and visit her mother on long holidays and vacations. Mike was a little bit more willing to consider moving, but basically, was also clear that he does not want to. Mike's reasons were essentially the same, though he included some other activities he has here in ____________ that make moving unacceptable. He looked more afraid of hurting his mother, however, resulting in his greater expression of ambivalence.
>
> In an effort to try to understand some of their resistance, however, I asked what would happen if both their parents wanted to move, especially if they were still married. They indicated that they would not wish to move anyway, but that they would learn to adjust. They acknowledged that if they are forced to move, they probably will adjust, but neither one wants to move. Again, they made this quite clear on

> numerous occasions in the interview. Both Brenda and Mike again emphasized that they wished to point out that neither wanted to hurt their mother's feelings, nor did they have anything against their mother; they simply did not wish to move.

D. Next the evaluator may report on any observations of the child and his parents together. In this portion, the evaluator might be quite specific about observations, again tying it in with the referral questions and concerns. For example, if the mother says that the father is mean and the kids do not like him, it is important to observe and note whether or not the kids were afraid of him, loving toward him, or ambivalent. Similarly, the evaluator will want to note how well the father was able to interact with the children and how he responded when they pushed his limits. We often see children who have too much power and parents who are overwhelmed with their children's acting-out behavior. This is important to note, especially when we later recommend parenting classes for the father and therapy for the child.

Example 12

> During the conjoint session with their father, they confronted him on a lot of this and were frustrated by his response. For the most part, as indicated before, he sat there with a strange smile on his face, saying very little to them and giving them very little understanding that he heard what they were saying. Whereas none of the children wanted to sit near their father when he came into the session, they all clamored to sit near their mother and were clearly affectionate toward her and very distant from their father. In general, their anger, their hurt, and their distance were quite apparent.

E. In this portion of the report the evaluator summarizes the findings about the children, often in a general way. The summary integrates observations of the child's interactions in the interviews, the child's perceptions of his parents and his relationships to the larger world, the child's feelings and concerns, and observations of the child's direct interactions with his parents. When there is more than one child, this may be done in a general way for all of the children (if warranted) or done specifically for each child (when there are differences). In essence, we should close our understanding of the children with a summary report of our perception of who the child is, how the child feels about the issues related to the evaluation, and how we perceive them to be functioning in their world.

Example 13

> These symptoms and emotions were evident in their play, in their drawings, and in their interactions with both of their parents. I suspect that the boys do not know that it is okay to love both of their parents. At its worst, the children's psychological splitting of their parents gets so severe that Fred has a difficult time thinking of anything positive about his father all. As is common in high-conflict divorce situations, especially when the children are quite young when parents separate, the children feel a strong need to choose between their parents. In this particular situation they both are choosing their mother as the good parent. Once they express those feelings and feel secure about talking more openly about both of their parents, they clearly express that neither parent is all good or all bad, though it is harder for them to view their father in positive terms than their mother for many of the reasons noted. Fred confronted his father a bit when they were in the session together. Once he did that, they were able to relax and draw pictures together in a more reasonable and positive way. Unfortunately, the tension he feels internally is just too high. Although his mother perceives that his father is solely responsible for this, and Mr. Jones perceives that Ms. Quincy is solely responsible for this, I suspect that both parents provide many messages to the children that increase the tension that they feel.

INFORMATION FROM COLLATERALS

Next in the evaluation report I usually write about the information from collaterals. Just as with writing about the children, however, this can be somewhat tricky because many teachers and day-care personnel, as well as others, wish for a degree of confidentiality. Similarly, if I talk to a therapist, there is a certain degree of confidentiality that must be maintained. Given this, most evaluators either write only a little bit or write quite generally about what was said by collateral sources. In doing so, they can protect the confidences of others, while simultaneously relaying only that information that is pertinent. As described earlier, it is very important to protect therapeutic confidentiality as an ethical concern out of respect for the individual's right to privacy.

Example 14

> The therapist reports that Fred has had a lot of problems with his feelings associated with the divorce. After visits with his dad, he was

> closed off emotionally and often felt that he could not share his feelings with his father. In many ways he struggled with expressing these feelings, though she noted that Fred felt safer communicating his feelings to his mother and stepfather than to his father. The therapist also noted that Fred was quite critical of his father and felt unloved and emotionally overwhelmed when he had been with his father. From her description, it certainly seemed that she also observed the splitting that was evident to me in this evaluation.

On the other hand, there is sometimes very important information from a collateral source that must be included in order to present a complete understanding of the family in the report. Pediatricians who report that a parent does not follow medical advice, teachers who report a child's consistently missing assignments when at the father's house, or the day-care provider who reports that the mother always initiates negative conversations with her about the father in front of the kids must be included in the findings. In general, I try to balance rights of confidentiality with the details of the information when I decide how much to report from collateral sources. I tend to report less where therapists are concerned because of therapeutic confidentiality and to be more open about others who provide necessary information. Some of this will be addressed in more detail in Chapter 9 regarding the professional issues involved.

SUMMARY

By the time the evaluator has completed the portions of the report on the parents and the children, it is time to integrate the report into a comprehensive understanding of the family dynamics and the needs related to the children. Thus, the next critical section in the evaluation report is the summary. Attorneys and judges rely on the summary section to integrate all of the information and provide a complete understanding of all of the family's issues. With this in mind, the summary needs to reiterate the main referral questions, but to do so now with the evaluator's understanding of the answers to those questions. Whereas the earlier parts of the report focused on the individual dynamics of the adults and both the individual and relationship dynamics with the children, a strong summary takes those dynamics and provides a clear picture of the intertwined dynamics of the entire family. Whereas the earlier section with the adults relayed a parent's concerns about the other parent, the summary provides a chance to address those concerns the evaluator may have, while explaining why he does or does not see things similarly with the parents. In essence, whereas the child's or parent's issues reflect a narrow view of the family, the summary paints a broad picture of all issues that are relevant to the custody evaluation and the needs of the children.

Example 15

In many ways this evaluation is about perfection. Ms. Quincy is highly critical of Mr. Jones and his parenting and portrays him as threatening, hostile, and highly derogatory of her and simultaneously vulgar and negative with the kids. Mr. Jones portrays that Ms. Quincy wants to have a perfect family with her new husband and that he is pushed aside as a result. The children are trapped into psychologically splitting their parents into good and bad and, because of their anxiety, are forced to make judgments as to which parent may be telling the truth and which parent may be lying. Certainly, by the time the police are called, they don't know what is going on. All too often, the truth lies somewhere in the middle of what both parents say. Along with this, there is no effective communication between the parents. Both Mr. Jones and Ms. Quincy externalize all of the blame onto the other. Although both seem to have a fairly good understanding of the children and their needs, neither sees his or her own role in the children's problems.

Mr. Jones is overwhelmed by his perception that Ms. Quincy is attempting to undermine his role as a father. This is a major factor in the problems between them. He seems to feel threatened emotionally by the close relationship that the boys seem to feel with their stepfather. In addition to this, however, I suspect that Mr. Jones also feels overwhelmed as a father (made worse by his perception of Ms. Quincy's judgment of him) and that he feels inadequate in the ways mentioned above. He is quick to react to her and, unfortunately, he does not see any way in which his own behaviors or emotions contribute to the problems between them. This, too, is a significant factor in the ongoing battles between them. Ultimately, I suspect that Ms. Quincy does less to cause problems with the boys than does Mr. Jones, though she sometimes overreacts in ways that send Mr. Jones through the roof (such as calling the police when he is at work and his girlfriend is watching the kids).

Overall, however, it does not appear that Ms. Quincy is as alienating as Mr. Jones believes, though, as indicated, I am concerned that Mr. Jones has a difficult time dealing with his anger at Ms. Quincy in a way that keeps it from the children. In spite of this, however, he does not appear to be as bad a father as Ms. Quincy seems to believe. Unfortunately, the children *are* struggling a great deal, probably more than either parent recognizes.

Ultimately, both parents want the same thing, that is, to be left alone to have his or her own relationship with the boys unaffected and unencumbered by the other parent. They want the boys to feel free and secure in their relationships with each other, and they want the boys to grow up free of the stress and tension that has been so much a part of their lives. Finally, they want a relationship with each other in which they can communicate about the boys and not get so worked up in the couple's issues as they have over the past several years. Although each believes that this calls for sole custody for him- or herself, I do not see a solution coming from giving Mr. Jones custody, or from giving Ms. Quincy sole legal custody and limiting Mr. Jones's time any further. In fact, if either of them had too much power, I think it would isolate them even more and create even more tension for the children. Instead, I see the solutions coming from both Mr. Jones and Ms. Quincy learning to understand his and her own role in the problems the children face, becoming the best parent each can be, and leaving the other parent alone to be a "good enough" parent to the boys.

Example 16

In many ways, Mr. Long is quite accurate in his portrayal of Ms. Long. She is extremely angry at him and likely has been for many years. Although the anger may be justified, she appears to be significantly alienating the children against him and she cannot separate her own feelings from theirs. This is unacceptable. She is both subtle and overt in how she dumps on the children, depending on the issue, and the children are clearly overwhelmed with their feelings. They would like to love their father, but feel that it would hurt their mother to do so. They *do* blame their father for the divorce. Some of this is their own feelings, though some of it is likely the result of the alienation. However, because the mother has such a strong tendency to project her feelings onto others, it is unclear how much of the feelings are just her own, and/or theirs, as well.

Ms. Long is also accurate in her portrayal of Mr. Long. He was quite withdrawn from the children through most of their life and left most of the child rearing to her. This contributed to their closer bond with her. Although he justified his isolation because of the tension that he experienced, he can't expect the children to simply change allegiance

> from their mother to him just because she is dumping her rage too much. In addition, he does not really accept their feelings that they might be angry or not like his girlfriend because he blames Ms. Long for all of it. He is somewhat cold and narcissistic, as well, though there is evidence that this is getting better than it used to be.
>
> With the divorce, the children are currently depressed, anxious, and clearly caught in the middle. By now, they cannot separate their own feelings from their mother's, in large part because they are so protective of her and because she dumps on them so much. They seem fairly isolated, both from their feelings and from others, as well. Ms. Long indicates that the kids would run away from their father if they were given more time with him, but it is unclear to me how much of this is due to their own feelings or her projected feelings. Tom is overparentified and seems to feel a strong need to take care of his mother. Cory appears to be the most overtly anxious, and Diane seems to be the least affected at the moment. She is the one most willing to like Mr. Long and his girlfriend, as well as Tiffany (Mr. Long's daughter from a previous marriage), who has also been alienated by Ms. Long. In fact, Tiffany reported that Ms. Long recently told her she could come and visit the children "one more time, and then you'll never get to see them again." This greatly upset Tiffany, who believes that Ms. Long is alienating the children from her, as well. Ms. Long, however, indicated that she said that Tiffany would see them only one more time this summer because Tiffany is about to go away to college. She did not feel she was alienating the kids against Tiffany, though Ms. Long acknowledges her anger at Tiffany, as well.

In the examples noted above, the summary specifies issues related to parental alienation, reality testing and truth telling by the parents, the children's fears, the nature and extent of parental hostility, the father's alleged rage, and so forth. In the summary, the evaluator brings in the specific criteria that lead to the conclusions and pulls together all the information in the report. Just as the narrative becomes a bridge between the referral questions and the summary, the summary becomes a bridge between the narrative and the recommendations. By the time the reader has completed a review of the summary, the recommendations that follow should be clear and obvious. A report that is written concisely, yet thoroughly, leaves nothing to the imagination and is essentially foolproof for cross-examination by an attorney. If the narrative and summary are vague, the judge will have no idea why the recommendations are being made, and the report will be subject to a higher degree of cross-examination, almost forcing the case to trial. In addition, if the evaluator has not presented his material thoroughly and concisely, the parents will not understand why the recommendations are being made. Thus, a summary that is clearly focused on the children and their needs, the parents' functioning and their ability to meet those needs, and all of the broad issues in the case is less likely to be questioned by each parent when the recommendations are being made.

RECOMMENDATIONS

Among various evaluators and attorneys there is some controversy about whether evaluators should make specific recommendations about custody. There are some attorneys and evaluators who believe that the knowledge base of evaluators is too limited to provide the necessary predictability related to the issues involved in custody disputes. Some attorneys take the position that it is a breach of judicial authority for evaluators to make recommendations about the ultimate issue of custody because that is meant to be within the purview of the law. They argue that judges often give up their judicial authority to evaluators by accepting recommendations without change, and they believe that the law does not allow anyone other than judges to make judicial decisions. Some evaluators take the position that making recommendations around custody and visitation is unethical because there is no scientific proof that the recommendations are valid and predictable for the family. Those attorneys and evaluators suggest that evaluators should provide all of the information without making specific recommendations and allow the attorneys and judge to infer recommendations from the report. They would rather let the judge use judicial authority to make orders based on the information and summary contained in the evaluation report.

The main purpose for using mental health experts to do a custody evaluation is to provide the recommendations to the family, attorneys, and court, giving direction for resolving the conflicts and providing an opportunity for the family to end the litigious process. If an evaluator does not make specific recommendations, there is less opportunity for resolution and a greater likelihood that the family will be forced to litigate, and thus force the judge to make a decision. Not only does such litigation add further anxiety and distress to all family members and overload an extremely burdened court system, but it leaves the decision in the hands of a judicial expert who has less to rely on from the mental health expert if there are no recommendations. Many family court judges have little training in child development and family dynamics and rely on the recommendations of an evaluator to assist them in the determination of a parenting plan that is in the best interests of the children.

In fact, I believe that the most ethical thing evaluators can do is to provide very specific recommendations that assist the family in resolving their conflicts and moving forward, utilizing knowledge of the family and integrating this information with divorce research and child development needs as a guide to recommendations. In my opinion, doing less would be the same as doing only half a job. If evaluators did not make recommendations to complete their reports, I believe there would be little purpose for having evaluations. The evaluation itself often provides the catalyst for change, compromise, and resolution of intense conflict. It would not serve that purpose without clear and specific recommendations.

With that in mind, it is important that recommendations make sense. The recommendations not only need to flow naturally from the material gleaned from the evaluation, but also must relate directly to knowledge of the law regarding divorce, child development, divorce research, and the best knowledge available related to the issues of custody and shared parenting. Frequently, when a family comes to a custody evaluation, each parent is afraid that one of them will win and the other will lose. It is quite common for parents to view things in this all or nothing way, and the litigious process is typically filled with people who view themselves as winners and people who view themselves as losers. It is very common for children to come to the evaluation wondering which parent is going to win. The entire process tends to reinforce everyone's divisiveness and competition.

Recommendations that are focused on the issues, that provide healing and an opportunity for both parents to gain a portion of what each is seeking, and that clearly identify how the solutions and recommendations are in the children's best interests are the most useful. Recommendations must be practical, fair, and child focused and be a logical consequence of the material found in the report. If the evaluator recommends therapy or mediation for the parents, it must be clear how such recommendations will benefit the child. With such recommendations, both parents can feel as if they have won something, and ultimately they can feel that their children have benefited from the recommendations made by the evaluator.

I believe that when an evaluation is completed, the evaluator knows more about the complete family dynamics than anyone outside of the family unit. The attorneys, as advocates for their clients, know what their clients tell them and have only limited contact with the rest of the family members. The judge has had little opportunity to see the parents and has very little understanding of the children and their functioning. With this in mind, it is my belief that the evaluation recommendations are necessary and should be as specific as possible to help the family resolve all conflicts. Sometimes recommendations are relatively arbitrary and are designed for nothing more than resolution. Evaluators know that it is in the children's best interest for settlement to occur and therefore work for the possibility of resolution in the recommendations.

For example, when we specify that a child should be transferred from the mother's home to the father's at 6:00 p.m. every Friday, with a return to the mother at 7:00 p.m. every Sunday, these specifics may be related more to logistics and the need for a settlement than anything else. Clearly, there is nothing in psychological research that says what time children should transfer between homes. But if we are trying to maximize time with the father and provide an opportunity for the child to be home in time to get settled for school the next day, and if we know that the father can realistically get to the mother's to pick the child up by 6:00 p.m. on Friday, we would be remiss if we do not make such a specific recommendation. In addition, it is important to recognize that some couples, if left to themselves, will fight over the most minute of details. Thus, if we were to leave a broad recommendation that stated that the child should be with his father every other weekend, they would argue on not only the definition of a weekend, but the actual time each weekend begins and ends. Then they would argue as to what to do if one parent is late at pickup or drop-off and whether there should be some punishment for messing up. With evaluations that have many problems and complexities and much tension between the parents, we can reduce the tension with very specific recommendations for drop-off and pickup and our rationale for the recommendation.

We may recommend parenting classes and/or therapy for one or more family member to help the child, and it will be most helpful if we outline the kinds of issues that need to be addressed in such classes or therapy. When we find significant animosity, we might need to be very specific when recommending the alternation of holidays, the specific dates and times of transfer, and how the holiday is to be defined. For such high-conflict families, we may recommend mediation or Special Master. In the evaluation report we will likely encourage both parents to avoid making disparaging comments about the other parent and make other such recommendations in order to reduce the conflict for the children.

The following two examples are representative of the type of recommendations I often make:

Example 17

1. Both Mr. Jones and Ms. Quincy need to look toward themselves to make changes regarding the children. I recommend that Ms. Quincy stop telling the children so much about divorce issues and being so quick to react to the children and their criticism of their father. She needs to understand the nature of the boys' emotional splitting of their parents into good and bad so that she can better understand them and how they are dealing with the divorce and the hostility between the parents. Similarly, I recommend that Mr. Jones learn to feel more secure in himself as a parent and work more on his own to solidify and improve his relationships with the children, separate from Mr. and Ms. Quincy and his perception of their behavior and the boys' relationship to each of them. Until each parent learns to look inward and end the externalization of blame, the boys will continue to struggle.

2. Given the nature of the children's difficulties, I recommend that they get back into psychotherapy. Each of them needs to learn to deal with his feelings differently and reduce the symptoms that they are exhibiting. Both parents need to participate in this therapy, as requested by the therapist, to better understand the children and their needs.

3. I recommend that Mr. Jones get into individual therapy to help him deal with the previously mentioned emotional difficulties. In particular, he needs to come to terms with his rage at Ms. Quincy associated with his loss of the relationship with her and his perception of intrusion by her onto his relationship with the boys. He needs to find a less destructive way of venting his anger than he appears to do with the boys. He must stop swearing in front of the boys and he needs to understand that they have legitimate feelings that need to be honored by him. Even from my own observations, this is difficult for him. Separating his feelings about Ms. Quincy and her husband and their relationships with the boys from the boys' needs will be a suggested goal of his therapy, as well.

4. I also recommend that Mr. Jones get involved in parenting classes to help him feel more secure and confident as a father. He is responsible for his parenting of the children and also the behavior of anyone else toward the children when they are under his care.

5. Given the nature of their extreme difficulties, I recommend that they get involved in coparenting counseling or mediation. It may actually be best if they could utilize the services of a Special Master so as to enable them to feel more confident that a trained third party could help them settle their differences.

6. At the present I recommend a very structured schedule, with no leeway. I recommend that Mr. Jones have the children every other weekend from Friday at 6:00 p.m. until Sunday at 7:00 p.m. In addition, I recommend that he have the boys every Wednesday from 3:00 p.m. until 7:00 p.m. If they have homework when they are with him, he is to help them with it or see that it gets done. He is to provide his own clothes for the children when they are with him and make sure that they get a bath at least once per weekend. If he has to work when they are with him, he can make whatever child care arrangements he needs; however, it will be better for his relationships with his sons if he works as little as possible during those times.

In addition, during the summer months, I recommend increased time with him and the boys. During times that he can be off work, I recommend that he have up to 2 weeks of vacation. All weekend visits should be able to start at noon on Friday and end at 9:00 a.m. the following Monday if his work schedule permits. On his weekends that have a Friday or Monday off from school, due to school or legal holidays, his time should be extended to include the Friday and/or Monday, as well. I also recommend that holidays such as Christmas, Thanksgiving, and Easter be alternated so that he has a regular schedule with the boys for each of those holidays. Finally, I recommend that the schedule guarantee that he have the boys every Father's Day (from 9:00 a.m. to 9:00 a.m. the next day) if it is not automatically his weekend. Similarly, however, I recommend that Ms. Quincy have the boys every Mother's Day at 9:00 a.m. if it is otherwise his weekend.

Along with this schedule, I recommend that the boys be able to call either parent whenever they wish and that Mr. Jones be able to call up to two times per week to talk with the boys. During weekends, I recommend that Ms. Quincy be able to call the boys once. Each needs to avoid any harassment of the other during phone calls that are meant for the kids. Until they learn to talk more amicably, I also recommend that all communication between them about the children be done in the presence of the Special Master or the children's therapist(s).

Finally, I recommend that all differences of opinion regarding the schedule be monitored and settled by the Special Master, as well.

7. I recommend that the police no longer be called by either of them. Instead, they should work with the Special Master, who can be a combination mediator and educator to both parents. In addition, the Special Master can work with the therapist(s), if necessary, to understand the progress (or lack of it) that everyone is making.

8. Given the likelihood that things will change over time, especially as the boys and Mr. Jones work out some of these issues in therapy and/or parenting classes, I recommend a brief reevaluation in approximately 9 months to see how everyone is functioning. If Mr. Jones has made sufficient progress in his relationships with the boys and is showing an increased ability to meet their needs and follow through responsibly, there could be a reason to increase his time in the future. On the other hand, if he continues to struggle in his parenting and/or shows continued irresponsibility regarding the above issues, there could be a reason to decrease his time, as well. I also hope that Ms. Quincy will have a better understanding of the nature of the boys' splitting and will have removed herself from the issues between the boys and their father.

9. Finally, I recommend that both Mr. Jones and Ms. Quincy do what they recommend themselves, that is, be adults who do not put their children in the middle of this war, who learn to respect each other as parents, on their children's behalf, and who grant each other the freedom to be responsible parents to their children when the children are with each of them. If they can respect each other, the children can learn to respect themselves and both their parents and free themselves of the turmoil that they feel. In the absence of this mutual respect and autonomy of each parent, the children will continue to struggle emotionally, split their parents in an unhealthy way, and remain prisoners in the war between their parents.

Thank you for allowing me to be of assistance with this family.

Example 18

1. It is critical that both Mr. and Ms. Long look toward themselves to make changes that the children need. The externalization of blame is quite high, with neither Mr. nor Ms. Long able to really see how either of their own behaviors are negatively affecting the kids. Most important, it is critical that both parents refrain from saying derogatory things about the other directly to, or in front of, the kids.

To meet this goal, I recommend that both Mr. and Ms. Long get involved in individual therapy. Ms. Long needs to reduce her rage and her blame of Mr. Long and learn to separate her own feelings from her children. Unfortunately, until she can truly see the negative effects on the kids, the prognosis is not very good. Mr. Long needs to become more responsive to the children's feelings, separate them from his perception of Ms. Long's rage, and learn to understand and deal with his own feelings better, as well.

Finally, with this, I also recommend that the children get involved in some level of therapy, as well. Tom, in particular, needs to work on his feelings of responsibility regarding taking emotional care of his mother. All of the children need to free themselves of the intrusion of their parents' feelings onto their own. With both parents and the kids in therapy, I hope that the children can learn to feel free to love both of their parents and not feel the tension that they do. Both parents must participate in the therapy to help learn the ways that each is negatively affecting the kids. Again, it is critical that they look only to what they, themselves, can change, without regard to the problems of the other parent.

2. At the present, I am reluctant to recommend a significant change in the custodial time with each parent because of the children's strong feelings, as well as the fact that Mr. Long has not really shown that he can manage the day-to-day needs of the kids. However, in order to give him some more time, both to offset Ms. Long's rage and to see how he takes care of the kids, I am recommending the following for the short term:

Mr. Long is to have the children every other week from Thursday at 5:00 p.m. until Monday morning at 9:00 a.m. (or until he gets them to school when they have school). In addition, I also recommend that he have them from 5:00 p.m. to 8:00 p.m. on the alternate Thursday evening, as well. During the school year, when he has the children he is to spend time with them on their homework and make certain that he gets them to all necessary activities.

When the children are with him, they must have the freedom to call their mother when they want, up to once per day. Ms. Long is to refrain from any behavior that might negatively intrude on their having a good time with their father. Similarly, when they are with their mother, the children must have the freedom to call their father when they want. In addition, he is to have the time to call them every Wednesday evening (after their activities but before they go to bed) and on Monday evenings, as well. Neither parent is to interfere with the phone calls.

Mr. Long must follow through on typical parent responsibilities. He must help with homework, get them to their activities, go to school meetings, and generally be more actively involved in their complete lives, not just their recreation, as he had been in the past. This will be critical as he works to include himself more in the children's lives and if he truly wishes to be less than a weekend dad. He must also learn to understand his children's feelings better and spend some quality time with them away from his girlfriend, at least until the kids get more used to the divorce and their feelings. I encourage him to work with the children's therapist to help understand this, if need be.

3. We do not know how any of the Longs will react over the next 6 to 9 months. If the children are improving in their relationship with their father, if he is doing a more thorough and effective job of meeting their needs, and if Ms. Long is handling her anger better than now, there could be reasons to leave things during the school year, while increasing some of the nonschool time that the children spend with their father. There might also be a reason for increasing the time with their father toward a more equal basis.

However, if Mr. Long is not following through on his need to better understand the children and their feelings or is not effective at meeting their significant day-to-day needs, or if Ms. Long is still inappropriately dumping her anger and alienating the children against their father, in spite of how well she meets their other day-to-day needs, there could be reasons to make other, possibly more drastic changes in the custodial time. Thus, I recommend an updated evaluation to better assess those issues within that time frame.

Thank you for allowing me to be of assistance with this family.

When the evaluation is complete, the thorough evaluator will have at her disposal a tremendous amount of information from which to write a report. Attorneys and judges do not wish to read reports of 20 or more pages, as they often find them too wordy and too vague. The evaluator should pare down the information into a comprehensive and concise report that provides the necessary information to answer the referral questions without overloading the reader with additional, but less than useful, information. The evaluator who writes a concise beginning that outlines the reasons for the evaluation, a complete description of the procedures used in the evaluation, a thorough assessment of the parents and children, and a summary that synthesizes and integrates all of the important information will end up with recommendations that make sense and that meet all of the needs of the children.

8

Complex Issues

Only a small percentage of divorces result in a custody dispute, and, in most jurisdictions, only a small percentage of the custody disputes are referred for evaluation. As social problems increase today, many of these problems find their way into evaluation work with divorcing families. With an increase in domestic violence; child, sexual, and spousal abuse; emotional abuse, drug and alcohol problems, mental illness; and so forth, evaluators are faced with the complex task of understanding these issues while simultaneously trying to address children's needs vis-à-vis their parents' divorce.

In addition to these problems of violence and abuse, there are other significant issues that also present themselves in custody evaluations. One or more family members may have a significant medical problem. Children are often increasingly outspoken and may be very angry. Children may refuse to see one of their parents. Some evaluations involve issues of gay and lesbian parents and the complications that these may bring both in the courts as well as for the children. A growing and significant problem appears to be the alienation by one parent against the other. In subtle or very overt ways, children may be discouraged from having a relationship with the other parent in a way that is damaging to the child. Many of the evaluations with false sexual abuse allegations involve such parental alienation. These child and adult issues often complicate the evaluation process, as well.

Most of the issues that I address in this chapter have a great deal of research and/or one or more books written about them. It is beyond the scope of this book to give much depth to these topics. I intend in this chapter to highlight many of the issues that we see as evaluators and the procedures and skills required to make sense of them. See the Suggested Readings for more complete writings on these topics.

In many jurisdictions there is a growing trend to evaluate custodial disputes resulting from a desire for relocation by one parent. As life circumstances change, one parent may wish to move away from the other. Historically, the custodial parent (usually mother) could do whatever she wanted. Traditionally this could lead to a growing distance between children and their noncustodial parent (usually father). In more recent years, with increased shared parenting responsibility and more frequent joint legal custody, if one parent wants to move, regardless of the reason, the other parent asserts his or her rights against the children being moved. Yet, in a mobile society, in which most people move every few years or so, parental relocation is becoming a significant issue. Courts are grappling with the individual's right to live wherever desired and a child's need to have an ongoing relationship with both parents. Some courts have begun to set a presumption against a move, unless the move can be seen to be in the child's best interest. A parent's economic well-being may require that parent to move (such as in the case of a job transfer or layoff). A parent is sometimes being forced to choose between economic well-being and a relationship with the children who might be ordered to stay in their community. In some ways, the relocation of a parent is the most difficult of all evaluations, as there are often two involved, very good parents who have arranged a fairly workable shared parenting arrangement and who are now competing for primary physical custody of a child when one parent is forced to move.

Because so many issues are complex and ongoing, many families will need an ongoing longitudinal evaluation. When an evaluator initially sees a family for a custody evaluation, it is a static observation of a family at a point in their life. It is frequently at a time of high stress and certainly a time of high conflict. With a thorough evaluation, the evaluator might make many recommendations for therapy, mediation, and other ways to improve things for the children. A follow-up evaluation will help see the extent to which either parent responds to the recommendations and improves things for the children.

In addition, as children grow, their needs change, and custodial recommendations made at one point in their life might be inappropriate for another point in their life. An updated evaluation will be able to focus on the developmental changes of the children and the parents' ability to understand and meet the changing needs of their children. Thus, as the family dynamics change (becoming less combative and stressed, it is hoped) and as the child's developmental needs also change, there is a frequent benefit in updating the evaluation, providing for the family a more dynamic view of their needs and updating recommendations to meet those needs. Especially as it relates to many of the complex issues addressed in this chapter, a longitudinal evaluation, in which there is a thorough initial assessment combined with one or more periodic updates, might be the best way to ensure that the children's needs continue to be met by their parents.

ISSUES OF VIOLENCE AND ABUSE

In the last several years, there has been a growing increase in the nature and extent of violence in society. Incidents of child and spousal abuse have dramatically increased, there has been an increase in sexual abuse, and there is a greater awareness of the negative effects of emotional abuse on children. With increased pressures and family stress and a society in which there appears to be growing characterological problems, abuse and violence have grown. With increased awareness of the negative effects of such abuse, more spouses are seeking divorce as a way to end the continuing spousal or child abuse. Such a parent cannot take it anymore, leaves the spouse, and seeks a refuge for the children.

Simultaneously, however, we are seeing a rapid rise in the false allegations of violence or abuse when no violence or abuse is taking place. Many studies in the late 1980s and early 1990s have raised the question of false allegations of emotional, physical, or sexual abuse in which one parent will accuse the other of such abuse with no real evidence of it. It is quite natural for a perpetrator of real violence to be in denial or to minimize the abuse. It is equally understandable that someone who is accused of abuse, yet who does not commit any abuse, will also be denying the allegations. These dynamics are very difficult for the courts to deal with, and many of these families end up being referred to custody evaluators to try to determine the truth.

With increased publicity of highly contested custodial disputes, today's society has even witnessed well-known members of the entertainment profession on the evening news claiming guilt or innocence of child sexual abuse. Certainly, the public watching the TV news cannot tell whether a father has molested his daughter or if a mother is exaggerating and falsely accusing the father. Yet when such families appear in the office for an evaluation, evaluators are asked to determine the truth about particular events that have been alleged. Sometimes the truth is just as hard to come by in evaluations.

The first step in determining the truth is for the evaluator to have a good grasp of the many issues involved. By the time the family gets to an evaluation, the child has often been interviewed by the police and/or protective services, has been seen by doctors, and may already be in therapy for the "abuse." Young children may not know what is going on, may not understand this very well, and may have already come to accept that something abusive has happened, even if it has not. A parent who has been abused and has weak ego boundaries may project onto the child the fear of molestation and may frequently check for signs of molest following each of the child's visits with the other parent. This hypervigilance creates a mind-set in which there is concern about everything, even when the parent-child interactions are completely appropriate.

Similarly, a somewhat histrionic parent may hear of something that took place when the child was with the other parent and may overreact in such a way that leads people to believe an abusive event has occurred. For example, a child still in diapers, who has been continually checked by a parent after visits with the other parent and who has been told that no one should ever touch him or her in the "privates" might come home after a visit saying that the other parent "touched my pee-pee." Rather than calmly trying to understand what happened, the parent might immediately call protective services and rush the child to the doctor, telling everyone, including the child, that there was a molestation. A social worker will come to investigate, interviewing the child and the parent together. The child, frightened by the parent's reaction and the person coming to ask questions, might say very little, except to nod when the parent tells the story to the social worker. The child is then taken to the doctor and gets even more frightened, refusing to be seen without the parent. The doctor notices genital redness and concludes that molestation is possible. The parent goes into court the next day, asking for a cessation of all visits with the other parent because there is evidence that a molestation has occurred.

With society's hypervigilance on this issue, I have seen such an event occur, even when a molestation did not happen. The above events might occur when a father molests his daughter. But they could also occur when the father bathes his daughter, changes her diaper, and puts on a cream for a diaper rash. With the real risk of children being hurt in our society, there is an increased perceived fear that any strange behavior of a child is symptomatic of child abuse. Given the dynamics and hostility in the relationship between divorcing parents, this perceived fear gets translated into allegations of abuse.

In order to get as close to the truth as possible, I recommend a very thorough evaluation in which there is a complete review of all the physical evidence, psychological testing of both parents, and both separate and conjoint interviews with the child and each of the parents. The timing of the allegations in connection to the custody dispute should be considered, as well. In false allegations, there seems to be a pattern in which the alleged event was discovered just when the custody dispute was erupting. Evaluators need to understand the psychological makeup of the parents and look for objective evidence that suggests that either the mother might be overreacting or the father might be in denial. We need to use our observations of the parents and child together to help us understand the likelihood of real fear—or fear that has been projected by one parent onto the child. Similarly, we need to know that some children who are abused show no fear when seen with their abusive parent.

Ultimately, the neutral evaluator needs to keep an open mind to the *equal* possibilities that the allegations are real, the allegations are false, or the allegations are exaggerated, as she explores the issues in this matter. All too often, as the evaluator begins an evaluation and talks to one parent, she hears a convincing and understandable set of circumstances that has her believing the story. By the time she interviews the other parent, however, she hears an equally credible story, which leads to the question, "Where does the truth lie?" In these most highly polarized of circumstances, it is almost as if the evaluator is talking to two people who have not experienced the same events. Frequently, there is some overlap between the events observed and reported by mother and the events observed and reported by father. In the most polarized situations, it is difficult for the evaluator to find any such area of overlap. By using a variety of tools and by maintaining an open, neutral position until the evaluation is completed, the evaluator can diligently search for the truth. All too often, the evaluator may not know whether abuse really took place even when the evaluation is complete. In those circumstances, it is important for the evaluator to be clear about what he does know and what he does not know when completing his report. Finally, I recommend that any evaluator working with questions of violence and abuse have a good grasp of all the research on real and false allegations associated with such abuse within the context of custody disputes.

As a way of illustrating the issues noted above, I offer the summary section from two of my reports:

Example 19

Overall, this is an extremely complicated evaluation. Facing this evaluation is the question of whether or not Jill has been molested, whether or not Ms. Hall has a personality disorder, and whether or not Mr. Sax is responsible for being an unsafe and/or abusive father. Although there is some clear and convincing evidence associated with Ms. Hall's being dysfunctional and there is evidence to support the likelihood that she has a personality disorder, there is little or no evidence to support the likelihood that Jill has been molested or that Mr. Sax is an unsafe parent.

After many phone calls with a variety of collateral people and a review of written materials supplied by both Mr. Sax and Ms. Hall, it appears that there is no concrete evidence that Jill has ever been molested by anyone. At times it appears that her behavior is oversexualized, though this is primarily when in the care of her mother. In addition, there is evidence that Ms. Hall has difficulties dealing with issues of personal boundaries and ego space, and it is likely that Ms. Hall overreacts to any sexualized behavior (even typical 4-year-old sexualized behavior) that Jill presents. Given the evidence in this evaluation that Ms. Hall is occasionally delusional and distorts reality, at least at times, it appears that her allegations are false. Although we will never know for sure, the preponderance of evidence suggests that Jill has not been molested.

Finally, there is the question of whether or not Mr. Sax is an unsafe parent. By his own admission, he engaged in some less-than-safe practices when Jill was younger, but there is no evidence to suggest that he is an unsafe parent at this time. Clearly, his awareness and understanding of Jill's needs appear to be secure, and there has been no objective evidence of any significant problems in his parenting of Jill for the last year or more. Certainly Jill's words bear some testimony to Mr. Sax's safety, and he certainly is willing to attempt coparenting mediation as a way in trying to help both him and Ms. Hall be on the same track regarding parenting. Given all of this, I suspect that his parenting is at least safe, if not reasonably positive for Jill when she is with him.

Example 20

> Overall, there are several issues that are most critical to address at this time. First, regarding the issue of molest, there is no clear-cut evidence in this evaluation to suggest definitively whether any molest behavior has occurred toward Amy and whether or not Mr. Cass is responsible for it. However, because Dr. May had fairly conclusive evidence that Amy showed anxiety and fear (via nightmares and play) around such behavior when Amy was at ——— Hospital, and because Ms. Star has seen evidence of such behavior in her initial therapeutic work with Amy, it is clear that Amy believes that "dookie" games have taken place between her and her father. Given that evidence, and the evidence of Mr. Cass's polygraph, we are left with two possible conclusions. Either Amy has been coached into believing that her father has done this, or Mr. Cass has "split off" (and thus passed his polygraph) any possibility of his having committed such emotionally damaging behavior due to his anxiety, fear, and need to see himself in a positive light. Given these two alternatives and all of the evidence in this evaluation, it is my opinion that the latter explanation is the most correct. Mr. Cass's significant emotional difficulties and his tendency toward paranoid projection, delusion, and the psychological splitting off of his negative behavior is the basis for this conclusion. However, I do not completely trust that Ms. Cass has not also exacerbated Amy's own feelings and made them worse. Her tendency toward histrionic overreaction and her denial and lack of insight are the basis for this possibility.
>
> Clearly, although any such behavior would be damaging toward Amy, I am actually also concerned about Mr. Cass's agitation, limited relationship abilities, and the effects of that on Amy if there were to be unlimited, unsupervised contact between them. Similarly, however, it is my opinion that there is an equally strong risk of damage to Amy if there is no contact between Amy and her father because of the way that fantasy (as that is all she will have left if there is no contact) will likely harden her sense of his being a bad object in her life. The only solution that makes sense to me in these situations is to provide adequate safeguards to Amy, while simultaneously helping her to deal with the reality of her father's agitation and awkwardness in their relationship.

If we believe in the equal likelihood that children are damaged by real abuse as well as by false allegations that exaggerate or imply abuse and that then result in a disruption of a relationship between a child and a parent, we can see how important such a neutral and thorough evaluation can be. If we find abuse has existed, it is clear that we need to supervise the visitation between the abusive parent and the child, get people into therapy, and begin a slow process of reunification that may or may not ultimately lead to unsupervised contact after we have worked through the issues of the abuse.

If we discover that allegations have been false (or that abuse was unlikely to have occurred), we can use this information to ensure that there is no disruption in the relationship between the child and the accused parent. In fact, it is often necessary for the accusing parent to become involved in therapy in order to separate his issues and needs from those of the child and to strengthen the ego boundaries to reduce the likelihood of projection or histrionic exaggeration. At its most extreme, as in the case example noted previously, we might recommend primary physical custody to the accused parent because the accusing parent's ego boundaries are so weak that she cannot effectively separate her own abuse issues and projects, oversexualizes, and damages the child.

The more we understand the exact nature of the allegations, the psychological dynamics of each parent, and the beliefs and experiences of the child, the clearer we can become in making at least short-term recommendations that can get the family unstuck and moving forward to meeting the immediate needs of the child. Later in this chapter I discuss the need for longitudinal evaluations as a way of gathering more truth and ultimately meeting the longer term needs of the child.

In this section I have focused heavily on the question of sexual abuse because it seems to be getting the most attention by the courts. These may be cases in which an evaluator should consider *not* taking the evaluation referral, either because of limited experience or certain biases. These cases are extremely difficult and emotionally loaded, and for most evaluators, they are the most difficult. Truth is the most difficult to discern, and we often do not know whether abuse has taken place, even after completing the evaluation. The risk of both false positives and true negatives is high in such cases. In addition, this risk is equally serious in questions of other physical abuse, emotional abuse, and spousal abuse. The processes of discovering the truth tend to be the same no matter what type of abuse has been alleged and are equally likely to need updated evaluations, as well.

DRUG AND ALCOHOL ABUSE

As is the case with domestic violence and physical or sexual abuse, we are also seeing a large number of people who accuse each other of alcohol or drug abuse. It is similarly important to keep an open mind to an equal possibility that neither, one, or both parents uses or abuses drugs or alcohol and to try to get as thorough an understanding of this allegation as possible in the context of the children and the parenting. Finding signs of depression in children, unmet dependency needs, and overparentification of children may increase the likelihood of suspecting such abuse. If parents are psychologically tested, results with signs of dependency and other characteristics that are common to addiction would also raise the suspicions. It is my opinion that whenever suspicions are reasonably raised, evaluators should consider referring both parents for a substance abuse evaluation by a certified counselor or physician who will provide specific information with specific test results designed to gauge dependence.

In the event drug or alcohol abuse does exist, we still must try to work with balancing the needs of the child's relationship with his parent and the need to protect the child from the parent's addiction. Usually, depending on the extent of the addiction, we can recommend reducing the amount of time the child is with the parent and/or supervising the time if need be. It is important to maximize healthy time between the child and the addictive parent while minimizing risk for the child. At the same time, we must recommend treatment for the addictive parent, as well. See the next example for summary and recommendations regarding this.

Example 21

In summary, it is my opinion that Ms. Yu has relapsed, is currently working to deal with her substance abuse issues, but has not shown herself to have sufficient long-term progress given the extent of her substance abuse problems over the last few years. In contrast, Mr. Yu is doing a good job of meeting Pam's needs. He is trying to help her deal with the emotions of what she is experiencing, the facts of what she is experiencing, and the overall situation. He is providing a place of stability and appears to be meeting her needs well.

Given the above, I offer the following recommendations:

1. Mr. Yu is to maintain primary physical custody of Pam while the couple continues to share joint legal custody.

2. Ms. Yu is to continue to have supervised visitation up to three times per week for an hour and a half each time at the day-care provider's. Ms. Yu is to follow the rules set up by the day-care provider for this supervision. In addition, I recommend that for weekend prearranged visits, Ms. Yu should be able to see Pam at her home supervised

by Ms. Baw. Ms. Baw is well aware of Pam's needs, has baby-sat for her for both Mr. and Ms. Yu in the past, and is a responsible professional in the health care field who can take care of Pam if need be. I would recommend that these supervised visits be up to 4 hours in length on either a Saturday or Sunday according to Ms. Baw's schedule. I recommend that she have legal authority to remove Pam from Ms. Yu's visitation if she has any concerns about Ms. Yu's functioning and its effect on Pam.

3. For these visits to continue, Ms. Yu needs to remain in her psychiatric treatment with Dr. Sen as well as continue on a regular program of 12-step meetings and after-care for her substance abuse. She must provide proof of this on a regular basis to the person assigned to monitor this situation (see below). Along with this, I recommend that Ms. Yu be ordered to maintain random drug testing and that the drug testing itself be monitored in such a way to guarantee that she cannot be faking a sample. We must keep in mind that Ms. Yu's knowledge of the health care field is extensive and all efforts must be maintained to ensure that she does not manipulate or misuse the system on her behalf, as she has done in the past.

4. I recommend the appointment of a Special Master to monitor the drug screenings, the treatment, and the supervised visits. The Special Master must have the authority to order drug testing as he or she sees fit, speak to the supervisors of the visits, review proof of attendance at 12-step meetings, consult with Dr. Sen and the other therapists, and make immediate changes in the visitation if need be for Pam's security. I recommend that the Special Master remain in place until such time that her drug treatment needs are terminated, more than likely at least 2 years from now. Given the circumstances of this case, I recommend that the Special Master be an attorney, and for that I recommend either ——— in ——— or ——— in ———, both of whom are attorneys trained in mediation and the dynamics of such situations and both of whom have expressed willingness to participate in such a role.

5. I recommend that the current visitation plan continue for 3 more months while Ms. Yu shows her long-term commitment to this program. By the second week in February, if things continue going well in her treatments, and she remains drug free on *all* random tests, I suggest that the Special Master consider recommending the discontinuation of the supervision if he or she is satisfied that Ms. Yu is fully prepared to meet Pam's needs. At that time, a different visitation plan will likely be needed (e.g., every other weekend and one midweek overnight) for Pam's smooth transition.

6. Finally, I recommend that there be no actual change in the physical custody of Pam for at least 12 months, pending Ms. Yu's continued progress at meeting her own, and then Pam's, needs. Prior to any such change in physical custody in the future, I recommend another brief update of the entire custody situation.

MENTAL ILLNESS

In custody evaluations we do not often see people with significant mental illness, such as schizophrenia. However, we often see people with significant psychopathology, ranging from bipolar disorder, depression, and more characterological personality disorders, including borderline, narcissistic, and paranoid. In doing custody evaluations, it is important to understand the dynamics of a parent's mental illness and its effect on the child involved. Some parents are simply not capable of meeting the day-to-day needs of their children. Some parents have significantly paranoid delusions that interfere with the healthy growth of their children. The divorce itself may throw an otherwise fragile but functioning adult into such a state of disarray that his ability to meet his child's needs are marginal. When history or referral questions suggest a possibility of such a mental illness, it is important to thoroughly assess this in order to understand its interrelationship with the parent's ability to meet the child's needs.

By understanding the mental illness itself and observing the interactions between the parent and the child, we can see evidence of the way in which the mental illness manifests itself in the relationship. The father with paranoid delusions acts in a very stilted, guarded manner in his relationship with his preschooler in such a way that there is limited healthy interactions between them. The depressed mother cannot talk about her child's needs very well and does not even have the energy to play a game with the child during the observed interaction between them. In that same situation, we can then see the child begin to take on characteristics of caring for the parent, trying to please the parent, and reducing the stress for the parent.

We are always looking at the mental illness in the context of parenting responsibility, the coparenting relationship, the effect of the mental illness on the child, and ultimately the relationship between the child and his parent. This is critical because there are also some parents who do a very good job with their children in spite of a degree of mental illness. Thus, depression in and of itself is not an indicator of whether or not a parent might be able to share the parenting of her child. Observations of how the parent interacts with the child and recognizes and meets the *child's* needs are important factors in this regard.

Clearly, the greater the degree of pathology in a parent, the more we need to be careful of the effect of too much time with that parent on the child. In the case noted previously in which one parent was accusing the other of molestation when it was the result of her own projective fears, it appeared that the child could spend healthy quality time with that parent for a day or two before that parent began to deteriorate. The more we understand this, the more we can maximize the time that the child spends with her mother, while minimizing the risk of contamination. In each particular instance, we need to better understand the interaction between the mental illness and the parenting style so that we can encourage the healthy relationship between the child and her parents, while simultaneously reducing the risk of contamination from the mental illness. As with cases of abuse and addictions noted earlier, it is important to understand the interaction between the mental illness and the relationship that the child experiences.

Example 22

Clinically, based on all available information, Mr. Hap presented as a very defensive, guarded individual who portrayed himself in a very self-favorable light in this evaluation. He is unable to see any ways in which he contributes to the problems with his children or his wife, externalizing all blame onto her. He shows a lack of insight into his own emotions and appears to be consciously defensive about any problems that he might have. It is clear that he is being accused of significant mental illness by his wife, and he has a strong tendency to understate the severity of any problems or disturbance he might have. There is evidence on this evaluation that he is emotionally detached, overintellectualized, and quite rigid in his self-control. Insight and self-awareness are very poor, and it appears that he rationalizes his behavior most of the time.

In spite of his statements to the contrary, there is evidence in this evaluation of significant emotional outbursts when he is overwhelmed, a tendency toward suspiciousness and paranoia, poor judgment, and a manic style in which he is likely to be overactive for long periods of time. Although there is no evidence in this evaluation of any current psychotic functioning, the overall evaluation suggests that he can be

> emotionally explosive, controlling, rigid, manic, and self-righteous. He seems to utilize defenses of splitting, projection, and denial a great deal. At its worst, I suspect he has shown evidence of delusions and grandiosity in the past, as well. Overall, he presents features consistent with a diagnosis of either paranoid personality disorder or manic-depression, yet, given his extreme defensiveness, his very favorable self-presentation, and the mixed nature of his difficulties, his psychological profile is somewhat ambiguous. Dr. Paz thought he should take lithium for manic-depression, but Mr. Hap refused. Mr. Alm (Mr. Hap's previous therapist) acknowledges the likelihood of manic-depressive symptoms, but supports his not taking medication because it might slow down his creativity needed in his work.

MEDICAL PROBLEMS

Just as significant psychopathology may interfere with the ability to parent, specific medical problems of either the parent or the child may also cause problems. In the event of a parent's medical problems, it is important to understand the nature of the illness and the way in which the medical problems affect the ability to parent. The parent who is HIV positive still needs to have an ongoing relationship with the child, whether symptomatic or not. There may be lengthy periods of time when the parent cannot be as much of a parent as she would like because of medical treatments, and then there will be other times when she can spend extended periods of time with the child and do a good job of meeting the child's needs. It is important to treat the parent's medical condition as only one factor in understanding the overall dynamics for a family. Just as with the other issues noted previously, it is the interaction between the medical details and the parenting that is important.

In other cases, one of the children may have a medical condition that will greatly affect the recommended parenting plan. Childhood illnesses such as diabetes, attention deficit disorder, and asthma, may greatly interfere with a parent's ability to meet the child's needs or a couple's ability to share the parenting.

For example, school-age children with attention deficit disorder and significant problems with distractibility may have a very difficult time being in a week/week parenting arrangement. In spite of one parent's request for 50-50 time with the child, both parents must understand that their child is likely to need one primary home. Such a child may have tremendous difficulty keeping track of his schoolwork, his things, and so forth, when compared with children who have more intact organizational abilities. In addition, when evaluating the circumstances of a child's medical condition, it is important to talk to the physician to understand how each parent has been consistent in following through on the medical needs of the child and to understand the particular dynamics of the divorce on the medical condition. All children with specific learning problems and developmental delays will require this high level of understanding.

SEXUAL PREFERENCE

In today's changing, complex world, we are often faced with custody evaluations in which the lifestyle of one of the parents may be in question. In some jurisdictions the sexuality of a parent may be viewed by the courts as a direct issue in that parent's ability to meet the child's needs. As recently as 1993, a Virginia court awarded custody of a child to a grandmother because of the mother's homosexuality. This decision was applauded by some and argued by others. As gay and lesbian issues continue to create controversy in society, the sexual orientation of the parents will also be used as an issue in custody disputes.

I find that the sensitivity of the parents toward the needs and the feelings of the children are most critical regarding this issue. It is my view that gay and lesbian issues are among many that may complicate or make more complex the evaluation, but do not in and of themselves reflect a parent's ability to meet the child's needs. What I have found to be quite important is that children, when confronted with the realities of their parent's homosexual lifestyle, may have their own reactions to this. Clearly, the children's needs, feelings, and understanding must be taken into account. Because of the risk of embarrassment with their peers, prepubescent boys may have a very difficult time with a father who is open about his homosexuality. It is important for the father to understand his son's concern, and he may need to be sensitive to the places in which he is open about his sexuality. This may require the boy and his father to talk about these issues in an open and direct manner, often in a therapeutic environment. Over the years, I have found that the best way to understand and manage these issues is with openness in such an environment. This enables both parent and children to express and understand themselves and learn to be heard by the other. Once we understand this process, we can again see whether the father is sensitive to his son's needs (even if they don't match his values) and can work with his son to feel secure about this sensitive issue. Thus, recommendations should reflect those issues that are critical for the child, rather than a response to the other parent's anger or the gay parent's "rights."

Example 23

Overall, it is my opinion that several things are somewhat obvious, several things are quite obvious, and some things are still somewhat unanswerable even after this evaluation. What is most obvious is that both Mr. and Ms. Flint spend a great deal of time and energy caring about and for their children, much to the children's benefit. Each is aware of the many complex issues and ways in which these issues affect the children, and each tries to help the children in his or her own way deal with and understand their feelings. Mr. Flint has a somewhat greater difficulty doing this, but this is likely to be as much a function of the limited time they have as due to any problem on his part dealing with the children's feelings in a sensitive way. In fact, I find Mr. Flint to be a fairly sensitive and aware individual who would like to help his children more, but feels stilted in his efforts. In addition, he is not asking for an unusually large amount of time, just an amount that is fairly common in the typical divorce.

A less obvious factor is the way in which Ms. Flint's discomfort, especially as it relates to possible feelings of overprotectiveness, is contributing to the children's emotional dilemmas. It is my opinion that in subtle ways she is likely to unconsciously transmit her own insecurities about Mr. Flint's inabilities to the children, increasing their concerns and contributing to their own insecurities about him. Certainly the issues themselves—Mr. Flint's homosexuality, especially as it relates to Sam's emerging sense of self and his own sexuality, and Paul's (Mr. Flint's partner) AIDS and any fears or insecurities associated with that—and the more common issues around parental divorce, loyalty conflicts, and so on are all contributing to the complexities and difficulties for these children.

What is left uncertain, however, is what is best for the children. In many ways, I can see rationales for maintaining the status quo and rationales for making changes in the amount of time that Mr. Flint has with his children. The primary reason to maintain the status quo would be to accept the children's wishes as being what is best for them. In some ways this is accurate because if we follow the children's wishes, they will feel a greater sense of empowerment and will be less likely to have any short-term anxiety regarding any change in the schedule. The risks we take, however, by maintaining this current schedule is that Mr. Flint will never have an opportunity to show whether or not he can, in fact, be a more real father to these children. He loses out, and ultimately they lose out because they have less opportunity for him to be involved in a more intimate way with them. The risks to an increase in Mr. Flint's time are that the children will feel increasingly anxious and possibly angry that their wishes were not heeded and that if they have more time with Mr. Flint and Paul, there will be more opportunities for tension building, complications from Paul's illness, and no resolution of the issues that may come up with the increased time together.

In short, we are left with no perfect solution. In addition, we are left with no clear rationale for making any particular recommendation. Nonetheless, it is important to make a specific recommendation knowing full well that there will be both pros and cons to every option available.

ANGRY, OUTSPOKEN CHILDREN

In custody evaluations we may encounter children who have very outspoken beliefs about each of their parents. They may be extremely angry at one or the other parent and, in many instances, do not want to see that parent. Although it is not uncommon to see such strong reactions in adolescents, who developmentally and by their nature tend to be outspoken and potentially rebellious, I have seen an increasing number of latency-age children who are equally outspoken and angry. Whereas children are often somewhat guarded and torn between loyalty conflicts to each of their parents, in highly contested custody situations often children may side with one parent while blasting the other.

There appear to be many reasons why children seem to be splitting their parents into all good or all bad categories. This has already been addressed to some extent in Chapter 4. In evaluations this splitting may take its form in the outspoken anger toward one parent. It is important to look for signs of ambivalence in the child or the child's ability to see some good things about the parent with whom the child is so angry. Similarly, it is very important to assess the relationship with the other parent and to see if the child can identify some negative about the parent who is viewed as all good. In all work with children, however, I believe it is critical to honor the child's feelings while simultaneously trying to encourage the child to understand a broader view of both parents. We are not the child's therapist, though our evaluation process can be therapeutic.

More than anything, it is important to make recommendations that take into account the feelings and beliefs of the angry, outspoken children. If a 15-year-old says that he will run away from home if placed with his father, we need to accept this as a serious concern. Even if the mother is not the best parent, it may still be prudent to recommend placement of the child with the mother while working therapeutically to improve the quality of the relationship with the father and simultaneously encouraging the mother to become a more effective parent.

Similarly, it may be very important to recommend therapeutic contact between a father and his 10-year-old son, who is very angry about the divorce and blames the father for it. Although we might recommend that the boy spend a certain amount of time with his father, we may need to start things in a therapeutic environment if the child is going to get over his feelings. In such a setting, the child, father, and therapist can work together to reduce the splitting and help the child with his anger and outspoken feelings. Often I have recommended limited time between a child and his parent for several months while the issues are worked on therapeutically, with an expansion of the time as the splitting settles and the boy and his father grow in their relationship together.

Finally, we are often faced with the child who absolutely refuses to visit a parent, even with therapeutic intervention. This is one of the more difficult situations to make recommendations because forcing the interaction without supportive services may exacerbate the problem. Allowing the child to avoid the parent, however, may also exacerbate the problem and reinforce the splitting that is so unhealthy. Under such circumstances, I have found that it is often helpful to periodically revisit the issue and slowly encourage the parent to request some time together, to engage in some positive activity together. With time, and especially with continued therapeutic support, in many cases a child will finally accept some form of a relationship with the parent with whom he is angry. It is very important in these evaluations, however, to assess the interaction between the parents as well, to be certain that the couple's conflicts are not so strong that the child can deal with these conflicts only by terminating the interaction with the other parent. In such highly volatile situations, it is very important for the evaluator to differentiate between the child's feelings and the possible blend of the parents' feelings onto the child.

PARENTAL ALIENATION SYNDROME

This leads into another very complex issue in dealing with custody evaluations. Just as it is beyond the scope of this book to focus on all of the issues connected to abuse allegations in divorce, it is also beyond the scope of this book to address all the issues of parental alienation syndrome. Much has been written recently on this topic, and there are varying philosophies as to how to deal with it. For the purposes of this book, it is critical to address some of the symptoms and patterns found in parental alienation syndrome, so that we know what it is and how to recognize it. I will also provide some of my suggestions about ways to correct it and how to help the children who are torn by the alienation of one parent against the other.

In a fairly classic pattern of parental alienation syndrome, one parent (often the mother) subtly and covertly gives messages to the children about how bad the other parent (usually the father) is. In and of itself, parental alienation syndrome is emotionally dangerous to children and the health of their relationship with the other parent. However, rarely is parental alienation syndrome seen without vestiges of inappropriate behavior on the part of the other parent. Just as it takes two parents to entangle children in their conflicts in the first place, it usually takes two parents to engage in behaviors that resemble the patterns found in parental alienation syndrome. In order to see and understand parental alienation syndrome, we must understand the role that each parent plays in the process and how this filters down to the children. By understanding this process and the role that each parent plays in one parent's efforts of alienation against the other, we can begin to provide recommendations for its remedy.

As seen in Example 16 in Chapter 7, there are many features that include a history of conflicted relationships between the children and their father, a degree of psychopathology in their mother, and angry, outspoken children. The only successful solution comes from forcing the issues in all areas. It was important for the mother to get into therapy to identify her *own* role in sabotaging the father's relationship with the children. Their outspoken 10-year-old son needed to be in therapy to begin to separate his own issues with his father from those of his mother and work on resolving them. The father needed to work with this process to improve his relationship with his son and to help show that he could be a more sensitive, understanding, and participatory father.

Just as we tend to see parents who *do* alienate their children against the other parent, we also see parents who falsely claim that the other parent is alienating their children. When his 8-year-old son refuses to visit, a father is quick to blame the mother, even when she did not do anything but encourage the child to express his own feelings. In such instances, the father remains angry and has a difficult time seeing and understanding his child's feelings. He may not recognize why his son is angry at him, always externalizing blame to the mother and discounting his son's feelings. This is just as significant a problem as the alienation by the mother, and in this instance it usually requires the father to be in therapy to understand his own role in his son's feelings and to allow him to reduce his externalization of blame onto the mother.

Ultimately, the more we understand the complete dynamics that are involved in the parental alienation, the more we can make recommendations that will help reduce its impact. Usually, it is a three-pronged approach that requires therapy for the alienating parent (to reduce the rage and help separate her issues from those of the children), therapy for the children (to encourage a greater understanding of both of their parents and help separate their own thoughts, feelings, and wishes from those of their mother), and forced time between the child and the affected parent to allow for a normalization of the relationship. If the alienation is not taking place, we make recommendations for the child and the other parent to learn and work together to improve their relationship together. Ultimately, the more we can understand all of the complexities under which parental alienation exists, the more we can provide appropriate intervention to reduce its negative impact.

RELOCATION

In my experience, there has been an increase in the number of referrals for evaluations associated with the request of one parent to move away from the other parent. In many of these evaluations, the couple has already been divorced for a number of years and has had an existing divorce agreement that provides the parameters for which a parent or the children may be moved. Typically, a divorce agreement may state something like "neither parent shall move the child more than 100 miles away from the other parent without an agreement between them or by further order of the court." Other agreements may narrow the distance even further to local counties or even to maintaining the child in his present school district. In general, when such an agreement is entered into, neither parent has a plan to move beyond the bounds of the agreement, and it is expected that no problems will develop over time. In reality, however, people's lives do change. As economies change, people get laid off or transferred in their employment. People remarry and may wish to move with their new spouse. This requires a growing number of families to work out these problems on their own, or else one parent takes the other to court to settle differences between them.

Similarly, as more families share the parenting of their children after their divorce, with both fathers and mothers actively involved in and important in their children's lives, it is common for neither parent to be willing to give up status as a complete parent and allow the child to move with the other parent to the new community. Long-distance parenting is difficult and is not viewed as the preferred option by most parents. With that in mind, when a family is confronted with the prospect of a move, there is a new opportunity to fight over custody of the children.

In doing an evaluation associated with relocation, it is very important to understand the state's laws associated with relocation. Legislation may not say anything about relocation, but there may be local court rules or state appellate court rules that have created a precedence or a presumption regarding this matter. For instance, in the state of California, the burden of proof is on the parent who wishes to relocate that such relocation will be in the child's best interests, not just in the parent's best interests. If there is a working shared parenting arrangement or a close relationship between the child and both parents, and if the move is not imperative for the child, there is a presumption in California against the child moving, regardless of the adult's reasons for wanting to move. A good evaluation on the issue of relocation will address these questions, as well as questions about the noncustodial parent's visitation with the child, the child's activities and stability, and ultimately, the child's preference.

More specific, we need to assess the strength of the attachments between the child and each of his parents. Looking at the developmental age of the child and the ability of the child to tolerate distance from one parent to another and making a determination about which parent will be more difficult for the child to be away from is a large part of the task in doing such an evaluation. In essence, it is difficult to say that any move is likely to be in a child's best interest, because there is both an adjustment period for the child with the move itself, as well as an adjustment related to the change in relationship with the other parent. However, it is important to keep in mind that if the parent is moving anyway, the child must be away from one parent or the other for a considerable period of time (except for periods of visitation). We then need to look at the child's best interests in relation to that move, looking to see which separation will be more difficult for the child to endure.

In practice, relocation usually becomes an issue when the mother wishes to move, citing employment, family, or educational reasons as the primary reason for the desire to relocate. In such instances, the father does not want to see his role with his child diminished. In doing our evaluation, we must look at the nature of the relationships with both mother and father and ascertain whether the child can tolerate a long-distance relationship with either of them. Because of a closer attachment, the long-distance relationship with the mother may be more difficult for a young child to tolerate than with the father. In contrast, the older child may be able to tolerate a long-distance relationship with either parent and may be unwilling to move away from her school and her peers. As with these other complex issues, we need to develop as full an understanding as possible in order to make appropriate recommendations for the child's best interest.

Ultimately, in doing an evaluation in which relocation is a primary issue, we are often faced with a Solomon-like choice, looking at two good parents, each of whom has been actively involved in the child's life and one of whom is going to be moved to a lesser role of long-distance parent. It is important that we, as evaluators, try to assist the family in creatively looking at ways to maximize the time with the long-distance parent and to assist that parent in maintaining an active, participatory role in his child's life. By framing a report that highlights the positive benefits to the child of cooperation and working together and that encourages the parents to be creative in maintaining a long-distance relationship, we can allow children to continue to grow free of the loyalty conflicts that they have been avoiding while the parents worked together prior to the relocation.

BENEFITS OF LONGITUDINAL EVALUATION

As shown by many of the issues addressed in this book, an evaluation of a family at a given point in time is like a snapshot. It reflects the emotions, behaviors, strengths, and weaknesses of the parents as they relate to the parenting of their children at a particular moment in time. With a good evaluation, recommendations are made for implementing change and resolving conflict in a manner consistent with the needs of the children. In many circumstances, this information is sufficient for a family to move forward and meet their children's needs in a healthy, productive way.

When an evaluation focuses on significant pathology, such as family violence, child abuse, sexual abuse, and mental illness, or when a child's developmental needs change significantly from one point in time to another, it is often very helpful to have an updated evaluation on the issues to assist the family and/or the court in understanding how change has benefited the family. Certainly, a significant goal for mental health professionals is to assist their clients in making change, growing, and functioning more productively. If we view our job as custody evaluators within that context, our goal is to provide recommendations that can assist the family to be more productive for their children and help the family with the difficult transition from a state of being married to a state of being divorced. We encourage families to learn ways to resolve their conflicts and differences and separate their couple's conflicts from the children and their needs. In these more difficult evaluations, we need an opportunity to view our recommendations in a dynamic way that allows us to see the quality of change and how people meet that change. Examples 17 and 18 in Chapter 7 both reflect a need for updated evaluations. Example 21 in this chapter was the report of an updated evaluation required after clear evidence that the mother had relapsed in her drug abuse.

We may be hesitant in our recommendations because we are uncertain of the family's ability to follow through on them. We may complete an evaluation in which the mother has significant emotional problems and may even require hospitalization, and we are faced with the recommendation of primary physical custody with a father who has had little time to be a parent in his child's life. A reevaluation 6 months to a year later provides an opportunity to see the progress that the mother has made in her therapy. It provides a chance to see the progress that the father has made in meeting the child's needs. In addition, it gives us an opportunity to view the child and the ability of the child to adjust to a change in custodial circumstances and to understand the nature of her parents' issues. By updating evaluations, we can fine-tune our recommendations to be more appropriate to the new circumstances that we are now seeing. In this way, we can make evaluations more dynamic, reflecting the realities of family life.

We often do evaluations in which the children are quite young. As their developmental needs change and as a parent's ability to meet those needs changes, it is often useful to do an updated evaluation to see if there are any necessary recommendations that might assist the family in continuing to meet the children's needs. For example, an evaluation with a 5-year-old child may lead to recommending short periods of time for the child to be with each parent, with more transitions than are needed for a 10-year-old whose developmental abilities are now different. The 10-year-old may be much more prepared to spend a week with each parent and to manage the complexities of homework, extracurricular activities, and family life in two different homes. By the time the child reaches adolescence, however, this same child, as indicated in Chapter 4, may very well want to have a primary home base so that her friends can find her most of the time—from which she can go to school, go to her work, and maintain her social life. Obviously, if parents understand their child's developmental needs, a reevaluation may not be necessary. However, for the family who wants assistance in understanding these complexities and in resolving ongoing differences about the child's time with each of them, an updated evaluation can often be quite helpful.

Finally, as mentioned in Chapter 2, there are times when a Special Master may need to be appointed to monitor an ongoing situation. In some ways, the work of a Special Master can be in lieu of an updated evaluation. On the other hand, there can be a time when an updated evaluation will be useful to crystalize the knowledge gained by the Special Master while at the same time remaining neutral. This can occur when the task of the Special Master specifically excludes orders regarding the ultimate question of custody. In such situations, the Special Master, like the therapist or mediator, needs to be kept out of the decision regarding this issue, and the updated evaluation will need to return to the original evaluator.

In all of these instances, whether because the initial evaluation led to tentative short-term recommendations for a fairly chaotic and dysfunctional family, because of a significant developmental change, or to gather in and pull together the knowledge of several people (therapists and Special Masters), an updated evaluation can be an effective tool in meeting the ongoing needs of the families. Evaluation updates provide the dynamic view of the family that is so critical as we try to understand the issues that continue to change over time, as all people do.

9

Professional Issues

Over the years, it seems as if additional concerns, sometimes just as important as the complex issues described in Chapter 8 or the more standard ones described in Chapter 3, have become critical to a custody evaluator. These matters have nothing to do with the clients themselves, but relate to the process of custody evaluations and the task of being a custody evaluator. Mental health professionals are not usually trained to work with courts and attorneys. In fact, many mental health professionals view attorneys as a nemesis and the courts as a scary place to be. Mental health professionals who spend considerable time in custody work need to retrain themselves to view the attorneys and the courts as allies, all with the same ultimate goal. Our goal is to work ethically with the courts and thoroughly understand the families, while helping children in postdivorce conflict.

Mental health professionals who are new to working in the legal arena face many challenges. State and national psychological associations and other professional associations are just now reviewing ethical principles and recommending new standards in work with litigious families. New standards are being developed about who our clients are and how we meet their needs. Certainly, the court may have one need, the attorneys another, and the individual family members themselves a third need. Questions of who has access to evaluation reports, confidentiality, payment for services, and testifying in courts are all major professional issues that need to be addressed. Evaluators who do a lot of custody work tend to feel overwhelmed and face burnout. Many psychologists are worried that they put themselves at greater risk for malpractice suits and ethics complaints as a result of working with angry, litigious clients. In 1992 and 1993 the public saw several courtroom shootings and increased family violence associated with the despair and rage of a parent in the midst of a custody and divorce dispute. Such experiences raise fear and concern in all of us who work with these high-conflict families.

To deal with this, mental health professionals who are trained in the role of therapist must rethink their training and become focused to think like investigators, while maintaining ethical and professional standards. We must be prepared to think of the many possible parameters of our work and how to work within the context of a legal system. As evaluators, we must respect our power and recognize that custody evaluations require the widest range of skills in our work. We must be knowledgeable in the areas of child development, working with children, diagnosing adult psychopathology, dynamics of divorce, and state and local laws and rules related to divorce. We must develop integrative skills to put all of the puzzle pieces together and write a comprehensive report that focuses on strengths and weaknesses of each parent, makes sense to parents and the courts, and most important, gets the children out of the war zone. Evaluators must work with people who hate each other and need to find ways to be comfortable and work with children who have learned to avoid sharing any information about themselves and their feelings.

The purpose of this chapter is to address these professional issues and the professional conflicts inherent in the evaluator's role and to provide some thinking about how an evaluator might approach them. There are task forces and committees across the country that are currently trying to address these very complicated issues. I offer a framework in which the evaluator can begin thinking about these issues, so that she can make her own working solution to these complicated, yet important, issues. In fact, it is my hope that, with a strong commitment from those who consistently do this work, the mental health community can develop guidelines and standards for training and competency in this increasingly prominent area of professional practice.

AN ETHICAL STANDARD FOR THE EVALUATION PROCESS

By its very nature, the custody dispute is an adversarial one. It involves the litigation between two parents. Although some jurisdictions are suggesting that a family court be established to change the process, until that happens custody disputes will often be contentious. When an evaluator is hired, she must understand that she is being brought into an adversarial system and that her role as an evaluator might be affected by this system. Judges and attorneys need to appoint a court expert who will be trained in the psychological dynamics of the family and who can make recommendations regarding those issues that are in the best interest of the child. The court needs specific recommendations and some rationale on which to base a court order. Some evaluators believe that specificity of recommendations is unethical because some recommendations cannot be based on psychological research. The evaluator must always balance her need to please the judge with her need to do what she believes is ethically correct. Because licensed mental health professionals are required by their license to uphold the ethical principles of their profession, we must always be diligent to be certain that our actions do not violate the ethical principles to which we subscribe.

During the years that I have been working with custody evaluations, I have been asked by attorneys to do assessments that I believe are clearly unethical. Most of the time, the request revolves around the question of seeing one family member and then making a custody recommendation. I think that the best solution is to politely say no, while explaining the ethical dilemma to the attorney.

In the past several years, a significant rise in malpractice claims against psychologists across the country has been caused by psychologists who have seen only one parent and then made a recommendation related to the custody of a child. Clearly, ethical principles indicate that an evaluator must not say diagnostic things or make recommendations related to someone the evaluator has not seen. Making such a recommendation is unwise legally, but is unwise ethically as well, because the evaluator compromises the rights of the parent not seen by making statements about him or that impact him. Unfortunately, there are evaluators who, in order to please an attorney, have made such statements in recommendations to the court. It is the position of most state and national organizations that address this issue that an evaluator cannot make a statement about custody without seeing both parents.

There are several ways to diffuse this issue. Frequently, one parent will absolutely refuse to participate, and the judge is not ordering an evaluation because he is not convinced that a problem exists. I have had attorneys ask if I can see a child to try to understand a question of abuse or a conflict in a relationship, or to substantiate a positive relationship between a child and her father when the mother is seeking primary physical custody. In the absence of a court order for a neutral evaluation and with the refusal of one parent to participate, we are limited in what we can do. However, I believe that we can see the child (if the parent who brings the child has the legal authority to do so) and write a report to the court of our observations of the interaction between the child and that parent and make some statement about our observations. We can even suggest that the parent is frustrated, and, if we believe it to be appropriate, we can recommend a neutral evaluation. I believe that neither of those actions is a violation of our ethical principles because they do not compromise the rights of the other parent because no statement has been made about either custody or the other parent. In fact, my major recommendation from such an undertaking is usually that a neutral custody evaluation be ordered. It is this type of situation in which the evaluator can try to meet an attorney's needs, yet maintain ethical principles.

WORKING WITH ATTORNEYS

Over the years, I have found that attorney styles vary greatly. Some are highly litigious and fight for their client's interests only, with little regard for the children and/or the cost of their work. Others are much more interested in mediation and working with mental health professionals to resolve conflicts for their clients. Some have little or no awareness of children and their needs; others are very sensitive to children of divorce and the effects that the parental conflict is having on the children. In all such work, I have found that there are certain guidelines that work well in dealing with attorneys, regardless of their focus or style.

As I previously indicated, mental health professionals have often viewed the attorneys as the enemy. Frequently, we portray attorneys as being highly litigious and complicating the mental health needs of individual family members. In contrast, I have found that many attorneys are simply trying to do their job to the best of their ability and are quite willing to rely on the expertise of the mental health professional to understand their clients and their families. More than anything, I have learned that it is highly beneficial for the mental health professional to listen to the needs of attorneys and, just as with our clients, focus on the ways that we might be of benefit to them. In many instances, attorneys are not really certain whether or not a custody evaluation, mediation, or therapy might be indicated for their families. In recognizing that we can be an ally to the attorney, we can assist the attorney in helping her judge the best roles for the mental health professional to undertake. Showing mutual respect and understanding of their tough role in domestic disputes is very helpful in building a working relationship with attorneys.

I have also found that it is very helpful to be very direct with attorneys. Attorneys are used to pleading their case before a judge, and it might be easy for novice evaluators to be steamrolled by effective attorneys wishing to plead their client's case. Although I believe it is important to listen to what the attorneys have to say, I also believe that it is important for the evaluator to be firm with regard to the evaluation process and ethical principles. I have never found an attorney who, even though he disagreed with me, would ask me to violate my ethical beliefs or give inappropriate preference to his client after I have made my ethical position clear. Yet I have experienced attorneys asking me to do lots of things that I find inappropriate or trying to give me information that is false or very one-sided. Just as we do not always know the real truth about what our clients tell us, we also do not know the real truth about what attorneys tell us with regard to their clients. If an attorney is zealously attempting to promote his client's interests, I recommend asking the attorney to hold off giving too much information until the evaluation has begun. In this way, the evaluator remains neutral and can develop her own understanding of the case, less biased by the attorney.

If an evaluator has a standard style for how an evaluation should be done, I recommend that this be explained to the attorneys at the beginning. Just as we explain to our clients the nature of our biases, I encourage evaluators to do the same with attorneys. Often there is a certain procedure that evaluators would like completed before they start an evaluation, and I recommend that the evaluator make this clear as attorneys make initial phone calls. For example, in California, there is a statute that provides for the evaluator to be a court-appointed expert. This grants certain powers and privileges to the evaluator. I have determined that it is in *my* interest to request that all evaluations be court ordered under this procedure. When a new attorney contacts me for a potential evaluation, I always explain this process to him or her. Similarly, I find that it is quite helpful to explain to attorneys my evaluation procedure, anticipated fees, and so forth, and to use the attorney as an ally in getting some of this communicated to the client. Ultimately, I believe in encouraging a relationship with attorneys in which we view ourselves as working together for the same goal, that is, the development of a greater understanding of the family for the purpose of outlining children's needs.

Mental health professionals should have clear rules in their communications with attorneys. I request communications in writing when an attorney wants to "bend my ear" about a case in which I am involved. Then I copy that information to opposing counsel. In this way, each attorney knows what information I am receiving, and has ample opportunity to respond in kind. Regarding phone calls from attorneys, if they are not too substantive and especially if they are for minor clarification of issues, I have no problem with unilateral calls. But for more substantive clarification of my recommendations or to get more specific information about the clients, I recommend that conference calls be arranged so both attorneys are on the phone together. In this way, ex parte communication (communication with one party while the other party is not present) is avoided. Finally, I often get requests after evaluations for recommendations for other professionals, such as therapists, mediators, or Special Masters, per my recommendations. In general, I ask that such requests be put in writing, with copy to opposing counsel, so that my response remains the clear response of the neutral evaluator. I have found that, for example, if I give the father or his attorney a couple of names, the mother or her attorney might view those people as "dad's therapist" and reject them outright. Therefore, I am careful in making recommendations to be sure that everyone knows that my recommendation is neutral and not for the benefit of only one party in the dispute.

One way to bridge the gap between attorneys and mental health professionals is to join associations that promote interdisciplinary understanding. I have been actively involved in several such associations over the years, the largest of which is the Association of Family and Conciliation Courts (AFCC). At the local level, there are many task forces and interdisciplinary groups that are designed for the same purpose. Inviting attorneys to local psychological association meetings and attending or speaking at local family law meetings also help bridge the gap between disciplines.

I have found that the more mental health professionals and attorneys can become allies in our work with clients, the better we can all become at meeting the needs of families. The attorneys that I know who are actively involved in these associations are very caring professionals who try to improve their base of understanding, especially around issues of child development and family dynamics, and they appreciate our assistance in this undertaking. Similarly, they reasonably expect psychologists and other mental health professionals who work within the purview of the court to gain an understanding of the court process, the needs and styles of the attorneys, and the intricacies of the law as it pertains to family issues. I believe that it is reasonable for an attorney to expect me to understand his or her job, the legal issues associated with custody, and all the intricacies associated with it if I am going to work in family law matters. By working together in small groups, by conferencing and networking, by teaching each other, and by actively pursuing the same goals, attorneys and mental health professionals can become allies rather than enemies in the work that we do.

WORKING WITH THE COURTS

In many jurisdictions, there are two different departments in the courts with whom we might work. One is the family court mediators who receive funding and direction from the judges and whose task often is to work with families to mediate solutions before families go to court. The other is the judges themselves, whose task it is to hear arguments, help families reach stipulated agreements, and ultimately hear trials and make orders for families, when necessary. In this section, I look at each of them separately, within a framework of an overview of the court system itself.

Courts are run by very specific rules that evaluators must understand if they are going to work with the courts. Some of the rules can be worked to our advantage, namely being the court-appointed expert. All of these rules are important for the mental health professional to understand. Each jurisdiction has its own local court rules that reflect not only how the judges process their divorce cases, but also how the family court services operate. I have worked closely with several jurisdictions, each of which has different family court systems and each of which I needed to understand in order to work more effectively.

I have found that it is quite helpful to meet with the staff and/or director of the local family court services (or similar court-run mediation services, if there is one) as a good way to understand local court rules. This not only provides an opportunity for the court mediators to understand the credentials and experience of the evaluator, but it clearly gives the evaluator an opportunity to learn about the needs and the rules of the court. One family court with which I work fairly regularly has a meeting once or twice a year for interested evaluators to learn about and understand the needs of that family court system. Some family courts do only mediation and refer all evaluations to the private sector. Others do both, but refer psychological testing to the private sector to assist the court-appointed evaluator in some evaluations. Some jurisdictions want brief, summary-type reports; others want fairly lengthy reports with more detail. Most court personnel request that evaluators avoid mental health jargon and the listing of test scores that are meaningless to the court in their reports. In general, I have found family court personnel to be very interested in our impressions of the family and want us to give specific recommendations regarding the family. Along with this, however, most family court personnel want us to consult with them prior to making these recommendations because they have considerable experience in working with the family. As with attorneys, it is important to be allies with one another, working for the good of the family.

In addition to working with mediators, it is common for evaluators to work with the judges, as well, who frequently need clarification of recommendations. It is important to note that most family court judges have limited training in child development and often come to family court work from outside the family court area. For newer judges in particular, it is critical that evaluators provide a clear foundation of their recommendations and the basis for them. More than anything else, however, it is important to recognize that courts have specific rules that evaluators must follow to avoid appearing partial to one side or less than neutral. Evaluators should learn about local court rules in the community by asking judges, attorneys, or their local family court. Although local rules may vary from jurisdiction to jurisdiction, it is usually unwise for an evaluator to talk to the judge on an ex parte basis. This means that the evaluator is talking to the judge without notifying the attorneys and having them be available for the conversation. Judges are not supposed to listen to testimony from anyone without attorneys present. Although there may be some local court rules that allow for an evaluator to talk to a judge directly without attorneys present, it is important for an evaluator to understand those rules before doing so.

It is important to understand the style of reports that the judges prefer. As I indicated, some judges like very specific and concrete recommendations and are less interested in the family history and the family dynamics. In contrast, however, some judges enjoy reading a thorough report, almost like reading a good short story, because it provides a thorough understanding of the family and the children's needs. Some judges never read the report itself, looking only at the recommendations and the bottom line. Other judges, although they care about the recommendations, wish to understand the evaluator's assessment of the family in order to make their own rulings. With thousands of family court judges across hundreds of jurisdictions, there is an endless array of possible local court rules and judicial preferences that need to be understood. I highly recommend that evaluators get to know their judges' individual preferences and the local court rules in order to better assist the judges in doing their jobs. If we remember that ultimately our primary purpose is to be the court-appointed expert with the task of assisting the court in the determination of children's best interests, we can recognize that our job can be accomplished most efficiently if we understand the needs of each particular judge with whom we work.

Courts are run by a schedule, and as evaluators, we must understand and meet the guidelines of that schedule. Although we cannot be expected to meet every request that comes to us, we need to be clear that we have deadlines in our work. Court dockets are full, attorney calendars are quite busy, and we must know what is expected of us when we accept a referral for evaluation. I recommend asking attorneys or the court to put in the original order the requested date for completion of the evaluation report and to be quite clear what the next step of the process will be.

Frequently the evaluation is to be completed as a step before a recommendation conference, at which the attorneys and the judge meet and try to settle the dispute instead of going to trial. At the recommendation conference the attorneys and the judge attempt to work out a solution to the custody dispute so that both parents can agree on a custody plan for their children. At times the evaluator is included to clarify ideas or to offer suggestions and clarifications related to questions from the attorneys and the judge. In my local jurisdiction the recommendation conference is the last step in the judicial process, as the parents, through their attorneys, usually use the information in the evaluation to draft a stipulated agreement, usually based on the evaluator's recommendations, at that time. If that fails, the next step will be the trial itself.

Another possibility is that, following the evaluation, the family will return to mediation to try to resolve their own dispute, without court intervention. Whatever the next step, the evaluator must be aware of the court process and deadlines. The evaluator can assist the family in transitioning to the next step of the process. If we find that scheduling prevents us from meeting a deadline, we must let the court and the attorneys know as soon as possible and give them an alternative date for our completion. In essence, I suggest that we act in a professional matter that respects the time deadlines of others and in which we work to meet their needs for completion. If we do this and the other parts of our job professionally, we are likely to continue to get the referrals that we want from the courts.

As with attorneys, I find it very helpful to meet the judges with whom I will work. The best place to do so is in local, state, and national association meetings. At the local level, family law attorneys usually have periodic meetings, and frequently evaluators can attend in order to have an opportunity to meet and discuss issues with attorneys, mediators, and the judges. At the state and national level, associations such as AFCC have meetings in which interdisciplinary groups can interact, learn from each other, and discover each other's preferences and needs. Just as it is important to understand attorneys in this way, it is very important to understand and meet with the mediators and judges in this way, so that we can best meet their needs. Through the years, I have found that the more I get to know specific mediators and judges, their needs, and their preferences, the more effective I have become in doing my evaluations. As is always the case, the more I know, the better I can do the work that I need to do.

COMPLETING REPORTS: WHO HAS ACCESS TO THEM?

As described in Chapter 7, the evaluation report is the vehicle through which we express our understanding of the family and its needs. The written report not only addresses the issues as we see them, but does so in a way that is appropriate to the family and responds to the questions that the attorneys, mediator, or the judge might have. In this section I address some of the issues that are often raised as to who should have access to the written report. Again, local court rules will often determine this issue, but the purpose of this section is to acquaint the reader with some of the concerns people raise about this question.

In many jurisdictions, local rules direct that the evaluation report is the property of the court and is not to be given either to attorneys or their clients. In such circumstances, attorneys may read the evaluation but may not take a physical copy of the evaluation with them. It is often felt that the material in a custody evaluation report is confidential and that the court is a holder of the privilege in these contested custody disputes. In such circumstances, the purpose for allowing attorneys to review the report is to help them prepare for their clients' needs, but they may not take the report with them because of this confidentiality.

In other jurisdictions, it is felt that the attorney's need to know what is in the report and the client's right to know what is in the report supersede these issues, and the court will often order that the evaluation is open and available to both attorneys and to the family members. In such circumstances, attorneys have the reports, clients get the reports, and everyone is completely aware of all of the information described by the evaluator. This means, however, that the mother will have access to and knowledge of all the information about the father, and vice versa, even though many people believe that this information should be kept confidential. Unfortunately, this availability can lead to the public disclosure of private information. I have seen situations where reports are distributed to friends as a way to slander a spouse or are left out to be read by children, who are always hurt by this.

The two main issues, as I see it, are confidentiality and the openness of the file. Information in a court proceeding is open to the public and having an evaluation in the court record means that anyone with reasonable cause will have access to all information in the court record and thus the information in the custody evaluation. In order to safeguard against this, many jurisdictions seal custody evaluation reports so that they cannot be open to the public. At the very least, this safeguards the confidentiality of clients from others outside the family matter. In this way, clients are at least somewhat protected against public exposure.

I am equally concerned, however, about parents having access to each other's clinical information and parents having access to statements made by children with an expectation of confidentiality. If attorneys and their clients are given copies of the report, there is no confidentiality with regard to each other and, as indicated earlier, children will need to know that anything that is in the report could not be kept confidential. However, if we exclude the report from the attorneys, attorneys cannot prepare a proper defense, nor can they assist their clients in fully understanding the issues and possibly avoiding a lengthy court battle. Often attorneys are adamant that they must have access to the reports, and, to my knowledge, even in those jurisdictions that prohibit attorneys from getting copies of the report, they always have access to review the reports. Parents often believe that because they are paying for the evaluation, they should have a copy of the report and are often frustrated when they are told that they will not get a copy.

I have found that there are several ways to respond to this issue that can ensure the confidentiality of all family members while at the same time helping the attorneys to do their job to their utmost and honoring the client's right to know. When local court rules permit, I believe that a copy of the evaluation should be sent to the court and to each attorney, but that the attorneys should be prohibited from giving a copy of the report to their clients. This will enable the attorneys to have the information they need to do their job, while providing a measure of confidentiality for their clients. I tell parents that they have not waived confidentiality with respect to each other, so I do not believe they should have access to the complete report. I am always willing to share the information with each individual client about herself, especially the psychological testing information as it applies to her. In this way, however, I maintain confidentiality the best I can, the court continues to hold the privilege, I have respected the confidentiality of the children and their needs, and yet I can provide each adult with the information that the individual or the attorney needs to understand my observations and recommendations. In the jurisdictions in which I work, I have found that this is the most useful style.

In one particular situation, however, greater care must be taken than in any other. This is when one or both parents are acting as their own attorneys and thus would have the same right to access that a licensed attorney would have in preparing for the case. In that situation, I either look to the court for direction (because sometimes the court is very clear about whether or not a report is to be open under such circumstances) or I explain the dilemma to the parents at the beginning. Sometimes parents will waive confidentiality with respect to each other and then both parents can have a copy of the report. My preferred practice is to be a bit more vague in my report in order to respect everyone's right to confidentiality. Thus, when I know the parents are going to get the report and when one parent is acting as his own attorney, I believe that both parents should get a physical copy of the report. I then include less information, so it is a bit more difficult to breach confidentiality in such circumstances. However, when a parent represents oneself, I believe strongly in informing each parent that both parents may be reading the report and in explaining the limits of confidentiality in this circumstance.

Aside from the issues of confidentiality, there are several other reasons why I believe that evaluation reports should not be in the hands of parents. All too often, I have seen angry parents abuse the information in the reports, show them to children, share them with friends, and so forth, all of which adds fuel to the conflict and hostility between the parents. Most evaluators have heard horror stories of reports being left on the coffee table and children reading them and learning information about the parents that had been family secrets. As a therapist, I am generally not in favor of maintaining family secrets, but I certainly do not believe that reading information in a custody evaluation report is a healthy way for children to discover them. In fact, it is my experience that only damage can be done by having children inadvertently or otherwise read the reports that we provide to the court. Thus, in order to safeguard the children, prevent abuses in sharing information, and uphold the sanctity of the evaluation and the process, I strongly urge that parents do not get copies of the report.

Parents often ask if their therapist can get a copy of the report to assist in their therapeutic work. Again, I am a strong believer in sharing appropriate information about each person with anyone chosen by that person. If a mother wants her therapist to have access to *her* information, I believe that is her right and I try to support that whenever possible. However, in doing a comprehensive report, the evaluator must be cognizant of each person's right to confidentiality. Luckily, with the advent of word processors, it is easy to share such information with a minimum of effort. In such instances, I delete all information from a report that is not directly related to the client. Along with this, I provide all the information, especially any test results if included in the report, to the therapist for the benefit of the therapeutic relationship. Whenever I delete material, in order to preserve the integrity of the report and to help the reader recognize that it is disjointed for a reason, I add the words "Material Deleted" in those spots. An evaluator should be able to edit a well-written report that is organized and structured properly in less than 15 minutes for such purposes.

PAYMENT FOR SERVICES

When an evaluation is court ordered, it is best if the court is clear in its direction regarding the payment for the evaluation. If an evaluation is to be done by a public agency, such as court-connected family court services, the agency will have specific guidelines about payment and its fee structure. In general, the rules and the fees of such a public agency are quite clear, and the expectation is similarly clear about how those fees are to be paid.

In my experience, it is best when private practice evaluators approach the fee structure in the same way. It is important that, right from the beginning everyone is clear about the amount of the fee, how and when the fee is to be paid, what the fee covers, and what might lead to an increased cost to the family. Evaluators should be definite about whether the fee is based on an hourly charge or a flat fee amount and answer any questions the clients have about how the fee is derived.

I find that there is a tremendous amount of work that we do that is often ignored when we consider the costs of doing the evaluation. Numerous phone calls, review of written material that the parents bring in, and the dictation, writing, and editing of the report all take time and cost the evaluator if he is not adequately reimbursed for this time.

In my own practice, I try to clarify the responsibilities for fees from the attorneys or the court prior to my phone calls with the clients. More often than not, the parents are required to split my fee equally, but on occasion, one parent or the other pays the fee up front, and the court will reserve the right to adjust this pending the outcome of the evaluation. I inform the responsible parent that I prefer the cost of the evaluation to be paid at the beginning of the evaluation. This is usually understood. At times, that does not work, and I am willing to negotiate a retainer of at least half at the beginning of the evaluation, with the balance being paid prior to the conclusion of the evaluation. I then follow the phone call about fees and the initial appointment with a cover letter to each client that repeats the understood agreement about fees.

Other colleagues and I have encountered numerous situations in which we have agreed to be paid over a period of time, but we have found that once the report is sent, the rest of our fee is ignored. Obviously, in doing our reports, we generally upset one, if not both, parents who do not like our observations and recommendations. Given the opportunity, many will avoid paying for our work, and, as such, given that reality, most evaluators expect full payment prior to sending the report to the court.

Many evaluators charge a flat fee for the evaluation, based on their expectation of the number of hours they will spend on a given case. I believe that this is the best way to handle fees, as it reduces the complications regarding billing and helps us to get adequately paid for our work. Sometimes we find that we are doing significantly more work than expected, either because a parent has an enormous amount of material for us to read, listen to (on audiotape), or see (on videotape) or because of complications that arise during the evaluation process. In such a situation, I find that it is best to inform the clients as soon as possible about the additional cost and the reasons for that and to expect the additional payment in full before sending the report.

Finally, there are times when an evaluator might have meetings with attorneys following the completion of the report or might be called to testify in a court proceeding. These events were not planned for before the fee was set and will require additional fees in most instances. Again, I encourage evaluators to be clear about the responsibility of each parent to pay for such fees and expect payment for such fees in advance. We might need to schedule a meeting with attorneys or go to court when we have not been paid in advance because of a desire to help the family settle their differences and an ethical responsibility to help the children. There are times when it is necessary to do this without advance payment, but I find that such situations create the greatest risk that we will not be paid.

CONFIDENTIALITY AND THE HOLDER OF THE PRIVILEGE

In order to do a thorough custody evaluation, it is important for the evaluator to have access to all appropriate information regarding a family. Although some evaluators want to talk to friends and family, it is usually necessary for evaluators to talk to professionals who have worked with the family and have prior experience in understanding the dynamics of the family situation. Because an evaluation is truly a snapshot into a family's life, talking with people who have known the family over time provides insight into a more longitudinal understanding of the family and its dynamics.

In every discussion of confidentiality, it is important to understand who holds the privilege as it relates to the release of information. Given the fact that most custody evaluations are court ordered, it is often stipulated that the court is the holder of the privilege related to all the issues involved in the release of such information. In many instances, if I wish to speak to a therapist and one of the parents refuses to allow it, the court will make a determination about the necessity of having me speak to that therapist. Certainly, once a parent signs a release of information, she has waived the privilege that allows me not only to talk to the person involved, but to report on that in my report to the court. The important part is to clarify with the court, attorneys, and clients at the beginning who is the holder of the privilege, whether or not there is confidentiality, and how to get information if someone is attempting to withhold it. By its very nature, a custody evaluation that is court ordered grants the evaluator a significant amount of leeway to get information and pass it along to the court, with sanctioning from the court.

In spite of this, I still believe that it is necessary to get complete releases of information signed by both parents. In my first interview, with both parents present, we discuss the various professionals who have been involved with the family and who might have information useful to the evaluation. Even before that, when talking with them on the telephone, I indicate that I will need to talk to these professionals and ask them to think about who might have reasonable information that will be useful for my evaluation. I indicate that I might not speak with all of them, but it is important for me to have a complete list of professionals who have worked with the family and who might have useful information. During that first appointment, I then have a release of information typed, which will enable me to receive information from all these people. I am quite clear with the parents from whom I will be getting information and to whom I will be giving information, and I inform them of the fact that they are not releasing information to each other. The court is the ultimate holder of the privilege. If the evaluation ends in a trial, the parents know that I will then be forced to give information about each of them to the court and therefore to each other and their attorneys; but otherwise, they know that the report will go only to the attorneys and the court.

Finally, as indicated earlier, I also focus on the fact that I do not believe it to be in anyone's interest and I feel it is a violation of confidentiality for parents to have copies of the report. I emphasize that during the time that parents sign releases. I make it clear to the parents what their rights are regarding confidentiality and the privilege, yet I also recognize that the court ends up being the true holder of the privilege in most of the evaluations that I do and that if a parent refuses to participate in the release of information, the court may so order it.

TESTIFYING IN COURT

For many evaluators, the scariest part of doing an evaluation is the prospect of testifying in court. In our own arena, the evaluator's office, we are confident and feel knowledgeable and secure in the work that we do. However, the prospect of courtroom testimony, and, in particular, cross-examination by a potentially hostile attorney, raises the anxiety of many evaluators. Custody evaluators need to know that they work in a system with lawyers, and we must assume that lawyers are "mini-experts" who will know about child development, psychological tests, evaluations, and other issues in our custody work. This means that, in order to testify effectively in court, we need to assume that the attorneys will know how we should do our job, and will look for ways to advocate for their client in their questions. This section is designed to provide information and techniques that will reduce the evaluator's anxiety about courtroom testimony.

Typically, the major source of this anxiety is the fact that trial advocacy is the attorney's arena, and is foreign to our arena. Most evaluators are uncomfortable with being in a courtroom and with the aura that surrounds judges and their court. Our scientific training does not prepare us for the adversarial system. If we understand the sources of our anxiety, and can prepare for the courtroom experience in advance, we can reduce our anxiety, and can better maintain our professional stature in the courtroom.

In my experience, the best way for an evaluator to prepare for courtroom testimony is to prepare a well-written, thorough report, that is clear, concise, and focuses only on the conclusions of the evaluator. A well-organized report of this kind indicates to both attorneys that the evaluator has clearly thought out her position, has looked at the complex issues, and has made a recommendation that is consistent with these findings. When the recommendations are clear and come from the material within the report, they are more difficult to question. In contrast, when the evaluator offers psychological test data that are meaningless to the judge and attorneys, and when the evaluator's report is relatively brief and limited in scope, it often appears that the evaluation recommendations come out of the blue. Not only will attorneys be less likely to trust that the conclusions make sense, they will have more opportunity for cross-examination in order to "attack" the legitimacy of such conclusions.

It is equally important that the factual information in the report be accurate. If an evaluator makes a blunder in reporting specific factual information, this will provide an opening for a good attorney to question the rest of the information in the report as well as the evaluator's judgment. It is important in the body of the report to separate facts from perceptions and perceptions from conclusions. When we make clinical judgments in our reports, it is best to describe things as being in the evaluator's opinion. When describing perceptions, it is often helpful to state that things "appear" to be a certain way. Finally, when stating conclusions and recommendations, it is important to be clear that such conclusions or recommendations are those of the evaluator and are based on all of the information we have received. As long as we relate our recommendations to the children and their needs, we can ensure that our opinions can be questioned but not destroyed.

Finally, I would caution evaluators not to put too much in a report, especially information that is not directly related to our recommendations. Although a report of 30 or more pages may provide tremendous detail to the court, it also provides more opportunity for a careful attorney to cross-examine. I have seen a situation in which an evaluator listed references he had used in trying to bring some understanding to a very difficult diagnostic case. Although his intentions were good, and he showed the thoroughness with which he does his work, it opened the door for the attorney to question him, and to show that one of the authors cited by the evaluator had more recently criticized another of the references. In this way, the attorney was able to make the evaluator look suspect, and raise questions regarding his recommendations.

In spite of our good efforts, however, some evaluations are not settled and it is necessary to provide testimony in court. The next important skill that I find assists the evaluator is to maintain a sense of purpose and understanding about everyone's job in the courtroom. The evaluator's job is simply to report on her evaluation and answer questions put forth by the attorneys and the judge. It is not her job to make orders, but rather to explain her understanding of the family and make recommendations to the court for the benefit of the children. It is the judge's job to hear all of the evidence, including the evaluator's testimony and that of the parents and others whom the parents bring to testify on their behalf, to gather all the information, then apply the law. The judge makes a ruling that he feels will best apply in the circumstances before his court. For many judges, the most important information is that provided by the evaluator, but it is still only a piece of the testimony before him. Just as an evaluator does not want to take the recommendations of others in forming her conclusions, the judge is not supposed to take only the recommendations of the evaluator in forming her ruling. By recognizing this, we can reduce our anxiety, knowing that we are not the ultimate decision maker. Even if a case does not go to trial, it has not been our decision, but our recommendation that has helped the attorneys and their clients to reach a decision among themselves. If we recognize throughout the evaluation process that our role is to observe, evaluate, and recommend, we can reduce our anxiety about stepping out of our role, beyond the scope of our knowledge.

Similarly, we need to know that it is the attorney's role to advocate for her client. As long as divorce proceedings are in a litigious courtroom setting, there will always be a plaintiff and a defendant. We, as mental health practitioners, may question the judgment of this, but it is the reality in which we practice. Within the context of this adversarial, litigious process, we recognize that a competent attorney will be doing her job with thorough and professional cross-examination. If we do our job to the best of our ability, we will be less anxious, and we can recognize that the cross-examining attorney is simply doing her job to the best of her ability. Because her job is to defend her client and advocate for what her client wants, not what the child necessarily needs, we have no need to take personally the cross-examination that we face. Just as our job is to make recommendations about the children's best interests and the judge's job is to make a ruling that is in the children's best interests, it is the attorney's job to defend her client.

If we testify, there are many things that we can expect. First, we will be asked questions about our education, experience and qualifications so that the court can make a ruling that we are, in fact, experts in the areas of child custody and divorce. This process is called "voir dire" and is the legal process for determining if we are really expert. One of the main benefits of having a court order before doing the evaluation is that it often stipulates that the evaluator is an expert in the court for purposes of completing a custody evaluation. If not, the opposing attorney may try and use cross-examination to show that we are not sufficiently experienced or knowledgeable and may try and get the judge to rule against our being an expert. This strategy usually fails but is a process that we must endure until we get known in our local courts.

Once qualified as an expert, the next step is direct examination by the attorney who has called us as her witness. If we have done a thorough and comprehensive report, this process is usually relatively brief. The attorney asks us questions about our evaluation, what we did, when we did it, and whether we reached conclusions. She will then ask us what our conclusions are, ask us if the report is ours, and submit the report as evidence. Sometimes the opposing attorney will object to something that we have been asked. If that happens, I sit back and watch the attorneys and judge go through their procedures regarding objections, trying to learn about it while maintaining my inner focus on my forthcoming testimony. Similarly, there may be times when the judge will ask for clarification regarding something we have said. For the most part, however, during this part of our testimony, things are straightforward, with little to cause us anxiety.

When the first attorney has finished her direct examination, the other attorney will begin his cross-examination. We must remember that his job during this process is to advocate for his client, and the best way he can do this is to make us look like we have missed something, or have not thought through our recommendations sufficiently. Although he may make personal attacks against us, that is relatively rare. Instead, he will look for inconsistencies in our report, or inconsistencies between our report and our testimony. He will ask about our procedure, trying to suggest that we missed something important, either something positive about his client or something negative about the other parent. He will question our interpretations, he may question our reliance on psychological testing (if used) and the validity of such testing in the context of custody evaluations. He will look for ways to discredit anything we have done. If he can succeed, he can suggest to the judge that our conclusions need to be discredited.

One technique that attorneys frequently use during cross-examination is the that of hypotheticals. He may provide us with a set of facts which differ slightly from those of our findings, and ask us for our opinion and conclusions regarding these hypothetical facts. Usually, these hypothetical facts are closer to his client's perception and the conclusions he is looking for are closer to his client's desired outcome. For example, if we have focused on a parent's drug abuse as a reason for recommending primary custody and limited visitation to the other parent, the attorney may ask us hypothetically if we would reach the same conclusion if the parent is found to no longer have a drug abuse problem. Similarly, if we have recommended a week-week time-share between the parents, and his client is fearful that it will be unstable for the children, the attorney may question us on research that shows some children have trouble with transitions, and then ask us hypothetically what we would recommend if the children begin to show signs of distress with the recommended time-share. In each instance, he is simply trying to suggest that his client's perception of the needs of the children may be better than ours. When he finishes his cross-examination, he hopes to have suggested to the judge that there could be other outcomes than the ones we recommended, outcomes that are closer to the wishes of his client for whom he is advocating.

Our job during both direct and cross-examination is quite simple. It is to:

1. remain neutral, impartial, and fair to both parents;
2. avoid adding to the splitting and polarization in the courtroom;
3. answer all questions honestly, clearly, and succinctly;
4. avoid overexplaining or getting too technical;

5. avoid arguing with anyone;
6. maintain our position; and,
7. be clear with the court if we do not know something or cannot be certain about an event.

If the evaluation relates to a question of sexual abuse, for example, and we cannot be certain if it happened, we have a duty to state our inconclusiveness. If we also have an opinion, based on other information, we also can state that. For example, if we cannot know for sure if a molest occurred, but we feel that the evidence supports the likelihood of a false allegation, we need to be quite clear with the court of what we do know, what we do not know, and what we suspect may have occurred.

If we are presented during examination with information that we did not have, we need to incorporate it into our findings and make an honest conclusion about its impact. We need to avoid rigidity, recognizing that there may be other interpretations than our own, yet we need to stand by our conclusions and maintain our recommendations given our interpretation of the issues and the needs of the children. We need to stay child-focused, no matter how much the attorneys try and change our focus to the other parent and his or her flaws. We need to recognize that we are being paid for our time, not our testimony. In this way, we need to recognize that our obligation is not to the attorney who called us to testify; rather it is to the children and the court.

In addition to being prepared, it is important for the evaluator to speak loudly, clearly, and slowly during our testimony. It is necessary for the evaluator to maintain calm and organization throughout her testimony. The evaluator should always take the time to understand the questions, and take the necessary time to answer all questions asked. It is perfectly acceptable to refer to one's notes; in fact it is preferable to making mistakes which must be corrected later. To do so, simply ask permission from the court for any necessary delay. Finally, it is usually best if the evaluator sits and waits during the challenges between the attorneys. Never get involved in the courtroom discussion about objections, because that discussion is between the attorneys and the judge and revolves around court rules and the rules of evidence, both of which are beyond the purview of the evaluator.

In spite of our best efforts, we may face very uncomfortable cross-examination. This is the time when we ask ourselves why we ever decided to do this work in the first place, and it is the time to take some control of the situation. When questions get uncomfortable, and I am not sure how I want to answer,

I might pause for a short time. Never pause for more than 30 seconds, though, or the attorney may see that as a sign of indecisiveness. During the pause, I take time to regain emotional control of myself and to decide how I want to proceed. If I need more time to answer the question, I ask the attorney to rephrase the question. While the attorney is doing this, I will have more time to formulate my answer to the question. I might begin to talk more slowly so I can think while I talk. By taking a little more time, I also take the steam out of the attorney's hostile cross-examination. I look for pauses by the attorney and use such time to recall my fundamental principles of testimony, and to remember what I want to say to the judge. Then, if I am asked questions that allow me to make my point, I do so, for I may never get the opportunity again. Finally, because the judge wants to get as much information as possible, if I have the opportunity, I might ask the judge for direction about how to proceed.

In all of these techniques, I recognize that my main job is to hold to my principles, present the facts and my opinions as clearly as possible, and remain neutral and focused on the children. If I do these things, I can be satisfied that I have done my job well. I need to respect the advocacy of the attorney and avoid arguing with him when he questions my opinions. If I can accomplish this, I will feel good about my testimony and know that I have done my job professionally, regardless of the outcome within the court.

ETHICS, BIAS, AND PROFESSIONAL RESPONSIBILITY

Throughout this chapter and throughout this book, I have focused on the paramount issues of ethics and professional responsibility. It is clear that the evaluator's primary job is to maintain a high ethical standard in his work. If we do nothing else, by maintaining such a high standard for ethical responsibility we can educate the court and the attorneys about these critical issues. If we do *only* evaluations that are court ordered (or agreed on) and if we refuse to take cases where there is even a hint of inappropriate bias, it is harder for one of the attorneys or one of the parents to question our recommendations as unprofessional.

For example, in my recent experience, a father continues to have a very hard time accepting the recommendations of an evaluator, in part because the mother's cousin is a psychologist who works on the same faculty as the evaluator. I do not even know if the evaluator knew this, but this was enough of a potential source of bias, at least in the father's eyes, to give him a reason to question the evaluator's recommendation that went more in the mother's favor. I will not take referrals from a close friend who is a family law attorney simply because of the potential for appearing to have a conflict of interest. Similarly, I recently knew of an evaluator who, at the end of the evaluation, concluded that primary physical custody should be with the mother because 4-year-old children need mothers in that capacity. The evaluator had not informed the parents or attorneys of that potential gender bias at the start of the evaluation, and, because it came out that way, the father had a hard time accepting the recommendations. In essence, it is critical for evaluators to pay attention to potential conflicts of interest and their inherent biases, know their source (research-based, theory-based, or value-based), and make them clear to the parties and attorneys before commencing with the evaluation if there is any doubt whatsoever.

I recommend that evaluators work with their local and state professional associations to promulgate guidelines and rules for conduct in custody evaluations. We need to adopt standards for the ethical practice of custody evaluations. Several state or local organizations have begun this process, and I have summarized their major points in Appendix 6. In today's litigious society, and in such a litigious area, it is critical that evaluators understand the potential risks to their practice and professional relationships. By taking the challenge to get involved in the development of guidelines, those who do the work of evaluation are in the best position to manage the task of maintaining ethical responsibility and balancing that with the needs of the courts and the families that they serve. This is an area of mental health practice in relative infancy, and over the next several years, we will see more clarity on these concerns. By working in the field and staying current in our understanding of such guidelines, we can guarantee that we maintain a high standard of professional ethics in our work.

EVALUATOR IMMUNITY

Anyone who works in this area knows that there are many risks to this work. One of the greater risks is that of being sued by a client who is angry and upset with our recommendations. Some states, like California, have statutes that can make the appointment of an evaluator more risk free. In California, if an evaluator is appointed by the court under the provisions of

Section 730 of the Evidence Code, the appointed evaluator is free of risk of civil suit, just as a judge is free of such risk by nature of that appointment. However, there is nothing in California law to prohibit a disgruntled parent from making a complaint about an evaluator to the licensing board.

The best way of reducing the risk of civil lawsuits or claims with the licensing board is to act ethically and professionally at all times. There are many ways a mental health professional can act irresponsibly, such as by making custody recommendations when he has seen only one parent in a dispute, by switching roles and agreeing to do an evaluation when he has already been the child's therapist, by agreeing to do an evaluation when one of the parties (usually an attorney) is a close friend and not divulging that information in advance, by having a value-based bias that he keeps secret in advance, or by ignoring his ethical responsibility to have signed releases of information when he talks with other parties. In essence, the best way of avoiding risk is by maintaining the highest of ethical standards.

The mental health professional needs to be responsible and held accountable for any inappropriate actions. However, I believe that we also must work with courts, legislators, and licensing boards to create an environment in which the mental health professional who acts ethically is free of risk of harassment from disgruntled, litigious parents. For example, in California the provisions of Section 730 of the Evidence Code is a start. Working to make similar rules in other states regarding civil liability, as well as working to strengthen rules regarding licensing complaints, will reduce this risk even further.

EVALUATOR BURNOUT

As can be expected given the high degree of tension and responsibility in such work, it is common for good custody evaluators to quit doing custody evaluations after a time. With all of the family tension that is seen and the litigious atmosphere in the courts, many skilled evaluators, as well as many skilled attorneys, are getting out of the business. The work of a custody evaluator is quite stressful, with many demands for time from the clients, the attorneys, and the courts. As indicated, we have deadlines to meet, and if we do a lot of evaluations, we often find ourselves pressured by these deadlines. Evaluators tend to work alone a lot of the time, which can add to the tendency to feel overwhelmed, as well. In his recent book on custody evaluations, Dr. Richard Gardner explained that he was quitting his work on custody evaluations largely because he tired of the burden it placed on him. He expressed the belief, and it is one that I share, that the system creates some of the problems for families and those who work in it. I have seen many skilled people burn out and selectively limit or quit doing this work.

Each evaluator must decide for herself what to do when she feels that she is starting to get overwhelmed by the nature of this work. It is important for those who get into this work to recognize that they are likely to feel symptoms of burnout over time. Possible symptoms of burnout can include anger at clients, feelings of being overwhelmed with pressure, getting numb to the conflicts that we see, not wanting to call clients back, and so forth. We must be cognizant of our own signs of pressure and burnout, and develop strategies for dealing with it.

I have managed to find a variety of techniques for dealing with my own burnout. Probably the two most successful activities are periodically sharing my feelings about difficult cases with a close colleague and participating in peer consultation groups, in which evaluators share experiences and feelings on a regular basis. Such sharing and participation helps us recognize that we are not alone in this difficult work and gives us an opportunity to strengthen our strategies for dealing with difficult clients, difficult attorneys, and the difficult court system. I have seen good evaluators begin to work as teams to reduce the stress, to balance the work load, and to give themselves an automatic sounding board on difficult cases. Sometimes this also enables them to do more work in a shorter and more productive time than either of them could have done individually.

Along with this, maintaining control of schedules and developing other time management skills, balancing the work load by doing other work that is not custody related, attending conferences and workshops in the field, taking vacations, exercising regularly, eating well, and participating in other stress reduction activities like meditation and relaxation can all assist in dealing with the stresses of this work. I find that evaluators who keep control of their schedules and limit the number of evaluations to a level that feels manageable can reduce burnout, as well. For myself, a manageable number of evaluations at any one time is related to my other tasks and the total number of hours I work. Usually, two or three per month is the most that many evaluators can manage. Finally, I find that those evaluators who have a purpose in their work and remind themselves during times of stress of that purpose, whether it be to serve an overburdened court system, to maintain their sharp skills as evaluators, or to work for the betterment of children in divorcing families, manage their burnout the best.

TRAINING AND COMPETENCY OF EVALUATORS

At the present, I know of only one program that is specifically designed to train evaluators in this demanding and difficult work. It is a private program affiliated with the California School of Professional Psychology that teaches the knowledge and skills of doing evaluations. In this program, future evaluators learn didactic information about custody evaluations and problems of divorce and then get intensive supervision in doing custody evaluations. Although this program trains new evaluators in doing custody evaluations, it also provides the court with low-cost alternatives for the court to appoint an evaluator. Organizations such as the Association of Family and Conciliation Courts (AFCC) present workshops and institutes on custody evaluations. AFCC is planning symposia and training modules for teaching custody evaluations, as well. Many evaluators learn their work as new employees or interns of court settings, with good supervision from more experienced evaluators.

At the present, I know of no licensing body that lists a specialty in custody work, or any other body that regulates evaluators. I suggest that state licensing bodies develop a specialty in this field and that organizations that promote guidelines and ethics work together to promulgate guidelines for the training and competency of new evaluators. Until that is done, I recommend that anyone who is new to custody work get adequate supervision in that work.

The American Psychological Association deems it to be unethical for anyone to practice in a field of psychology in which he or she is not adequately trained and competent. I find that the best way to get competence in this field is to work under the direct consultation and supervision of someone who has significant experience. The Academy of Family Mediators has specific guidelines for mediator training and ongoing supervision before someone can become certified. I hope that similar guidelines for evaluators will be developed, with training courses and supervision available in custody work, as well. I support the standards of AFCC that give specific direction regarding the training, qualifications, and experience of custody evaluators (see Appendix 6).

CONCLUSION

I would like to close this chapter by stating that anyone who works in the field of custody needs ongoing training in child development, family assessment, problems of divorce, the workings of the court, and the special ethical issues this work brings. We need to network with one another to learn as much as we can about this burgeoning field. We need to develop interviewing skills, and we need better research on what makes a good parent. We need to develop new instruments that help us understand the tasks of parenting and find ways to integrate them into our comprehensive evaluations.

It is our duty as professionals to understand the dynamics of divorcing families, maintain an understanding of the needs of children and the changing laws of the states in which we work, and maintain the highest of ethical, professional standards if we are going to work in this dynamic, highly conflicted, litigious, yet rewarding area of our fields. We need to be cognizant of the power that we have and use it wisely. We need to respect parents and their children, respect the process of the courts, and continue to grow in our skills. We must always work for the betterment of children, who remain the victims of divorce unless their parents can learn to free them from the battles of parental conflict. If we meet these standards, maintain our professional integrity, hold to our ethical principles, and write reports that empower parents to strengthen their parenting skills, we will benefit from the rewards of helping families reduce the divorce conflict for their children.

Glossary of Legal Terms

Appeals court The court that hears an appeal after a trial court has made a judgment. The appeal is usually based on a determination that the trial judge misinterpreted the law or misused judicial authority when rendering a decision.

Case law Law that is formed by the aggregate of cases rather than by statute.

Code A collection of laws or statutes that are classified according to subject matter.

Conciliation court A court that aids in resolving marital disputes and provides counseling services for couples considering divorce.

Court order Direction of a judge entered in writing.

Cross-examination The examination of a witness who has already been questioned by the opposing attorney.

Custodial parent The parent who has the physical control, care, and custody of a minor child.

Custody The care, control, and maintenance of a child.

Custody evaluation An investigative procedure to gather and analyze facts regarding the family for the purpose of making a recommendation to the court regarding child custody and/or visitation. A custody evaluation may be initiated by order of the court or by stipulation of the parties, pursuant to local court rules.

Deposition The questioning of a party or witness, under oath, outside of the courtroom, usually in one of the lawyer's offices.

Dissolution of marriage The act of terminating a marriage by divorce.

Divided custody Arrangement in which each parent is custodian of the same child for different periods of time, with cross rights of visitation.

Domestic violence Physical or mental abuse of a family member.

Evidence Testimony, writings, objects, or other material offered to prove the existence or nonexistence of a fact.

Evidence code A section of state law that governs the procedures under which evidence can be obtained in a legal proceeding. In California, Section 730 of the Evidence Code sets the rules for appointing child custody evaluators.

Ex parte A judicial proceeding, order injunction, or conversation undertaken for the benefit of one party only, without a full hearing or both sides present.

Expert witness One who by reason of education or specialized experience possesses superior knowledge of a subject and is therefore determined by the court to be an expert on a specific area, such as child custody.

Family court services County-run programs for mediation and evaluation services, usually under the auspices of the local courts and by rules promulgated by state agencies or laws.

Family law Legal matters involving family issues—divorce, paternity, guardianship, dependency, adoption, and domestic violence.

Finding A determination of a fact by the court based on the evidence presented.

Guardian ad litem A special guardian appointed by the court on behalf of a minor child.

Hearing Public administrative or judicial proceeding, usually less formal than a trial, with definite issues to be tried, in which witnesses may appear and parties have the right to be heard.

Joint custody Joint physical and legal custody of a child.

Joint legal custody Custodial arrangement in which both parents share the rights and responsibilities to make decisions regarding the health, education, and welfare of a child. A parent who shares legal custody cannot have his or her rights of parenthood terminated.

Joint physical custody Custodial arrangement in which the child spends time with each parent for significant periods of time.

Judgment The final decision of a court determining the rights and obligations of the parties.

Legal custody The right and responsibility to make the decisions regarding the health, education, and welfare of a child.

Local rules of court Rules adopted by individual courts to define more specifically the general procedural rules that are set out in the various state rules of court.

Mediation The process by which parents voluntarily discuss and try to settle disputes, often related to child custody and visitation, with the assistance of an attorney or mental health professional trained in mediation skills.

Noncustodial parent The parent who does not have physical custody of a child.

Order to show cause (OSC) An order to appear in court and present reasons why a particular order should not be executed. If the party fails to appear or give sufficient reasons why the court should desist, the court will take the action requested.

Petition A formal application to the court requesting judicial action on a certain matter.

Petitioner The person who initially files a petition to the court.

Physical custody The right of a person to have a child reside with him or her and make the day-to-day decisions regarding the child's care during the time that the child is in his or her care.

Precedent A rule of law established for the first time by a court for a particular type of case and thereafter referred to in deciding similar cases.

Presumption An assumption of fact that the law requires to be made from another fact or group of facts. It is either conclusive (not subject to opposition) or rebuttable (capable of being rebutted by presentation of contrary proof).

Privilege The right not to disclose confidential statements made between certain persons who have protected relationships. These include statements between a husband-wife, patient-physician, attorney-client, psychotherapist-patient, and priest-penitent. For a child, the court usually becomes the holder of the privilege during a litigious divorce action because parents cannot agree.

Recommendation conference In some jurisdictions, the process in which the judge and attorneys review the recommendations of a custody evaluator and try to reach settlement on the issues.

Respondent The person who answers a petition in the form of a response.

Restraining order An order of the court forbidding a party from committing particular acts, either until a hearing can be held (temporary) or for a specific period of time (such as 3 years).

Settlement An agreement by persons who have been in dispute.

Sole legal custody Custodial arrangement in which one parent has all the rights and responsibilities to make the decisions regarding the health, education, and welfare of a child.

Sole physical custody Custodial arrangement in which the child resides primarily with one parent, with specific visitation rights to the other parent.

Split custody Custodial arrangement in which each parent has the physical custody of at least one child of the marriage, with specific visitation rights by each parent with the noncustodial child or children.

Statute A law established by the legislature.

Stipulate To agree.

Stipulation An agreement made by the parties and/or their attorneys, settling some or all of the contested issues or procedural matters. Often the appointment of a custody evaluator is made by stipulation between the parties.

Subpoena An order to appear at a certain time and place to give testimony or produce a document at deposition or trial.

Supervised visitation Arrangement in which a court orders a parent to visit a child only in the presence of a designated third person.

Temporary restraining order (TRO) An emergency remedy of brief duration that a court may issue in exceptional circumstances until the court can hold a hearing on the matter.

Tender years doctrine The outmoded presumption that custody of children of "tender years" (usually under 7 years old) should automatically be awarded to the mother.

Trial A judicial examination and determination of issues of law and fact between parties to a lawsuit.

Trial court The local court that initially hears all cases in dispute. If an attorney or party believes that a trial court judge has exceeded judicial authority or inappropriately applied the law, an appeal can be made to the appeals court.

Visitation rights Permission granted by the court to visit children. Visitation rights may be granted to parents and any other person having an interest in the welfare of the child, including but not limited to grandparents, stepparents, and other relatives of the child.

APPENDIX 1

Sample Forms, Letters, and Court Orders

This appendix includes:

Sample Custody Evaluation Face Sheet

Sample Referral Form/Special Master Appointment

Sample Cover Letter

Sample Child Custody/Parenting Evaluation (Agreement)

Special Master Program: Parent Information Sheet and Agreement

Sample court order for private custody evaluation

Sample court order for appointment of Special Master

CUSTODY EVALUATION FACE SHEET

Full name:_______________ Birth date: ______ D.L.# __________ S.S.#_________

Address: City: _______________ State: ______ Zip: _______ Phone: ___________

Employment: Address: _______________________________ Phone: ___________

Reason for referral: _______ Custody: ___________ Visitation: ______ Other:____

Referred by whom: ___________ Phone: ________________________________

(Ex)Spouse's full name: ___________ Birth date: ______ S.S.#: _______________

Address: City: _______________ State: ______ Zip: ___________ Phone: _______

Children: Name Birth date School/Grade Current living arrangement

1. ____________________
2. ____________________
3. ____________________
4. ____________________
5. ____________________

Others living in home Age Relationship/Status

1. ____________________
2. ____________________

Date of marriage:________ Separation:________ Date divorce filed: ___________

Who filed: __________________ Date of divorce (if applicable): _____________

Court action: (use back if necessary)

1. Date:____ Initiated by? Father: ____ Mother: ____ Reason: _______________

Result: ____________________

2. Date:____ Initiated by? Father: ____ Mother: ____ Reason: _______________

Result: ____________________

3. Date:____ Initiated by? Father: ____ Mother: ____ Reason: _______________

Result: ____________________

4. Date:____ Initiated by? Father: ____ Mother: ____ Reason: _______________

Result: ____________________

Father's attorney: ________________________________ Phone: _____________

Mother's attorney: ________________________________ Phone: _____________

Family court evaluator: ____________________________ Phone: _____________

Previous marriages: ____________________

Father: _____ Dates(s) of marriage(s): ___ Divorce: _______ # Kids:_________

Mother:_____ Dates(s) of marriage(s): ___ Divorce: _______ # Kids:_________

Employment history: (list most recent first)

Father: ____________________

Father: ____________________

Mother: ____________________

Mother: ____________________

Previous mediation/evaluation? Yes: __ No: __ Date(s) seen: ______________

Name of mediator/evaluator: ______________________________

Recommendation: ______________________________

Who cares for your child(ren) when you are not at home: ______________

Describe your child(ren).

____
____
____
____
____
____

Describe your relationship with your child(ren).

____
____
____
____
____
____

Describe your (ex)spouse's relationship with your child(ren).

____
____
____
____
____
____

How do you discipline your child(ren)?

____
____
____
____
____
____

How does your (ex)spouse discipline your child(ren)?

____

____

____

____

____

____

Describe your strengths as a parent.

____

____

____

____

____

____

Describe your weaknesses as a parent.

____

____

____

____

____

____

Describe your (ex)spouse's strengths as a parent.

____

____

____

____

____

____

Describe your (ex)spouse's weaknesses as a parent.

____

____

____

____

____

____

What will your (ex)spouse say about you?

____

____

____

____

____

____

How would you recommend sharing parenting with your (ex)spouse?

____

____

____

____

____

____

Any other comments/questions (use back of form, if necessary): __________

____

____

____

____

I authorize ________________ to evaluate me and my children to assist the court in determining the most appropriate parenting plan for our "family."

Signed: ______________________________Date: __________

REFERRAL FORM
MARIN COUNTY SUPERIOR COURT
SPECIAL MASTER APPOINTMENT

CASE NAME: ________________ CASE NO.: ____________________

Special Master ______________________________________

Address ____

Phone # ____

FAX # ____

Mother's name ________________ Father's name ________________

Address ____________________ Address ____________________

Phone # Hm. ________________ Phone # Hm. ________________

Wk. ________________________ Wk. ________________________

FAX # ______________________ FAX # ______________________

Attorney ____________________ Attorney ____________________

Address ____________________ Address ____________________

____________________________ ____________________________

Phone # ____________________ Phone # ____________________

FAX # ______________________ FAX # ______________________

Mediator ____________________ Phone # ____________________

FAX # ______________________

Previous Special Master____________________________ Phone_________

FAX # ______________________________________

Previous Evaluator ________________________________ Phone_________

FAX # ______________________________________

Date of proposed appointment________________________

Term of appointment ______________________________

Allocation of costs: ______ %Mother _______ %Father

Children's names Date of birth

1. ____________________________ ____________________________

2. ____________________________ ____________________________

3. ____________________________ ____________________________

Other caretaking figures______________________________________

Current custody and visitation arrangement

1a. Joint legal __________ 1b. Sole legal__________________ with___

2a. Joint physical ________ 2b. Sole physical ________________ with ___

3. Other ____

4. Current access plan (describe or attach order) ______________________

____

____

____

Mother's concerns

1. Cooperation level
   - A. Not a problem ______
   - B. Doesn't communicate ______
   - C. No follow-through ______
   - D. Harasses ______
2. Fitness to parent
   - A. Emotional disturbance ______
   - B. Substance abuse ______
   - C. Disability ______
   - D. Other ______
   - ______________________________
   - ______________________________
3. Child abuse
   - A. Emotional ______
   - B. Physical ______
   - C. Sexual ______
   - D. Neglect ______
4. Spousal violence ______
5. Alienates children ______
   - From other parent ______
   - From self ______
6. List strengths seen in the other parent
   - ______________________________
   - ______________________________
   - ______________________________

Father's concerns

1. Cooperation level
   - A. Not a problem ______
   - B. Doesn't communicate ______
   - C. No follow-through ______
   - D. Harasses ______
2. Fitness to parent
   - A. Emotional disturbance ______
   - B. Substance abuse ______
   - C. Disability ______
   - D. Other ______
   - ______________________________
   - ______________________________
3. Child abuse
   - A. Emotional ______
   - B. Physical ______
   - C. Sexual ______
   - D. Neglect ______
4. Spousal violence ______
5. Alienates children ______
   - From other parent ______
   - From self ______
6. List strengths seen in the other parent
   - ______________________________
   - ______________________________
   - ______________________________

Special needs of the children (please indicate which child)

1. Attachment concerns ____________________
2. Specific developmental issues (e.g., developmental lags) ____________________
3. Educational concerns ____________________
4. Mental health concerns (e.g., withdrawn, pseudomature, acting-out) ____________________
5. Medical concerns ____________________
6. Other ____________________

General caretaking arrangements

Please attach copy of current parenting plan.

Perceived problems with current arrangement ____________________

Brief description of each parent's proposed solution to perceived problems:

Mother ____________________

Father ____________________

Immediate conflicts to be resolved, known areas of likely dispute (please list issues that need to be immediately addressed and those issues/disputes that are likely to become problematic)

Immediate conflicts ____________________

Future issues ____________________

Please attach copies of pertinent court orders, custody/parenting agreements, current motions pending, and current time-share if different from order.

SAMPLE COVER LETTER

December 17, 199___

Ms. Jane Doe
123 Main St.
Caldwell, CA 91234

Dear Ms. ___________________

As we discussed, I plan on seeing you and your ex-husband for an evaluation related to your divorce beginning on ______. I will be scheduling a future appointment with each of you and appointments with you and your son after we meet. I am enclosing a form that I would like you to complete prior to the appointment and bring with you to the office. The information that you provide will allow me to do a more thorough job in assessing your family and your needs.

In order to do a thorough evaluation, I will need to know information about each of you. In addition to the time that I spend with all of you, I will be administering psychological testing as part of the overall evaluation. You will be asked to sign a release of information form that will provide me with access to medical, school, legal, and other information to acquire a complete understanding of you and your family.

I believe that it is in a family's best interests to develop their own postdivorce parenting arrangements whenever possible. I become part of the process when a family's own attempts to resolve these issues has reached an impasse and an evaluation is needed to assist the attorneys or court in determining the children's best interests. It is my belief, and research shows, that it is best for children when parents can agree on parenting arrangements. My evaluations are designed to promote resolution of conflicts in this area. Along with this, it is best if neither of you discusses this evaluation with your son until after we meet, so that it does not become a source of further anxiety for him.

As we discussed, the fee for this evaluation is expected to be $______, and I expect this to be paid when we meet. As I understand, you are each responsible for one half of the fee and will each be paying $______. In the event that I spend significantly more time than anticipated, I will inform you of any further charges. When I have completed my evaluation and all fees have been paid, I will mail my written report to your attorneys and the court. In the event that I am required to testify in court, I will testify only to my evaluation and I will bill my usual and customary hourly charges for all time associated with the testimony and its preparation.

I hope this addresses a few of the questions that you may have. Please bring the enclosed form with you to the appointment. If you have any questions in advance, please do not hesitate to contact me.

Licensed Psychologist

Enclosure

CHILD CUSTODY/PARENTING EVALUATION

In order for this evaluation to be of help to you and your family, the following conditions must be met. I recognize that these conditions may seem very stringent and formal. However, it has been my experience that very clear agreement at the start of this kind of evaluation will help you and your family by ensuring the fairness of the evaluation and by minimizing potential confusion or disagreement.

INTERVIEWS

1. The evaluator will need to interview all members of the immediate family. This includes the mother, father, and children. The evaluator may also need to interview other parties who are important for a full understanding of your family and the current situation. These might include present or prospective parent surrogates (e.g., stepparents) and closely involved grandparents or other relatives. Usually the interviews of the parents and surrogate parents will require 2 to 3 hours each; interviews and testing with children will require 2 to 4 hours each. The evaluator will also need to observe the family as a whole or in subgroups at the office and/or at a prearranged time at each home. By mutual agreement, the following people will be available for interviews:

______________________________ ______________________________

______________________________ ______________________________

______________________________ ______________________________

______________________________ ______________________________

______________________________ ______________________________

CONFIDENTIALITY

2. In order to allow exploration in depth of issues concerning your family, the parties must agree to a modification of the traditional rules of confidentiality. Specifically, the evaluator, at his or her discretion, must be able to reveal to one party what has been said by another. This does not mean that all information will be automatically revealed or that certain information cannot be discussed in private. It means only that the evaluator reserves the right to share the information that is needed in order to explore important or disputed issues thoroughly.

3. Prior to beginning the evaluation, the parties must agree on all sources of information to which the evaluator will have access. I must have signed releases from all the adults allowing my office to obtain reports from other professionals who have been involved with your family. This would include, at the evaluator's discretion, medical doctors, hospitals, counselors, therapists, teachers, schools, and other agencies. A release form is attached for you to fill out and sign.

4. Unless otherwise specified as an addendum to this agreement, all parties waive their rights to claim privilege with respect to the proper use of this evaluation and report. That is, the report and any information supplied to the evaluator by any party in the course of this evaluation will be available to the court and to both attorneys.

FEES

5. The cost of this evaluation is: ________________________

6. Should your case require them, the fees for depositions and court appearances are: ________________________

7. In order to ensure that financial factors do not delay or complicate the evaluation, I require a payment of ________________ at the time of the initial interview. Payment in full is required before the report can be released.

TIMING

8. I will attempt to do the entire evaluation as quickly as possible. It is usually (but not always) possible to provide the written report within____________ days of the date of the initial interview.

WHAT TO EXPECT

9. The initial interview will usually be with each parent separately. Each adult will usually be interviewed in two or more office visits. The children will then be seen individually and family sessions then scheduled. Please note that the findings will include psychological observations, discussions of your strengths and weaknesses as parents, as well as current and future-oriented recommendations concerning the issues that are in dispute (e.g., recommended form of custody, amount and timing of contacts with the children, where the children should live, etc.)

10. Following those meetings, the final report will be prepared and sent to the court or family court service. The judge or conciliation worker will then make the report available to both attorneys. Because of the potentially sensitive nature of the report, both attorneys are requested to respect the report's confidential nature and to refrain from sharing it with either of you.

These agreements are necessary in order to allow me to work with your family in a fair and effective way and to provide to you, to your attorneys, and to the court a thorough and objective evaluation.

Having read this document carefully and discussed it with your attorney, please indicate your understanding of it and agreement to its terms by signing it below and returning it to me, along with your share of the initial costs. Following receipt of the signed agreements, release forms, and fees from all of the parties involved, I will contact you in order to schedule your interviews.

* *

AGREEMENT

I have read the above, discussed its provisions with my attorney, and agree to proceed with the evaluation as described. I am attaching $ _____, representing my _______% of the initial costs, and I agree to pay the same percentage of any reasonable costs above that amount, in accordance with the payment schedule described above.

Dated: ______________________ By: ______________________________

(Signature)

Attached: Release forms

SPECIAL MASTER PARENT INFORMATION SHEET AND AGREEMENT

Dear Parents:

I am writing this letter as an introduction to what you can expect in our Special Master work. When I get appointed as a Special Master, either through court order or stipulation of the parents, it is usually following disputes related to custody and visitation which have become intractable, often lasting for many years. This takes a heavy emotional toll on both you, the parents, and your children. It will be my job to try and help you reduce the future toll on all of you. By explaining my philosophy, it will be clear to you how I intend to work, how I set my priorities, and I hope it will clearly set out your responsibilities and mine in this process.

As a Special Master, I have a multifaceted job in which I am part detective (as parents tell me different stories, it is my job to try and understand the "whole truth"), part educator (I try and help parents understand how to share their children, understand their child's developmental needs, resolve problems, and move on in their lives following the divorce), part mental health professional (I try and understand your feelings and attitudes about your experiences and understand your childrens' feelings about their experiences), part judge (I make decisions), and part advocate for your children (their needs will be my first priority in the decisions that I make). I will often need to talk with other professionals, such as doctors, therapists, school personnel, or others, and may need to meet with your children to understand their feelings and opinions. The task is a complex yet important one, because of the ongoing dispute between you and the other parent.

By the time you have decided on a Special Master, you have probably spent thousands of dollars on attorney fees and court costs, and are reluctant to spend more money in this process. It is likely that several thousand dollars were also spent in a custody evaluation before my appointment. My fee is __ per hour for all of the work I do. By your order, I will bill each of you 50% for my services. When you see a bill, it will reflect your personal charges, and an identical bill will have been sent to the other parent. I ask for a retainer of $_____________ before starting my work, and as I continue my tasks and you incur new fees, I expect bills to be paid by the 15th of the month in which you receive them. If bills are paid promptly, no further retainers will be required, but if not, I reserve the right to request a continuing retainer once the previous retainer is used up. In general, I bill for all my services, including phone calls with parents, attorneys, the judge, and other collateral people; letter writing; sessions with parents, children, or anyone else who I might see; and any other peripheral work that I do for your families. If you have any questions about my bill, or any of my charges, please do not hesitate to ask about them. I will charge only one of you for missed sessions, and if the order allows for it, I reserve the right to allocate a different percentage on my billing if it appears that one of you is generating the vast majority of my work. Even with this in mind, most people find that my costs are significantly less than the cost of two attorneys and court costs.

In order to balance my availability of time, it takes a while to understand your family and its needs. I prefer not to waste your time, your money, or my time and it is my hope that all work in which I am involved is used productively. For some families, this might mean that I do little or no work for several months at a time while things are moving smoothly. For other families, there is an ongoing need to make decisions, provide for conflict resolution, and give direction regarding other problems that you encounter. In general, I respond to phone calls within 24 hours, but if you have an urgent matter, please inform my answering service of the urgency. If you ever wish to leave a very detailed message for me, simply tell the answering service that you would like to put the message yourself into my voice mail, and they will connect you directly to my voice mail. Otherwise, all messages will be taken by my answering service. On occasion, it may take more than 24 hours to return your call, and if it has taken more than 48 hours, please call again, as there could have been some mix-up. There are times when I am out of town or expect to be unavailable for several days, and I generally inform my answering service of all such instances. Although I have no control of whether they communicate this to my clients, I have found that most of the time the answering service will inform you if I am out of town when you call.

In order to reduce wasted time, I try and determine relatively early whether or not I can provide mediation services that, while somewhat more costly, enable you, as the parents, to make decisions for your children. If it looks rather quickly that you will remain at odds with one another, I will attempt to listen to each of you about your ideas and your concerns on issues pertaining to your children and then make a decision as quickly as possible. Hopefully, this process will feel very different than the court process, which has probably been emotionally and financially costly, and which may have taken months for decisions to be made. In general, when an issue is presented to me, I will make decisions rather quickly. If they are about more complex issues, I will inform you of a deadline in which I intend to make decisions, and then I will make every effort to meet that deadline. By reducing the time it takes me to make decisions, we can reduce fees, and hopefully the emotional and financial costs of your experience.

In general, the scope of my work is best identified by the court order or stipulation. Typically, Special Masters work to solve disagreements about such issues as schedules, overnight visitation, choice of schools, extracurricular activities, troubles at transfers, holiday scheduling, parenting differences, health issues, children's therapy, and/or problematic behaviors on the part of one or both parents. To the extent that your order allows, I will be happy to address issues related to any of the above, or any similar issue that ultimately affects your children. Under current

Contra Costa County Guidelines, if the two of you have stipulated to this Special Master agreement, it is my expectation that, when I make a decision, it is binding. In contrast, if you have been ordered into this Special Master agreement by the court, you have the right of appeal to the judge. Irrelevant of how I was appointed, I would like to set forth my guidelines for making decisions. When you reach an impasse on something, I expect you to contact me and let me know as soon as possible. I will then discuss the matter with each of you, and if there is something in the court order that sets a precedent and helps to define the issue, I will take that into account as I think about my decision. My other priority is to understand how the issue affects your children. I will always look to the impact on your children for any decision that I make before I look to the question of fairness for either of you. Because it is my belief, and California law is clear in its intent, that the "best interests of the children" are paramount, if there is a clear way of determining what is best for your children, I will use that as my first choice.

If there is no clear understanding how the issue impacts your children, and there is nothing in the order that gives me direction, I am likely to make decisions based on what seems "fair." In such circumstances, I am likely to alternate between you based on other decisions I have made. Because I keep extensive notes of all my contacts, and a record of all decisions made, it will be easy for me to determine what seems fair once I have been involved with your family. Over time, it is likely that each of you will take turns being pleased with, or being upset with, my decisions. This is an expectation that I have when I start working with high-conflict families of divorce. With that reality in mind, I certainly encourage you to ask questions about my decisions and how I reach them, but I also expect you to learn to accept and go along with them if we want this experience to be more successful than your previous experiences in the courts.

Finally, it is important to recognize each of our responsibilities in this work. My primary responsibility as Special Master is to help educate the two of you and make decisions that are in your children's best interests. My responsibility is to respond to your calls as quickly as I can, and unless I am out of town, this will usually be within several days. My responsibility will be to set timelines for which I will make decisions, and then make every effort to meet those timelines. Ultimately, my responsibility will be to adhere to the scope of my role as outlined in your court order or stipulation and assist in the process of conflict resolution.

On the other hand, your responsibility is to keep me informed of your concerns. Although I cannot read your minds, I can read your letters and respond accordingly. If you have questions about the Special Master process or my understanding of your family situation, please do not hesitate to contact me. If you have concerns about the other parent, please do not hesitate to contact me. Although it is my belief that each of you needs to have the opportunity to do the best job of parenting that you can without concern about the other parent's interpretation of your parenting job, it is clear that each of you needs a place and an opportunity for voicing concerns, and I am the one to whom you need to voice them. Another responsibility of yours is to follow both the court's and my orders. Ultimately, it is your responsibility to act in a way that promotes conflict resolution and eases the pain and burden on your children. By statute, it is your responsibility to promote a healthy relationship between your children and the other parent and to avoid interfering in any negative way in that relationship. This is not only part of the California law, but it is clearly in your children's best interests. Finally, as indicated earlier, it is your responsibility to pay your bill on time in order that I can continue working in this capacity with your family.

It is my hope that, as we work together, we can find a new way of resolving conflicts and moving on in your post-divorce life successfully. If we all work as outlined, I hope that your children can be raised with less emotional trauma than they have already experienced.

By your signature below, you acknowledge receipt of this letter and agree to pay for all services performed by Dr.___________ as Special Master for your family.

_____________________________ _________________________________

Mother Date Father Date

IN THE SUPERIOR COURT
OF THE STATE OF CALIFORNIA
IN AND FOR THE COUNTY OF CONTRA COSTA

____

Petitioner, No. ____________________

and STIPULATION FOR ORDER AND ORDER FOR PRIVATE CHILD CUSTODY EVALUATION

____

Respondent.

____________________/

The parties stipulate that the following agreements may be made an order of the court. Local Court Rule No. 13B sets the policy and procedure for child custody evaluations. This stipulation and order supplements those procedures and policies.

1. __________ is appointed the Court's expert for purposes of conducting a custody evaluation in this proceeding pursuant to Evidence Code §730.

2. The parties shall cooperate in the evaluation. As part of the evaluation, the parties shall participate in such testing and interviews as the expert directs, including making themselves and the children available as needed for testing and interviews. Interview schedules and administrative details of the evaluation are at the sole discretion of the evaluator.

3. The parties shall make financial arrangements with the expert forthwith. The evaluation will not commence until after the parties have made financial arrangements for payment acceptable to the expert.

4. The costs of the evaluation shall be advanced by

(a) ______________ subject to allocation at the time of trial OR

(b) Paid in advance as follows:

____________________ ____________________

FATHER to pay ($ or %) MOTHER to pay ($ or %)

Failure to attend scheduled sessions and or failure to cooperate shall be subject to court review in allocating costs or reimbursing the cooperating spouse.

5. No party or attorney for a party shall initiate oral or telephonic contact with the evaluator other than for purposes of scheduling or administrative details, or in response to a request from the evaluator, unless by conference call with both attorneys or pro per party(ies) on the phone simultaneously with the evaluator or all parties and their attorney(s) present. No communication shall be made in writing by any party or their attorney unless data or information in writing or background materials are specifically requested by the evaluator. The parties shall comply with the request of the evaluator for documents or correspondence as long as it is with notice to the other party and his or her attorney and providing that copies of all

documents and/or correspondence are provided to all parties or their attorneys. Only documents as specifically requested are to be provided, and all parties shall have an opportunity to rebut or present opposing documents on a time schedule to be set by the evaluator with copies provided to the other party and/or his or her attorney. A person in propria persona shall have no advantage by his or her status to speak to the evaluator without the represented party being included in the communication as part of the process. Any such communication shall be limited to relevant issues or facts about which the evaluator has specifically requested information. The same process shall be utilized in the event the evaluator wishes to initiate contact with a party in propria persona or the attorney(s). The evaluator is free to ask for whatever information or documents are felt appropriate and necessary to conduct the evaluation. All parties and the evaluator are free to call each other about scheduling or other nonsubstantive matters. The evaluator is free to call any witnesses he or she wishes in order to get information about the evaluation, but any documents supplied as a result of the inquiry shall be copied to all other parties and/or their attorneys. Nothing in this section shall preclude the evaluator from calling a party or any witness to clarify a point raised during an interview or to answer questions as needed to corroborate information or to complete the evaluation. That contact is at the evaluator's sole discretion. The evaluator may conduct individual interviews or sessions as he or she sees fit.

6. At the conclusion of the evaluation, the expert shall prepare a written report. An original shall be sent to the Family Court Services with copies to the court and both counsel. Pending further order of court, counsel for the parties may permit their clients to read and review the report in the presence of the attorney. Parties in propria persona may review and read the report at Family Court Services. No party may be provided a copy of the report without court order. No report may be attached to a pleading without leave of the court. Any violation of this provision may be the subject of sanctions and/or contempt to the attorneys and their clients.

7. The parties are restrained and enjoined from discussing the evaluation or the written report with the children or discussing the report and evaluation in the presence of the children.

8. The parties are enjoined and restrained from discussing in the presence of or with their minor children specific facts, issues, or positions relating to custody or visitation in a manner that disparages the other party or with the intent to influence the child with respect to custody and/or visitation.

9. As part of the evaluation, by executing this stipulation, the parties waive the psychotherapist-patient privilege as to the children's therapist(s), section 1014 Evidence Code. The parties are also waiving any psychotherapist-patient privilege as it relates to their own therapist(s). If the children's therapist wishes to raise the privilege on behalf of his or her patient(s) because of a concern relating to the best interests of the minor child/children, the therapist may request and obtain an in

camera hearing with the court for purposes of showing why otherwise confidential information should not be disclosed. If there is a conflict relating to the release of information, the court may appoint an attorney for the children to protect and represent the children in the proceeding limited to the release of information, or for such other purposes as the court deems appropriate. If the court appoints an attorney for the children or if there is an attorney for the children, the attorney may also raise the issue of privilege and disclosure as set forth above. The judicial officer hearing the in camera proceeding relating to privilege shall not be the same judicial officer that will hear the trial or other matters in the case. The best interest of the child/children shall be the criterion for determining whether the questionable information should be released to the evaluator or to determine the terms and conditions of the release and use of information presented.

10. The court reserves jurisdiction over the evaluation process to resolve any disputes that may arise. The attorneys and/or party(ies) in propria persona shall meet and confer prior to contacting the court for resolution over problems that arise during the evaluation. If the dispute is not resolved, the parties shall schedule a conference call with the court giving the court at least two (2) days advance notice. If the parties wish to submit documents in writing, a formal hearing may be scheduled in the usual manner, which may or may not include an order shortening time for hearing.

11. Any violation of the above provisions may be cause for monetary sanctions or may be punishable by contempt, or both.

12. ADDITIONAL PROVISIONS:

____

____

____

____

____

____

____

____

____

____

____

____

____

____

____

____

SO STIPULATED

Dated: ____________________ ______________________________
Petitioner

Dated: ____________________ ______________________________
Respondent

Dated: ____________________ ______________________________
Attorney for Petitioner

Dated: ____________________ ______________________
Attorney for Respondent

UPON GOOD CAUSE IT IS SO ORDERED:

Dated: ______________________________
JUDGE (PRO TEM) OF THE
SUPERIOR COURT REFEREE

SUPERIOR COURT OF CALIFORNIA, COUNTY OF MARIN

In re the Marriage of | No. FL MARIN

Petitioner: | STIPULATION AND ORDER APPOINTING SPECIAL MASTER

and

Respondent:

________________________/

Pursuant to the stipulation of the parties hereinafter set forth, and good cause appearing therefor,

IT IS ORDERED, ADJUDGED, AND DECREED THAT:

APPOINTMENT:

1. ______________ is appointed Special Master under Evidence Code §730, Code of Civil Procedure §1280, et seq., and Code of Civil Procedure §638 until resignation of ________________ or written agreement of the parties, further Court Order, or ________________, whichever first occurs.

2. This appointment is based on the expertise of the Special Master as a licensed mental health professional. The Special Master shall have authority to make decisions on the following issues:

AUTHORITY:

[ ] Legal custody of minor child(ren)
[ ] Physical custody of minor child(ren)
[ ] Time-sharing/visitation actual schedule
[ ] Vacation and holiday schedule
[ ] Education and schooling
[ ] Child care, day care, and baby-sitting
[ ] Religious training, affiliation, and attendance
[ ] Daily routines and issues: bedtime, diet, etc.
[ ] Restraining orders
[ ] Clothing use and allocation
[ ] Recreation
[ ] After-school and enrichment activities
[ ] Discipline
[ ] Health care issues
[ ] Other

QUASI-JUDICIAL IMMUNITY:

The Special Master is a Court Officer/Referee. The Special Master has quasi-judicial immunity. The Special Master cannot be sued based on his or her actions in this matter. The Special Master cannot be compelled to testify and is not subject to subpoena pursuant to Evidence Code §703.5. However, the Special Master may choose to testify if the Court so requests, or upon application of the Special Master to the Judge notifying the Court of the Special Master's desire to testify. Such testimony shall not constitute a waiver of the Special Master's quasi-judicial immunity.

PROCEDURE:

Both parties shall participate in the dispute resolution process as defined by the Special Master and shall be present when so requested by the Special Master. The Special Master shall conduct hearings as an Arbitrator, that is, they may be informal in nature, can be by telephone or in person, and need not comply with the rules of evidence. No record need be made, except the Special Master's statement of decision or order. Upon the request of either party, the Special Master shall allow testimony to be taken or either party to be represented by an attorney, or other actions required by Arbitrators.

The Special Master shall have the authority to determine the protocol of all interviews and sessions including, in the case of meetings with the parties, the power to determine who attends such meetings. The Special Master may order the child(ren) of the parents to participate in adjunct services including physical and psychological examinations and assessments and psychotherapy; alcohol and drug monitoring/testing and _________ .

The Special Master may utilize consultants and/or assistants as necessary to assist the Special Master in the performance of the duties contained herein.

DECISIONS:

If the Special Master is appointed by agreement, then, unless his or her powers are limited in some way by the agreement, or unless the agreement provides for an alternate method of judicial review, the Special Master may make all decisions subject to the following forms of judicial review.

a. If the decisions relate to conflicts between parents that do not substantially affect the best interests of the children, the Special Master may make direct orders, approved as made by the court, and reviewed only by a standard of abuse of discretion. These orders will be effective when made, and continue in effect until set aside by a court of competent jurisdiction. These types of decisions include, but are not limited to, dates and times of pickup and delivery for visitation/time-share, division of vacations and holidays, method of pickup and delivery, transportation to and from visitation, participation in visitation (significant others, relatives, etc.), child-related issues such as participation in the selection and provision of child care, day care, and baby-sitting, bedtime, diet, clothing, recreation, after-school and enrichment activities, discipline, health care and management, and alterations in schedule that do not alter the basic time-sharing arrangement or percentage.

b. If the decision relates to any other issue of parenting or time-share that does not substantially alter the previous time-share, does not alter an award of physical or legal custody, or does not substantially interfere with a party's relationship with his or her child(ren), the decision shall be made by statement of decision or arbitrator's award. Such types of decisions include, but are not limited to, large alterations of vacation and holiday time-shares, religion and religious training, private school education, mental health care and management, or major health decisions. The decisions shall be submitted to the court, which shall approve them as made and enter them as orders. These decisions may be reviewed on such grounds as would permit review if the underlying decision had been made by a subordinate judicial officer or referee, that is, by the filing of objections that set out the issues to which exception is taken, and the filing of a motion comparable to a motion for new trial under C.C.P. §57. The motion may be made to the Special Master or to the Superior Court and shall be determined in the same manner as a motion for new trial. The statement of decision/arbitrator's award is effective when made and remains in effect until set aside or altered by a court of competent jurisdiction.

c. If the decision alters an award of physical or legal custody, substantially alters a previous time-share, substantially interferes with a party's relationship with his or her child(ren), or allows one parent to move with the children to a distance that would interfere with currently existing time-share arrangements, the decision shall be approved by the court. The decision is not effective until entered by the court as an order, and may be presented in the form of an Order to Show Cause why the recommendation should not be adopted. The objecting party shall carry the burden of proof as to why the recommendation should not be adopted.

d. Hearings granted to review the decisions of a Special Master should, in general, be submitted on declaration, subject to cross-examination, as any other family law motion, unless oral testimony is requested pursuant to local rules.

COMMUNICATION WITH SPECIAL MASTER:

1. The parties and their attorneys shall have the right to initiate or receive ex parte communication with the Special Master. Any party may initiate contact in writing with the Special Master, provided that copies are provided to opposing counsel simultaneously.

2. The Special Master may communicate ex parte with the Judge, at the discretion of the Special Master and the Judge. The Special Master may request that the Judge appoint counsel for the child(ren).

3. The parties shall provide all records, documentation, and information requested by the Special Master, and if unavailable, shall sign any and all releases for records and information requested by the Special Master.

4. [ ] counsel for [ ] Petitioner [ ] Respondent shall provides copies of all:
[ ] pleadings
[ ] orders
[ ] correspondence (between_____________)
related to the issue assigned within________ calendar days of the date this order is filed.

DATA COLLECTION:

Special Master may interview all members of the immediate or extended family of both parties.

Special Master may interview and request the participation of other persons who the Special Master deems to have relevant information or to be useful participants.

The parties consent to release of records and information from and shall sign appropriate releases there for:

a. child(ren)'s current/previous pediatrician
b. child(ren)'s current/previous psychologist/psychiatrist
c. child(ren)'s current/previous teachers
d. hospital and medical records
child(ren)'s current/previous physician
mother's current/previous physician
father's current/previous physician
e. police department
f. mediator
g. prior Special Master(s)
h. mother's current/previous therapist
i. father's current/previous therapist
j. custody evaluator(s)
k. other

CHILD(REN)'S THERAPIST:

The Special Master is appointed guardian ad litem of minor child(ren) for limited purposes of whether any minor child(ren)'s therapeutic privilege should be waived by the court for the purpose of obtaining information [the testimony] from the child(ren)'s therapist.

a. The Special Master may obtain information from the child(ren)'s therapist outside the presence of the parties and their counsel.

b. The Special Master may refuse to disclose to the parties the details of the information received from the child(ren)'s therapist if revealing the information will be detrimental to the child(ren) or the child(ren)'s therapy.

c. This waiver of the therapeutic privilege shall not extend to any other proceedings except those before the Special Master and may not be used to compel the therapist to testify in court.

FEES:

Charges and Costs

The Special Master's fee for serving as Special Master is $_________ per ______minute period (per session). Time spent in interviewing, report preparation, review of records and correspondence, telephone conversation, travel, court preparation, and any other time invested in association with serving as Master other than for court appearances and settlement conferences will also be billed at the $______ per session rate. The Special Master's fee for court appearances and settlement conferences is $ _________ per session while in court and at the conference and $ ___________per session travel time to and from his or her office.

It is understood that despite the fact that the Special Master may prepare reports and/or testify in support of one party, both parties will continue to be responsible for the payment of fees associated with such services at the allocated percentage designed below. In the event that the testimony and/or written report of the Special Master is required for any hearing, settlement conference, or court action by one or both parties, the Special Master's fees for such services shall be paid by both parties, in advance, according to an estimate provided by the Special Master, according to the specified share of cost percentages. Ultimately, the court shall determine the proper allocation between the parties of the fees of the Special Master for such services and may require reimbursement by one party to the other for any overpayment to the Special Master.

The Special Master shall be reimbursed for any expenses he or she incurs in association with his or her role as Special Master. These costs may include, but are not limited to, the following: photocopies ($__________/page), messenger service, long-distance telephone charges, express and/or certified mail costs and excess postage to foreign countries, parking, tolls, mileage, travel expenses, and word processing ($___________/hour).

Payment shall be expected at the time services are rendered and must be made no later than ________ business days from the receipt of an oral or written statement from the Special Master of the outstanding balance unless otherwise approved by the Special Master, in order to avoid an interruption of services and/or letter to both attorneys and/or the court regarding noncooperation and/or any other relevant action deemed necessary by the Special Master. The Special Master shall provide written monthly billing statements to both parties.

Prior to the initial interview, the parties will provide the Special Master with an advance deposit totaling $ _________. This advance deposit (without accrued interest) shall be returned to the parties after the Special Master has received a letter from both attorneys that his or her services are no longer being enlisted and requesting return of the deposit balance. This deposit will not serve as an advance retainer, in that the aforementioned fees will not be drawn against it, unless there has been a failure to pay the Special Master's fees. In the event either party fails to pay the Special Master's fees, the entire advance deposit may be used by the Special Master to cover the outstanding balance of either or both parties, regardless of their percentage contribution.

Any objection to the Special Master's bills must be brought to his or her attention in written form within _______ business days of the billing date; otherwise the billing shall be deemed agreed to.

The parties assign to Special Master a lien in the amount of his or her fees.

In the event that arbitration proceedings or a legal action becomes necessary to enforce any provision of this order the nonprevailing party shall pay attorney's fees and costs as may be incurred. The Special Master may proceed by noticed motion to the court in the event his or her fees are not timely paid.

Allocations

Except as otherwise provided herein, the fees of the Special Maser shall be shared by the parties in the following manner:

_____________shall pay______% of the Special Master's fees, expenses, and advance deposit, and_________________shall pay _______% of the Special Master's fees, expenses, and advance deposit.

The Special Master shall have the right to allocate payment of his or her fees at a percentage different from the above if he or she believes the need for his or her services is attributable to the conduct and/or intransigence of one party.

Telephone calls to the Special Master by either party are part of the process and appropriately paid for by the parties according to their percentage share as ordered, unless otherwise determined by the Special Master.

In the event that either party fails to provide twenty-four (24) hours telephone notice of cancellation of any appointment with the Special Master, such party shall pay all of the Special Master's charges of such missed appointment at the full hourly rate, at the discretion of the Special Master.

GRIEVANCES:

The Special Master may be disqualified on any of the grounds applicable to the removal of a Judge, Referee, or Arbitrator.

The Special Master's decision or action taken may be vacated or corrected on any of the applicable grounds specified in C.C.P. § 641, 1286.2, and 1286.6.

Any complaints or grievances from either party regarding the performance or actions of the Special Master shall be dealt with according to the following procedure:

a. A person having a complaint or grievance regarding the Special Master/Expert must discuss the matter with the Special Master/Expert *in person* before pursuing it in any other manner.

b. If, after discussion, the party decides to pursue a complaint, he or she must then submit a written letter detailing the complaint or grievance to the Special Master, to the other party, to both parties' attorneys (if any), and to the attorney for the child(ren), if one exists. The Special Master/Expert will then provide a written response of the grievance to both parties, both attorneys, and the attorney for the child(ren).

c. The Special Master will then meet with the complaining party and his or her attorney (if any), to discuss the matter. The complaining party must then submit a letter to the Special Master stating that the grievance is satisfactorily resolved, or detailing the reasons why the grievance is not resolved, within ten (10) business days of the above meeting. If the grievance is resolved, no further action shall then be taken regarding the grievance by the complaining party.

d. If the grievance is not resolved, a meeting to include all involved attorneys, both parties, and the Special Master shall then occur. Subsequent to this meeting, the complaining party must submit a letter to the Special Master stating that the grievance is resolved or listing the reasons why it is not, within ten (10) business days from the date of this meeting.

e. If the grievance or complaint is not resolved after this joint meeting, the complaining party may proceed by noticed motion to the court for removal of the Special Master/Expert as specified above.

f. Complaints and grievances referred to above shall include, but not be limited to, allegations of bias, unethical conduct, unfair billing practices, overcharges, unprofessional conduct, "malpractice," or any other complaints regarding the performance of the duties of the Special Master/Expert.

The Special Master may submit a bill to reflect his or her time and costs involved in defending against the complaint, which shall be paid by the parties within ten (10) days of receipt thereof.

The court shall reserve jurisdiction to determine if either or both parties and/or the Special Master shall ultimately be responsible for any portions or all of said Special Master/Expert's time and costs spent in responding to the grievance and the Special Master's attorney's fees, if any.

SUBSTITUTION OF SPECIAL MASTER:

The Special Master may resign at any time he or she determines the resignation to be in the best interests of the children or the Special Master is unable to serve out his or her term, upon thirty (30) days written notice to the parties. The remaining term of the Special Master shall remain in full force and effect and shall be filled by a new Special Master unless otherwise mutually agreed by the parties, or unless the Special Master determines that the Special Master process is not in the best interests of the child(ren). Upon notice of impending resignation, the Special Master shall recommend to the parties at least three (3) qualified Special Masters. The new Special Master shall be chosen by agreement of the parties or, if the parties are unable to agree, the Judge to whom the case is assigned shall choose a new Special Master to fulfill the remaining term of this stipulation.

Submitted for signature and signed: ____________________ , 199___ .

____

JUDGE OF THE SUPERIOR COURT

APPENDIX 2

Sample Questions to Ask Parents

GENERAL QUESTIONS DURING THE EVALUATION:

Why are we here?—Used to generate discussion about all of the issues, especially the conflict between the parents. In almost all evaluations, it is the first question I ask parents in the initial individual interview. From that single question, I find myself asking other leading questions based on the information that I hear. Sometimes in the first interview, there is no other formal question asked, as I take the answers from the parent and go where they lead me.

What was your marriage like before the problems began?—Gets the parents talking about their historical relationship with the ex-spouse. It provides an opportunity to find out if there were times of peace before the discord and to find out when things started to go awry.

Tell me about your children.—Obviously, used to begin talking about the children. I often ask this question when a parent is in the middle of complaining about the other parent. In this context, I use the question to see if the parent can stop talking about flaws in the other parent. Look for changes in affect; for example, does the parent smile more and relax when talking about the children, or stay angry and demeaning?

What do you like about (other parent)?—Again, often used to see if the parent can focus on anything positive about the other parent.

How does your arguing with (other parent) affect (child)?—Gives a clue to parents' ability to understand the effects of the couple's conflict on the children.

How do you suppose your feelings about (other parent) affect your child?—Provides sense of parents' ability for insight into this issue.

Given what you say, I don't understand why you stayed married to (other parent).—Used to confront some of the issues being raised. See if the parent can accept any responsibility for problems between them.

What do you sometimes do to contribute to the problems between you and (other parent)?—Same as above.

QUESTIONS REGARDING PARENT-CHILD RELATIONSHIP AND PARENTING STRENGTHS AND WEAKNESSES:

What does (child) need?—Gives overview of parents' ability to conceptualize and verbalize their child's many needs, including the need for a relationship with the other parent. I try and use the answer to that question to confront something that I have heard in other interviews, especially with parents who tend to idealize themselves or their children. Useful in determining which parents truly understand children and their needs as opposed to those parents who want to control, hurt, or punish the other parent by taking the child away from them. Pay special attention to parents who answer this question by staying focused on the negative qualities of the other parent rather than their own positive understanding of the children.

What gives you pleasure as a parent?—Gives a clue about how the parent benefits from the relationship with the children.

What were your mother's (father's) good qualities as a parent?—Gives a clue to the feelings associated with the parenting that each parent received and some insight into the relationship between the parenting received and the parenting given.

What were your mother's (father's) bad qualities as a parent?—Same as above.

Tell me about (describe) your children.—As before, look for affective indicators of joy in the parent-child relationship.

Tell me about a typical day when the children are with you.—Helps to understand about the structure a parent follows, if there are typical times for meals, bedtime, rules, and so forth.

What are some things you would like to change about (child)?—Helps find out about the relationship with the child, openness regarding problems, or idealization of the child, a sign of defensiveness.

What are some of your rules that (child) doesn't like?—Same as above.

How do you discipline (child)?—Same as above.

What can you do to make things better for (child)?—Same as above.

What would you like to change as a parent?—Gives a clue to parents' willingness to look inward regarding their flaws.

What concerns, if any, do you have about (other parent's) relationship with (child)?—Gives the parent an opportunity to express his or her concerns.

What can (other parent) do to satisfy those concerns?—Gives a clue to a parent's ability to view the other parent as capable of growth and change.

What will (child) need in 5 years? In 10 years?—Shows parents' ability to look forward to the future developmental changes of their child.

How is (child's) health?—Obvious.

What are your child's favorite activities and interests?—Gives a clue to parents' knowledge of child's activities and interest. Used to compare what parents say about the child with the child's own description of favorite activities and interests.

What makes (child) feel sad (happy, excited, scared, worried, etc.)? Gives a clue to the parents' ability to understand the child's feelings and respond on a feeling level with their child.

What is your child's favorite foods? What is the bath routine in your house? What is the bedtime routine in your house? Where does your child sleep? Tell me about your child's early development. Were there any problems with toilet training? Does your child have any speech problems or show other signs of regression or anxiety? Has your child started to play with friends?—Typical questions I ask parents of children of preschool age in order to understand their ability to deal with age-appropriate issues.

How does your child like school (teachers)? How does your child get along with his peers? How does your child express himself if he's angry? Is your child afraid to be alone for a short time? Does your child have nightmares or other signs of emotional distress? Has your child started to sleep over at friends' houses? How does your child follow rules (deal with authority)?—Typical questions I ask parents of school-age children in order to understand their ability to deal with age-appropriate issues.

How does your child deal with authority? Do you think your child is excited (afraid) to get more independent? Does your child push your rules and limits very much? Is your child open to talking with you about sex (drugs, peers, school, etc.)? Is your child responsible for her age? Does your child have any ideas what she will do when she is finished with high school? Does your child have a job outside the home?—Typical questions I ask parents of adolescents in order to understand their ability to deal with age-appropriate issues.

QUESTIONS ABOUT THE COPARENTING RELATIONSHIP:

How do you and (other parent) make decisions about school (doctors, vacations, religious training, etc.)?—Explores the ability to make joint decisions, or not, between the parents on behalf of the children.

When you were married, how did you make decisions about school (doctors, vacations, religious training, etc.)?—Explores any change in the coparenting relationship from when they were married.

How are the rules in your household the same (or different from) the rules in (other parent's) household?—Gives clue to the way in which the parents are aware of the style of parenting in the other parent's household and whether there are major differences that the child must encounter during transitions.

When you try to talk with (other parent) about (child), what happens?—Gives a clue to the quality of the communication between parents.

If you have school or medical information for (other parent) about (child), how does it get to him or her?—Provides an idea of the style of sharing information (over the phone, in writing, through the child, or not at all).

How does (child) treat you in front of (other parent)?—Gives a clue to the quality of the child's loyalty conflicts when the parents are together.

Who attends (child's) events and how does (child) deal with it when you and (other parent) are at the same event?—Same as above.

From material I have heard from the other parent or the children, I will always ask questions to confront things I have heard from each parent. This is critical in my understanding of truth for the family.

What can you do to help disengage from (other parent) to help your children?—A good clue for how each parent understands this necessary step for ending the conflict.

What can you do to share in the parenting with (other parent) more cooperatively?—Indicates how each parent understands this next step in cooperative parenting.

FINAL QUESTION:

Finally, at the end of my last interview, I always ask the following:

We've talked about a lot of things. Is there anything else you want me to know or is there anything you would like to ask me?—Gives parents a last opportunity to make sure I know everything that is important to them and to ask me questions that are on their minds. For those parents who are extremely critical, it usually gives them one last time to criticize the other parent. For those who are child focused, it gives them a final opportunity to express feelings and thoughts about their children and their needs.

APPENDIX 3

Sample Questions to Ask Children

Do you know my name? Why you are here? Do you know what I do (what psychologists do)? What did your mom (dad) tell you about me? How do you feel about being here?—The first questions I ask children are used to break the ice, to provide the children with some information about me and what they are here for, and to begin to understand if their parents have been open with them or have given them propaganda about the evaluation. I am quite suspect when I hear in the first few moments statements about custody (e.g., "I want to live with my mom"), especially when I am asking these quite general questions.

Where do you go to school? What grade are you in? How are your grades? What do you like (dislike) about school?—Gets the focus off of the divorce, turning it onto the child's own life.

Who is your best friend? Tell me something about your friends. What do you like to do with your friends?—Same as above.

What are some of your favorite activities? Do you play any sports (music)? What are some things that you love to do? What are some things that you sometimes have to do that you don't like doing? Do you have any favorite video games (TV shows, movies, etc.)?—Same as above.

Who gets you up in the morning? Who else is up then? How do you get breakfast? How do you get ready for school? How do you get to school?—Basic questions about the morning routine.

How do you get home from school? What do you usually do after school? When do you do your homework? Who helps you with (or supervises) your homework?—Basic questions about the after-school routine.

What time is dinner? Who fixes dinner? Where do you eat dinner and with whom?—Basic questions about the evening routine.

What time is bedtime? What do you do to get ready for bed? Does anyone read to you at bedtime?—Basic questions about the bedtime routine.

Do you know what divorce means? How do you feel about your parents' divorce?—Gives a clue to the child's understanding of divorce and how much parents or friends talk about divorce. This question helps to begin an understanding of the child's feelings about the parents' divorce.

Tell me something you like (don't like) about mom (dad).—May indicate the child's ability to talk openly about feelings toward each parent. Very important in understanding the nature of the child's psychological splitting of parents into good and bad, if any.

Who do you talk to when you get scared (worried, happy, etc.)?—Gives a clue to the emotional connectedness of the child with either parent and/or other people in the child's life.

How do you know when mom (dad) is mad? sad? worried? happy?—Indicates how parents express their feelings.

What does your mom (dad) do to help with homework?—Gives a clue to the parent-child relationships.

What happens when you get mad at your mom (dad)?—Same as above.

What does your mom (dad) do when she gets mad at you?—Same as above.

What kinds of punishments does your mom (dad) use?—Same as above.

How do you feel when your mom says bad things about your dad (and vice versa)?—Gives a good clue about how the child handles angry parents and loyalty conflicts. My question assumes that this goes on. In those instances when it does not, the children are quick to tell me so.

How do your parents treat/feel about each other?—Similar to above; also gives a clue to how much parental stress or animosity the child witnesses.

If there was one thing you could change about yourself, what would it be?—Provides an opportunity to assess self-esteem, fantasy life, and other inner feelings of the child.

If you could have three wishes for anything in the world, what would you wish for?—Same as above.

If there was one thing you could change about your mom (dad), what would it be?—Gives a further clue to the parent-child relationship. (Asked again when seen conjointly with parent.)

How do you like to spend your time with your mom (dad)?—Same as above. (Asked again when seen conjointly with parent.)

Do you and your mom (dad) have any favorite things to do together?—Same as above. (Asked again when seen conjointly with parent.)

What ideas do you have about how to split your time with mom and dad?—Gives a clue to the child(ren)'s thoughts about this question, without asking with whom they want to live. Especially useful for older latency, preadolescent, and adolescent children who have their own thoughts and ideas and may want the evaluator to hear them.

With young children, I tend to ask fewer questions and to observe them more in their play. I use a dollhouse to set up various situations and encourage their interaction. By observing their affect and their play responses, I get a clue to parental availability and emotionality. If there are siblings, I ask similar questions about sibling relationships, differences in their perceptions of how the parents treat each of them, and the amount of support the siblings provide one another.

In addition to the questions that I ask children and parents when seen together, I often encourage them to engage in an activity together (such as play with Legos, draw a picture, play a board game, or do some other task). This gives me a chance to directly see their one-on-one interaction and support of one another, as well as the parent's level of directiveness or freedom toward the child. Sometimes I see parents who claim to be active participants with their child who have little idea how to freely interact with their child in my office. While doing all of this, I look for clues to the affection between the parent and child and how much their interaction resembles what both parents and child have been telling me.

APPENDIX 4

Sample Reports

The following are two entire sample reports from custody evaluations that I have completed. They are presented to give readers a sense of how reports flow from beginning to end. As with all other examples, names have been changed and dates omitted to protect confidentiality.

SAMPLE 1

Custody Evaluation

Name: Cooper, Judy and Jim

Dates of evaluation:

Evaluated by: Philip M. Stahl, Ph.D.

REFERRAL INFORMATION

This evaluation was requested in order to assist in diagnostic understanding and to aid in determination of appropriate custody and visitation planning for minor children Meredith, age 12 (b. __/__/__) and Kristen, age 7 (b. __/__/__).

BRIEF BACKGROUND AND HISTORY

According to information available to me, Meredith and Kristen currently spend one week with each of their parents and have been on a similar schedule since the parental separation in 19__. History reveals that Mr. and Ms. Cooper met when Ms. Cooper was married to another man and that their affair produced a pregnancy with Meredith. Soon after Meredith was born, Ms. Cooper and Meredith went to Baltimore with Ms. Cooper's first husband but they separated and divorced, and Ms. Cooper came back to California. This couple was married in 19__, and Kristen was conceived soon thereafter. Apparently, the marriage was never a good one, and within 3 years Mr. Cooper had filed for divorce after Ms. Cooper alleged that he was physically abusive to her. Mr. Cooper denies all allegations of physical abuse made by Ms. Cooper.

Both Mr. and Ms. Cooper report that things were going reasonably well for a while. However, each gives a different story as to what began to go wrong. Ms. Cooper indicated that she developed concerns about Mr. Cooper's functioning and that circumstances in her life caused her to want to move up north. She was working toward establishing herself in business, living up north while the children were at their father's and then living back here when the children were with her. This past summer, she wanted to move up north, but Mr. Cooper blocked this because of their joint custody. Over the next few months, problems continued to increase, with Ms. Cooper alleging renewed abuse by Mr. Cooper and Mr. Cooper being frustrated by his perception of her anger at him. Whereas Ms. Cooper is beginning to express concerns about moderately neglectful behavior by Mr. Cooper, Mr. Cooper is concerned that she is attempting to alienate the children from him and is creating a situation in which the girls are reluctant to love him as they used to. Each is beginning to blame the other for the problems that the girls are experiencing, and each reports different kinds of problems with the girls at this time.

In order to better understand all of this and assist in determination of appropriate custody, visitation, and other possible needs for the children, this evaluation was requested.

EVALUATION PROCEDURE

Conjoint interview, Mr. and Ms. Cooper, __/__/__.
Individual interviews, Mr. Cooper, __/__/__ and __/__/__.
Individual interviews, Ms. Cooper, __/__/__ and __/__/__.
Conjoint interviews, Meredith and Kristen, __/__/__ and __/__/__.

Phone calls with attorneys; Dr. Jones, therapist; and Ms. Julia Smith, mediator.

Review of written materials supplied by Mr. and Ms. Cooper.

In addition to the above, I administered the following psychological tests to each of Mr. and Ms. Cooper:

Bender Gestalt

Projective drawings

Rorschach

MMPI

PSYCHODIAGNOSTIC INTERPRETATION

Ms. Cooper presented as a generally cooperative, somewhat frustrated woman who expressed many concerns about Mr. Cooper and his relationship with the girls. As she talked, affect was somewhat anxious, but she maintained relatively good eye contact with me. For the most part, she expressed a great deal of concern about Mr. Cooper and seemed to suggest that he was responsible for most of the problems between them. On the other hand, she was able to acknowledge that sometimes she can be stubborn and unwilling to compromise. She also acknowledges that she possibly overreacts at times, as well.

Ms. Cooper presented two major themes about her concerns regarding Mr. Cooper. First, she is concerned that he has been controlling and emotionally and physically abusive to her throughout their relationship. She expressed concerns about two incidents of physical abuse, one at the time she separated from him and one quite recently. (Please note that Mr. Cooper has denied both of these allegations.) Even more than this, however, she presented a strong case of emotional badgering and control that she felt she has experienced throughout their relationship. She expressed frustration that this has been very difficult for her and that it has taken her a considerable amount of time to recognize that he is wrong when he is badgering her and that she no longer needs to put up with his emotional abuse.

It is Ms. Cooper's assertion that Mr. Cooper also treats the girls in this demeaning and controlling way and that, just as he never listened to her feelings, he doesn't listen to theirs, either. She believes this because of things the girls tell her as they frequently complain about him to her in this way. She fears for the girls because she knows how difficult this was for her as an adult, and she believes it must be even harder for the girls, who are children.

Along with this, Ms. Cooper expressed concern that Mr. Cooper does not provide reasonable structure for the girls. Although she is not claiming that he is negligent, she does not trust his judgment. For example, he will let Kristen and a friend skate to the park by themselves, which she feels is unacceptable. She is fearful that he allows them to engage in behavior that ends up risky, especially with problems in today's society. In contrast, she would rather they be left alone in their home, where she feels they are under less risk. She described an incident in which the girls and some friends were at Mr. Cooper's river cabin and a man exposed himself to the girls. Although she acknowledges that Mr. Cooper's response was appropriate (apparently he yelled at him and was very upset with the man, and he was very comforting to the girls), she believes that he does not prevent such problems by paying attention to where they are and what they are doing sufficiently. In general, Ms. Cooper would rather that Mr. Cooper use better judgment to prevent any risk to the girls.

Ms. Cooper also indicated that the girls have frequently expressed frustration to her that they spend too much time with their paternal grandmother. Although they enjoy some of their time with their grandmother, they express that it is too much time. She also said that the girls are frustrated that their grandmother is sometimes mean to them, as they report that she calls them names, and so forth. Ms. Cooper feels that Mr. Cooper's business comes first and that he is not as focused on the girls and their needs as she is. She made it clear that much of this is the result of things the girls say to her rather than her own perceptions of Mr. Cooper. In spite of this, she acknowledged that she has had her own conflicts with Mr. Cooper's mother for years, as she used to feel that her former mother-in-law would simply intrude too much in their lives. Ms. Cooper currently feels that Mr. Cooper will listen to his mother more than to her about the girls. Thus, although Ms. Cooper asserts that these issues are the children's and not hers, it is clear that she harbors a tremendous amount of resentment toward Mr. Cooper and his mother for their behavior during and since the marriage.

Ms. Cooper indicated that she originally did not want to make a big deal about these issues and has not wanted to change the custody arrangement until now. She says that she always regretted the fact that she was a party to her older son (currently age 21) having little to do with his father (her former husband). She does not want to take the girls away from their father, nor does she want to be perceived as such, she just wishes that things could change. She acknowledges that Mr. Cooper has wanted to try therapy as a way to solve some of the problems, but she does not trust him. He had picked a previous therapist several years ago, and Ms. Cooper felt betrayed by both Mr. Cooper and the therapist. Thus, although she will go along with therapy at this time, she wants to make sure that he is not in control of it. In fact, she acknowledges that it may be necessary for some therapeutic assistance to focus on the girls' wishes and concerns.

The more Ms. Cooper talked about some of the issues, the more balanced she sounded. Although there was a way in which she initially sounded histrionic as it related to her concerns regarding Mr. Cooper, as she began to talk about the children and their feelings she certainly seemed more in touch with their needs. For example, she said that Mr. Cooper will often refuse to allow the girls to call her, and she believes that this is wrong. Second, she feels that adults do not listen to the girls and their feelings very much, and that the real outcome of this evaluation must be that the children feel heard. She talked about Meredith's and Kristen's anxiety and stress and focused on some symptoms that she believes reflect this anxiety. She talked of her perception that there is too much instability in their lives, caused not only by the shared custody arrangement, but by her perception of the instability in Mr. Cooper's own life. She reports that, all too often, the children spend the night overnight or very late at night at their grandmother's because of Mr. Cooper's work. She described the girls' perception that their father is inconsistent and tends to have angry outbursts. Ms. Cooper is quite concerned about all of this and does not feel that there is any stability in his life. As she talked about these concerns, affect was more appropriate and there was a much less histrionic quality to her description of these concerns. Similarly, she showed a good understanding of the children's need to have a good relationship with their father; she just wishes that he was more in touch with their feelings and less prone to outbursts.

As she talked more about the children and their needs, she expressed the belief that they must learn to feel good about themselves. She is concerned that they feel powerless about their situation in life. That is one of the main reasons she hopes that they get listened to in this evaluation. She recognizes that the children probably do need therapy, and she would be more than happy to participate in such therapy as long as it is not controlled by Mr. Cooper. She seemed to understand that it is up to each parent to work out with the girls the things that they do wrong. She believes she tries to understand the children and their feelings, but fears that their father does not. Ultimately, Ms. Cooper believes that the children need consistency, stability, and fairness in their lives.

Ms. Cooper grew up in a family of five children. Her father was in the military. Apparently, he was very authoritarian, and as a child, she grew up hating authority. She described two different periods of her childhood in which things were very different. Prior to age 13, she said that her mother was very responsible and "taught me to have lots of self-respect." However, around age 13, her father began philandering, and her mother began drinking. She acknowledges that this led to a lot of conflict for her and probably contributed to some of the inconsistencies she has had in her own personal life. However, she believes that she is trying to move forward in her life and let things be so that the children can grow more naturally. She also seems to recognize that some of the frustration and anger that she felt in her childhood is likely to impact her feelings toward Mr. Cooper, especially as it relates to her perception of his control and demands.

Clinically, based on all available information, Ms. Cooper presents somewhat of a mixed picture. On the surface, she shows evidence of mild anxiety and insecurity. She tends to struggle with issues of control and passivity, which is probably contributing greatly to her difficulties in her relationship with Mr. Cooper. There is a mildly histrionic quality to the way she approaches him, though there is no evidence that she is like this in general. She has a tendency to lack insight into her emotions and appears to be mildly constricted regarding her own emotions.

Underneath, however, she also shows evidence of strong feelings of vulnerability and inadequacy in comparison to others. This shows up largely in her Rorschach responses, and I suspect it also contributes to the ways in which she feels so vulnerable as it relates to the girls' structure with their father. There is a tendency on her part to project her own feelings onto the children, especially as they relate to Mr. Cooper. In many ways, it is difficult for her to see her own role in the problems with Mr. Cooper. In spite of this, there is evidence that she shows good awareness and understanding of the children's feelings. Together, this mixture makes it somewhat difficult to separate her own needs and feelings from theirs. I see no evidence that she is alienating the children from their father. I do suspect that as the children express their concerns to her, she exaggerates these concerns in her own mind because of her own issues.

Mr. Cooper presented as a generally friendly, cooperative man who also was reasonably anxious throughout the interviews. As he talked, he was somewhat defensive, noting that he has been put on the defensive by many of Ms. Cooper's allegations. In general, he denies all allegations that he is physically abusive, either to her or the girls, and denies allegations that he has been neglectful of the girls. He acknowledged a couple of incidents in which Ms. Cooper alleged abuse, but he indicated that she was assaultive of him and then blamed him for being assaultive. He feels that she often overreacts to situations and that this makes it very difficult for him a lot of the time. He believes that he has been a good father to the girls, and although he acknowledges frustration and insecurity in being a single parent and that he has made mistakes at times, he feels that overall both he and Ms. Cooper are relatively equal in their parenting ability.

In fact, his major theme throughout the interviews was that he believes that the custodial situation should remain as is. Although he expresses some concern that Ms. Cooper is attempting to alienate the girls against him, he does not believe that either one of them should be removed from equal time in the girls' lives. Instead, he would like to see them in therapy, with both him and Ms. Cooper working with the therapist to improve things for the girls. He fears that any change in the custody would be detrimental to the girls because they are used to the weekly alternating schedule and both parents have something to offer the girls. He disagrees with Ms. Cooper's assertion that the girls are having difficulty with their homework or misplacing things, and even if they do on occasion, he feels that it is not enough reason to change the shared custody arrangement.

In addition to this, Mr. Cooper spent a great deal of time talking about himself and many of the issues present in this evaluation. He acknowledged that, as a child, he had significant problems growing up in a dysfunctional family and that at as an adolescent and young adult he did have some run-ins with both alcohol problems and the law. He was assaultive at that time, and it got even worse after his brother was killed. However, Mr. Cooper indicated that he went into therapy for about 3 years at that time and began to work on many of the issues in his life. He says that he has learned to be less constricting of his emotions and is trying to express himself better than he used to. He acknowledged that he has significant difficulty with this when he has to deal with Ms. Cooper, but he denies that he is assaultive to her. Although he acknowledges that Ms. Cooper believes that he might not be a good enough father, he fears that her main motive is one of money and that she is very angry at him for interrupting her possible chance to move up north with the girls. He says that the girls have been more distant with him since this, for which he blames her. He is concerned that her anger at him is spilling over to the children and causing them to change some of their feelings about either the shared custody or their relationship with him.

Mr. Cooper acknowledged that he is quite angry at and distrustful of Ms. Cooper. He recognizes that some of this goes back to the beginning of their relationship together but also feels that much of it is connected to the behavior currently. He believes that Ms. Cooper is extremely angry at him because he prevented her move up north this past summer and that she is trying to control him now as a result. He feels very torn by all of this, because he always wanted to do what was right for the girls and fears that ultimately this is going to backfire for the girls. He recognizes that the girls feel frustrated by him some of the time, but does not believe that taking time away from him is the correct answer. Instead, he sees therapy as the more appropriate solution. He feels stymied by Ms. Cooper's refusal to go along with this in the past.

As he talked more about the girls, it became clear that he frequently feels insecure and inadequate as a parent. He acknowledges that he and his daughters often get into power struggles, which do not get settled easily. As he put it, "Either they run over me or I run over them." He knows this is hard on the girls, and he struggles with how to improve things. He has taken two parenting classes on communicating with children. He believes that he has learned a lot from these classes about how to deal with his daughters. He does not believe Ms. Cooper knows about or cares about these efforts that he makes, or else she might be more accepting of him as a father. In a way, he goes back and forth between his own insecurity and his need to show Ms. Cooper that he knows what he is doing and that he is a good father. It is interesting that when he talked about the girls' safety, he sounded as if he truly believes he is correct. He described the amount of independence he allows the girls and the watchful eye he carries at other times. He knows that he and Ms. Cooper have differing views, but he believes that he has done a careful job of assessing risk and monitoring the children for safety.

Ultimately, when asked what the children need, he replied "two parents who can get along and make decisions for their benefit and who don't display hostility that they see from both of us." He talked more about this and was easily able to acknowledge his own role in some of these problems, but feels that Ms. Cooper does not see her own role in the problems between them. (As indicated earlier, I feel that he is correct in this assessment.) Yet, as he talked about this, he was unable to talk about how he sometimes prevents the children from calling their mother or sometimes gets too angry at them. He also believes that they need stability and both parents actively involved in their lives and fears that the mistake will be made to solve the problem by cutting his time with the girls. As he talked about this, however, although it was clear that he was concerned about the children and their needs, there was a somewhat narcissistic way in which he was also concerned about his own loss of the girls if they are taken away from him for some of the time. This is connected not only with the loss of time, but apparently with his sense of insecurity about his own role as a father, which he fears will be diminished if the girls are with him less.

Clinically, based on all available information, Mr. Cooper presents as a man with a very poor self-image who feels highly insecure and inadequate about himself in many ways. This is revealed both in the testing as well as in the interviews. There are simultaneously strong feelings of vulnerability noted, as well. Mr. Cooper was able to deal appropriately with his feelings of insecurity and there was no defensiveness noted, but there is strong evidence of conflicts with hostility and aggression, self-confidence and personal insecurity. As indicated, he often feels conflicted and insecure in his relationship with his girls and has a very hard time dealing with stress as it increases. Unfortunately, he tends to bring about some of this stress, and at such times he tends to feel emotionally overwhelmed. As this occurs, he tends to get constricted emotionally and then struggles with his typical defenses of rationalization and intellectualization, becoming more suspicious and impulsive at times. Although there is no evidence that he is abusive to the girls, at such times I suspect he becomes scary to the girls and less rational in his discipline. Meredith gave an example in which he had gotten quite angry at Kristen—grounding her and ordering her to do 150 sentences. He ultimately backed down and had her do only 25. In this way, he tends to react impulsively at first, but then tries to pull back and utilize his healthier defenses in a more appropriate way. This is a struggle for him, however, and appears to be endemic to his personality rather than simply a function of situational stress. Finally, because of his limited insight into all of this, even though he is highly motivated for therapy, his ability to use therapy in a productive way is hindered by his excessive rationalizations and limited insight into the intensity of his feelings of vulnerability.

Meredith and Kristen were seen conjointly for the first appointment. Meredith was seen alone for the second interview because Kristen was sick. Both of the girls were quite open when seen conjointly, and Meredith was also quite open when seen by herself. In general, they talked about several themes. For the most part, they made it clear that they hate it when their parents fight and argue and that they are really tired of it. As one of the girls said, "Divorce sucks," elaborating that her parents fight too much. They made it clear that they do not blame either one of their parents for this and that they feel that both parents need to take responsibility to stop the fighting. Unfortunately, they feel caught up in the midst of it because they hear about it from both parents and also because they often feel that their parents fight because of them. This causes the girls to get depressed at times and to feel somewhat powerless to change anything.

Another theme that was consistent throughout the interviews was their perception that their father yells too much. Clearly, they perceive him as an angrier parent than their mother, and they have a hard time dealing with this. Although both parents get on them and at times they get frustrated with each of their parents, the general perception was that they have a harder time with their father because his outbursts are too often. In addition, they get the feeling that their father's outbursts are less connected to their inappropriate behavior and more connected to his mood. This makes it harder for them, because they never quite know what to expect from him. They also seem to feel that he puts them in the middle a little bit more than does their mother, in large part because he often refuses to allow them to call their mother when they want to. They find this extremely annoying and frustrating. Finally, the girls also expressed frustration with the equal division of time with both of their parents. Although they made it clear that they would like to be with their father some of the time, both of the girls expressed the desire to live primarily with their mother. This is mostly because of their perception of their father's anger and their belief that when they talk to him about it, he may change for a little while, but then always goes back to the old way of acting. They have a very difficult time with this, and they are tired of waiting for him to change. In fact, they're afraid that he may never change.

In general, as the girls talked about all these issues, affect was mildly sad and anxious. There was no evidence as they talked that these were feelings of their mother. Instead it was quite clear that these were their own feelings that they were expressing. They have told both of their parents a lot of these feelings, and there was no real evidence of emotional constriction noted. In fact, there was a very healthy quality in the way in which the girls were able to talk about their frustrations with their parents and their desire for change. The biggest source of frustration appears to be their perception that even though they express their feelings, they do not get heard very well. Nonetheless, this does not lead to constriction, only frustration, which they seem to handle reasonably well most of the time.

SUMMARY AND RECOMMENDATIONS

In a way, both Mr. and Ms. Cooper are accurate in some of their observations, especially about each other. Mr. Cooper is accurate in his representation that Ms. Cooper overreacts somewhat to his parenting and does not like him. He is accurate in recognizing that she is easily angry at him and on occasion says negative things about him to the children. Ms. Cooper is accurate in her perception that Mr. Cooper is somewhat inconsistent in his parenting in that he struggles with discipline and is all too often impulsive or angry toward the children. Unfortunately, neither parent seems to have a very good understanding of his or her own role in the problems between them and the way they tend to escalate their hostilities in a way that is very painful to their children. They get locked into power and control struggles and stimulate each other into overreactions. Although we will never know, for example, whether or not Mr. Cooper pushed Ms. Cooper off the porch, the fact that hostilities escalate to the conflict point is a reflection of the critical level that their friction reaches.

Regardless of parental behavior, however, the children's feelings are very real. They are overwhelmed by the hostility between the parents, and as conflicts mount, children tend to choose sides, right or wrong. They cannot tolerate the conflicts and the ambivalence that they feel. Because they perceive their mother as more fair and more even toward them, they are choosing her side in this conflict. They need to be with her more because they believe that if they are with their mother more, the conflicts between their parents will reduce. Along with this, it appears that they also believe their guilt about being in the middle will also diminish.

Unfortunately, just because children see things a certain way, it does not mean that it is best. Like Mr. Cooper, I am concerned that if the girls are with their mother more, it will only reinforce the feelings that he is a bad parent and the greater cause in these problems. That will be tough to break, and in essence, we will end up with a good parent and a bad parent, something that is not in the children's best interests. Similarly, like Ms. Cooper, I am concerned that if we do not honor the girls' feelings, they will continue to grow in their sense of powerlessness and will begin to feel more inadequate just as each of their parents do. In short, there are no good solutions here.

Nonetheless, a choice must be made as to what is in the children's best interest. Clearly, there needs to be an opportunity to help resolve the issues in this situation and to reduce everybody's source of tension. In addition, the children need to begin to view both their parents in more real ways, though they do seem to recognize the good and bad in each of their parents. Whereas equal shared parenting is often an advantage for children and their parents, it is my opinion that it is currently contributing to the problems that the girls are experiencing as they become embroiled in the parental conflicts. In addition, although Mr. Cooper does try hard to be a more effective parent and is taking classes and other steps to improve his parenting of the girls, the girls remain fearful and overwhelmed by his angry outbursts and by the inconsistency in his discipline.

Given the above, I offer the following recommendations:

1. I recommend that the girls get involved in outpatient psychotherapy designed to help them continue to understand their feelings and learn to express them better to both of their parents. Both parents need to participate in this therapy to learn more effective parenting techniques and to better understand their children and their feelings.

2. I recommend that Mr. Cooper continue in his individual psychotherapy with the hope that the therapist can confront his defenses in a way that enables him to get more in touch with his strong feelings of vulnerability, his poor self-confidence, and some of the other issues noted above. I also recommend that Ms. Cooper be in her own therapy to help her work on separating her own issues with Mr. Cooper from those of the girls.

3. Mr. and Ms. Cooper need a vehicle through which they can talk about the children. They need to develop a certain amount of trust in each other and have a place to talk about issues of safety and disagreements between them. Left to their

own devices, they remain distrustful and angry and the children suffer. I recommend that they get involved in periodic mediation with someone who will help them understand each other's positions and reach some formal compromises.

4. I recommend a change in the schedule, although I believe that if significant changes could be made in the parental behavior, this would not be necessary. Until these changes are made by the parents, I am reluctant to recommend continuing the existing schedule because of the effect this has on the girls' feelings of powerlessness. Instead I recommend that for the present the girls be on a schedule with their parents as follows: Week 1, the girls with their mother from Monday morning until the following Monday morning. Midweek, one evening when their father is free, he should have them for a few hours for homework and dinner. Week 2, girls with their mother from Monday morning until Wednesday morning, girls with their father from Wednesday after school until the following Monday morning.

5. Along with this, I recommend Mr. Cooper manage his work in such a way that he can be home evenings when he is with the children. The children should have the unrestricted opportunity to call the other parent whenever they want. Even if the children are being disciplined for something, calling the other parent is not to be used as a privilege to be withheld. I hope that through the mediator, continued parenting classes, and with the therapists, a more appropriate form of discipline can be developed.

Thank you for allowing me to be of assistance in this case.

____

Philip M. Stahl, Ph.D.

Licensed Psychologist PSY 10272

SAMPLE 2

Custody Evaluation

Name: Hall, Dennis and Ann

Dates of evaluation:

Evaluated by: Philip M. Stahl, Ph.D.

REFERRAL INFORMATION

This evaluation was requested in order to assist in diagnostic understanding and to aid in determination of appropriate custody and visitation planning for minor children Rebecca, age 13 (b. __/__/__), Molly, age 9 (b. __/__/__), and John, age 6 (b. __/__/__).

BRIEF BACKGROUND AND HISTORY

Some of the early history of this couple is a bit unclear, as each parent has a different perception of their history. Mr. Hall reported that they were married before Rebecca was born, in November 19—, whereas Ms. Hall reports that they were married in November of the following year, after Rebecca was born. Similarly, Ms. Hall reported that they separated in January 19—, whereas he said it was the next year. One of the few things on which they agree is that the divorce was filed in 19—.

Since the separation there have been numerous changes in the ways in which the children spend time with each of their parents. Currently the children are on somewhat of a convoluted schedule in which Ms. Hall picks the children up every day after school, even when they are on Mr. Hall's time. The schedule was a bit difficult for me to fully understand, but it appears that, if one parent has the children for the weekend, the other parent has the following Monday and Tuesday. It is unclear what happens with Wednesdays and Thursdays, but then the following weekend the other parent has the children. Neither parent is happy with the schedule. Both feel that the kids do not like the back-and-forth arrangement. They have attempted other schedules, and there was a period of time in which all the children lived primarily with their father when Ms. Hall had house problems. He feels things were more stable for the children then. He believes that the children would do better if they were on a primary schedule with him with regular visitation with their mother. In contrast, Ms. Hall believes that the children should remain in some type of 50-50 arrangement, but wonders if maybe a different schedule would be better for the kids. She acknowledges that Rebecca wants to live primarily with her father, but she believes that Rebecca is quite angry at her and that Mr. Hall is bribing Rebecca to live with him.

Along with these concerns around schedule and time, Mr. Hall talked a great deal about some concern regarding John. He feels that John has had difficulties with aggressive behavior for much of his life and that the only real improvements he ever made was during the time that he lived primarily with his father. He believes that John gets a great deal of inconsistent parenting between the two households and believes strongly that his style is better than is Ms. Hall's. He feels that she is much too haphazard in her parenting style and that he is more structured, believing that this is important for John. Mr. Hall also raised concern about Ms. Hall's partner, Jim Little, as he says that Mr. Little is abusive verbally to the children and is extremely angry at him. He is upset that Mr. Little expresses his anger in front of the children.

Similarly, Ms. Hall expressed concerns about Mr. Hall's new wife (I will refer to her as Andrea), wondering if Andrea is physically abusive to John and not a very good role model. She expresses concern that Andrea's children, Kelly and Jason (ages 8 and 6, respectively), add to some of the trouble for the children and feels that there is too much chaos in Mr. Hall's home. She also feels that Mr. Hall is too harsh on John.

Both parents agree that there is little or no communication between them. Both parents acknowledge that Mr. Little contributes to some of the difficulty. Ms. Hall stated to Mr. Hall, "You left me, were seeing another woman, and Jim can't understand how any man could do what you did." Mr. Little does not believe that Mr. Hall appreciates his relationship with the kids and all that he sometimes does for the kids. Ms. Hall appears to continue struggling with her sense of loss in relation to Mr. Hall. Both parents recognize that the children are caught in the middle of loyalty conflicts between them. This evaluation was requested in order to understand all of the dynamics involved and to assist in determination of the children's needs.

EVALUATION PROCEDURE

Conjoint interview, Mr. and Ms. Hall, __/__/__.

Individual interview, Mr. Dennis Hall, __/__/__.

Individual interview, Ms. Ann Hall, __/__/__.

Conjoint interview, Mr. Hall and his wife, Andrea, __/__/__.

Conjoint interview, Hall children, __/__/__. During this session, Molly was seen individually for a period of time, as was Rebecca. In addition, all the children were also seen conjointly with Mr. Hall, Andrea, and Andrea's children.

Conjoint interview, Hall children, __/__/__. During some of this session, they were seen conjointly with their mother and her daughter Grace.

Conjoint interview, Ms. Hall and Mr. Little, __/__/__.

Review of written materials supplied by Mr. and Ms. Hall and/or their attorneys.

Brief phone calls with Mr.________ and Ms. ________, attorneys.

Phone calls with:

Mr. _________, mediator

Mr. _________, John's school counselor

Ms._________, John's teacher

Ms. ________, Ms. Hall's therapist

In addition to the above, I administered the following psychological tests to each of Mr. and Ms. Hall:

Bender Gestalt

Projective drawings

Rorschach

MMPI

PSYCHODIAGNOSTIC INTERPRETATION

Mr. Dennis Hall presented as a generally friendly, cooperative man who related reasonably well with me. He has an idiosyncratic quality in that he does wood carvings and frequently worked on his wood carvings as we talked. He did this in individual sessions, in the conjoint session with his wife, and during some of the time with his children. Although this may appear distracting at first, it became clear through the interview process that he pays full attention to what is going on and does this wood carving almost in the background. Another tendency is for him to get up and walk around in the middle of a session. This seemed to occur more often at times of stress, but it was difficult to fully understand this. Given other details, I suspect that both of these behaviors serve in some way to allow him to distance himself emotionally from the material being discussed.

Aside from this, however, Mr. Hall was generally open and friendly throughout the interviews. He talked freely about his perception of many of the problems, as well as his sense of many of the necessary solutions. He focused largely on the children and their issues, but did so in a way that reflected his perception that Ms. Hall is not doing a very good job during the time that the children are with her. He expressed numerous concerns about the children and their functioning, including John and his aggressive behavior, Molly and some school difficulty, and Rebecca and his perception that she is mistreated emotionally at her mother's. In all instances, the concerns he expressed about Ms. Hall and Mr. Little were directly and appropriately connected to issues for the children.

As indicated, he is quite concerned about John and his aggressive behavior. He said that John was removed from his regular kindergarten class last year because of aggressive behavior and reports that John has similar problems this year. He feels John is doing better and did much better during the time when the kids lived primarily with him. He is extremely concerned that Ms. Hall does not provide a structured enough home for John, and he resists the charge that he expects John to be a robot. In contrast, he talked of his efforts at discipline for John, which used to include spanking, but no longer does, because spanking had no impact. As he talked about these issues, he certainly seemed to have fairly good insight and understanding into John and his needs.

Similarly, he talked about his perception of Molly's academic trouble and his belief that her mother does not help her enough with her homework. He feels that Molly does not read very well, and he would like to see Ms. Hall work with her more. In contrast, he believes that he and his wife read with Molly a lot (along with the other children). He is frustrated that on at least one occasion, Molly was made to feel bad for calling him during a time when Molly was frightened. He related an incident in which Molly came home, no one was there, and no note had been left for her. He feels that Molly is too young to be left this way and that it was appropriate for Molly to call him because she was scared. Soon thereafter, Ms. Hall and Mr. Little ridiculed and disciplined Molly for calling him because she was scared. Mr. Hall is concerned not only about the message this gives to her about her relationship with him, but also about this apparent lack of empathy for Molly's feelings by her mother and Mr. Little.

For Rebecca, there were numerous concerns. He feels that Rebecca is often scapegoated by her mother. He believes that Ms. Hall and Mr. Little frequently call her a "name of the week." Recently, Rebecca had been referred to as a "back-stabbing slut," according to all the children. This was because Rebecca wants to live with her father. He feels that the message this provides the children is quite negative, and, as indicated, he feels it is wrong of Ms. Hall and Mr. Little to be critical of him and Andrea and the children themselves. He is concerned that the children have been told that he never wanted them. Mr. Hall reports that John was told that he was never wanted by him. According to Mr. Hall, Ms. Hall excused this by saying, "Well, even if he heard it, I didn't say it to him directly." He believes that Ms. Hall is insensitive of the children's emotional needs, lacks structure and discipline in her household, and does not meet the needs of the children very well.

In contrast, he feels that all three of the children did quite well when they lived primarily with him and visited their mother. Apparently, when Ms. Hall and Mr. Little were having trouble in a trailer park in the fall of 19__, the children lived with Mr. Hall for 3 months. He believes that during this time John improved his behavior a great deal and both Molly and Rebecca were more relaxed. They felt much better about their relationship with their mother, as they saw her every other weekend and a couple of times after school during the week. As indicated, he is concerned about the confusion to the children with the current schedule and the very strong differences in the two households. In addition, he continually expressed concern that problems are exacerbated by Mr. Little's extreme hostility toward him and Andrea. He believes that a joint custodial arrangement could work better if they were not so critical of him and if they were willing to talk with him or Andrea about the children more frequently. If that were the case, he might then see that an equal sharing of the time would work better. However, he feels that under the circumstances, he should have primary physical custody of the children.

When Andrea talked about some of these issues, she also focused on another phenomenon about which she is concerned. She perceives (and Mr. Hall agrees) that Ms. Hall views relationships in an "all or none" kind of way. For example, she believes that Ms. Hall is so unable to tolerate her own sense of rejection by Rebecca that Ms. Hall is willing to not see Rebecca at all if she goes to live with her father. Both Andrea and Mr. Hall expressed concern that Ms. Hall and her entire family deal with things in this way. They fear that this adds to some of the loyalty conflicts between the children and their parents. She believes that it would be much healthier for Rebecca if Ms. Hall could express her sadness at the possibility that Rebecca might live mostly with her father, but then maintain a room for her, keep her on a regular visiting schedule, and encourage Rebecca to feel wanted by her mother. Andrea is concerned that currently Rebecca is feeling rejected by her mother because of her mother's sense that Rebecca is rejecting her. In these ways, both Andrea and Mr. Hall express concern that Ms. Hall's emotions negatively affect the children.

In contrast, both Mr. Hall and Andrea talked positively about what they have to offer for the children. Both were able to focus quite well on the children and their needs, not only in their own terms, but in relation to their own individual relationships with both parents. They expressed concern that even Ms. Hall has talked to them about Mr. Little's drinking problem. Although Mr. Hall acknowledged that he used to smoke pot, he indicated that he has stopped. He believes that Ms. Hall has also stopped (he reports that they used to smoke pot together), but he does express concern that Mr. Little drinks too much. In relation to all the parenting issues, both Andrea and Mr. Hall were positive in their approach, showing evidence of good structure, discipline, and a desire to understand and talk with the children at a level appropriate to their development.

Clinically, based on all available information, Mr. Hall presents somewhat of a mixed picture. On one hand, he shows fairly good insight into his emotions and their effect on his behavior and seems to have a good grasp of the children's emotions and their needs. He is clearly able to separate his own needs and feelings from those of the children and appears to have a fairly structured approach to discipline. Relationship capacity appears to be fairly good. There is no evidence in this evaluation of any significant psychopathology.

In contrast, however, Mr. Hall does show evidence of a certain amount of internal anxiety and a desire to portray himself in a favorable light. He is somewhat defensive at times, though he is willing to look at his own role in some of the problems. He appears to be less polarized than many of the individuals usually seen in custody evaluations; however, he also seems to be somewhat distant from his emotions and their effect on his behavior. There is evidence that he has made considerable growth in the past year, probably connected to his marriage with Andrea. They appear to be good for each other. I suspect that Andrea has helped Mr. Hall emotionally confront many of the issues that he has. It is likely that she has helped him work on issues of hostility, aggression, and control, which probably were bigger issues during his marriage with Ms. Hall. In general, it is my opinion that Mr. Hall is continuing to grow and do better emotionally than in the past. Although he maintains a certain amount of defensiveness, he appears to be improving over time. There is no evidence in this evaluation to suggest that he would have difficulty dealing with the day-to-day needs of his children.

Ms. Ann Hall presented as a generally cooperative, somewhat sad-looking woman who struggled a great deal with some of the issues in this evaluation. It is clear that she is tired of Mr. Hall's accusations and continued criticism of her, yet she also seemed to have a difficult time dealing with the children and their emotional needs. Instead, she focused on her perception that Mr. Little is good to the children and said that she is tired of the criticism that he gets. However, she did acknowledge that he can be very critical of Mr. Hall in front of the children, which she does not like. As she talked about the variety of issues associated with this evaluation, it seemed as if Ms. Hall had some good understanding of what she thinks is needed, but has a very difficult time with any real follow-through for the children. Thus, although she would like Mr. Little to stop drinking or to stop being derogatory about Mr. Hall, she seems to have little or no ability to really effect this for the children.

Ms. Hall believes that the best solution for the children is a different type of 50-50 schedule. She feels that much of John's behavior problems were the result of the confused schedule and believes that he and Molly both would do better with an alternating week schedule. She does not understand why Rebecca wants to live with her father, saying, "We don't have the horrible relationship that Dennis thinks we have." She was not able to talk very positively about their relationship, just that it was not "as horrible" as Mr. Hall has made it out to be. In this way, things are again worse than she would like, but she cannot do much about it. Ms. Hall projects all the blame for all these problems onto Mr. Hall and Andrea. She has little awareness of her own role in any of the problems that she has in this situation, seeing herself instead as a "good enough mother" who should be able to have the children half of the time.

Ms. Hall denied some of Mr. Hall's allegations regarding her lack of time with the children. She believes that she does help Molly and John with their homework and feels that she does a good job with the structure with John. In contrast, she believes that Mr. Hall has been too hard on John and that John is doing a lot better as he gets older. Again, she began to act frustrated when talking about Molly, believing that Molly would do fine if Mr. Hall and Andrea did not keep harping on her to call them whenever there was a problem. She acknowledges having been angry one time when Molly called her father when she was "5 minutes late" picking her up. She did not think she was blaming Molly, but acknowledged being angry at Mr. Hall and Andrea for encouraging Molly to call every time something is wrong. In this same way, however, she continued to express her frustration about Mr. Hall and Andrea without really acknowledging what she is doing to contribute to the problem. Similarly, just as Mr. Hall described, she did not really seem to understand how the children might feel when Mr. Little is derogatory to them or if she is late or not home.

As Ms. Hall talked, it became clear that she has had a very difficult life. Her childhood was a scary one, as she has discovered that she was molested by both her father and uncle. She reports that she had a fairly difficult relationship with her mother. Her first husband was abusive to her. Mr. Hall was the first man who ever treated her well. However, over the years, she came to feel that even he was emotionally abusive and controlling of her. She feels that this continued through the relationship. She talked of some of the difficulty she has in her relationship with Mr. Little. As she focused on all these issues, I had the impression that she has been generally passive and emotionally dependent on the men in her life for a long time.

When seen with Mr. Little, Ms. Hall was clearly feeling caught in the middle. She gets frustrated with his angry outbursts, while simultaneously understanding them and feeling hurt because of the way she feels in relation to the children and her ex-husband. However, as she talked more about these issues, it became clear that Ms. Hall has a very good understanding of the children and their needs, especially the need to bring peace and calmness to the situation. However, there was also continued evidence that she feels overwhelmed by the issues in this evaluation, especially the anger between her former husband and Mr. Little and its effect on the children. She does not know how to stop Mr. Hall from harassing her, and she does not know how to stop Mr. Little from being so angry.

Away from them both, she clearly can be very loving to the children, has a very good understanding of their needs, and certainly seems to be a "good enough mother." She talked of the conflicts that John probably feels, as he is caught between her more laid-back style and Mr. Hall's more strict style. She does not feel that either is inherently wrong for John. She acknowledged concern for the current schedule sharing the parenting and seems to recognize that the schedule itself adds to some of the problems. In essence, she recognizes that there are good and bad in both households, but she feels that there are no significant problems in either household and that the children need to be able to spend time with both of them.

It is important to point out that Ms. Hall is concerned about losing Rebecca. She wants to have a close relationship with Rebecca, but she feels tremendous distancing from Rebecca. She talked about her efforts of trying to get close or help Rebecca with homework, but believes that Rebecca is resistant to any efforts of hers. She does not know whether to blame Mr. Hall and Andrea for this or something else, but she is hurting as she does not understand why Rebecca is distancing herself from her. As I talked about polarization and how common it is in conflicted divorces for children to feel a need to choose between their parents, Ms. Hall seemed to understand and was able to reduce her frustration. She made it clear, however, that she wants Rebecca to have a good relationship with Andrea, but she fears losing her child "to a man who says bad things about me." She clearly does not want to be left out of Rebecca's life.

Unfortunately, Mr. Little *is* quite angry. He denies calling the children names, but acknowledges that it is possible and that he does not remember. In a way, it was difficult for him to acknowledge his own role in the problems. This was a problem that both Ms. Hall and Mr. Little had. They were quick to externalize blame to Mr. Hall and Andrea, even more than Mr. Hall and Andrea did to them. When I was finally able to get them to focus solely on their role in the issues and what the children needed, both Ms. Hall and Mr. Little were able to talk quite succinctly and directly about the needs of the children and how to meet those needs. In fact, in spite of the obvious tension that often occurs between the four adults, Mr. Little suggested that I meet with all four of them to explain my findings as a way of helping them all hear what needs to be said. This is primarily because Ms. Hall and Mr. Little both believe that the children need the arguing to stop and for all the adults to be actively involved in the children's lives.

Clinically, based on all available information, Ms. Hall presents somewhat of a mixed picture. On the surface, she shows some insight into her emotions and their effect on her behavior, as well as some awareness of the children's needs, especially as it relates to the issues in this evaluation. Ego organizational skills appear to be fairly good. There is no evidence in this evaluation of any significant psychopathology.

On the other hand, however, Ms. Hall does show evidence of difficulty dealing with her emotions and appears to be defensive emotionally. She gets overwhelmed easily, especially when caught in the cross fire between Mr. Hall and Mr. Little. She loves the children very much, but feels somewhat inadequate at meeting their need for peace, because the men in her life are in such conflict with one another. Along with this, she is certainly feeling overwhelmed and hurt by Rebecca's attachment to Andrea. Although I do not believe it is because of jealousy, it seems connected to her feeling shut out of Rebecca's life. Whereas Mr. Hall and Andrea seem to portray that Ms. Hall is dealing with Rebecca's issues in an "all or none" manner, it is my belief that Ms. Hall has a fairly balanced approach and would like to have an active participating role in Rebecca's life while sharing her with her father and Andrea. She might have difficulty communicating this to Rebecca. Overall, however, when she gets stuck emotionally, her tendency is to become passive and dependent, probably as a result of the many issues that she has experienced in her own life. Unfortunately, with the high degree of conflict between her, Mr. Little, and Mr. Hall, her passivity makes it difficult to meet all of the children's needs for peace.

The children were seen in many combinations. Rebecca, Molly, and John were seen conjointly with each other and Rebecca and Molly were seen individually. They were also seen conjointly with their father, Andrea, and Andrea's children, as well as conjointly with their mother and her daughter Grace. Essentially, there was little change in how the children related to me or the evaluation process whether they were seen individually, conjointly with their siblings, or with adults.

As a group, all of the children are extremely frustrated with the current schedule. Along with this, they are tired of the parental fighting and seem to feel that both of their parents are responsible for some of the problems. In addition, as a group, they all feel that Mr. Little is too angry; they wish that he could learn to deal with his anger in a different way. They are very tired of his making derogatory statements about their father, but they are also tired of their father's and Andrea's derogatory statements about their mother. It appeared throughout the evaluation that the children feel pulled between their parents, feel a tremendous loyalty conflict, and seem to be caught up in the polarization of their parents. It appeared that none of the parents have been able to effectively shield the children from the conflicts that they are all experiencing.

Along with this general view, Rebecca presented as a somewhat angry girl who is struggling a great deal with her mixed feelings toward her parents. On the surface, she is distant from her mother and angry at Mr. Little, feeling closer to her father and Andrea. She has expressed for several months a desire to live with her father, and she perceives her mother's hesitation as a rejection of her feelings. This causes her to view her mother in more negative ways, solidifying her feeling that her father and Andrea are supportive of her while her mother and Mr. Little are not. She is extremely angry at Mr. Little for his behavior a lot of the time, either when he is critical of her father or when he calls her names. She indicated that on at least one occasion he has referred to her in vulgar terms, which angers her greatly. Rebecca is the most polarized of the children, primarily viewing her father and Andrea as mostly good and her mother and Mr. Little as mostly bad.

Underneath this, however, I suspect that Rebecca is feeling a lot of hurt. I suspect that she feels sad about the deterioration of her relationship with her mother, while simultaneously being angry at her mother for her perception that she favors Mr. Little over her. As Ms. Hall thinks, Rebecca sometimes gets annoyed with the younger children in both households and feels she has more privacy and believes her feelings are more honored at her father's. It is important to point out that, in addition to all of this, Rebecca mothers the younger children a great deal in both households. This is something that she has done for much of her life, and she comes by it naturally. However, it is my opinion that this contributes to some of the splitting and polarization that she feels. She gets angry at her perception that she has to mother Grace, despite the fact that she could choose not to mother her at all. Contrary to Rebecca's belief, Ms. Hall is willing to do the mothering of Grace and prefers that Rebecca would not take on this additional burden. Nevertheless, at the present time, Rebecca feels this responsibility on her own, which adds to her feeling drawn toward her father. Overall, it is my opinion that Rebecca is confused, overwhelmed by her feelings of polarization and splitting between her parents, and sad about the nature of her relationship with her mother. It is also clear that she wants to live primarily with her father and change the quality of her relationship with her mother. She would like Mr. Little to finally treat her nicer and be less derogatory of her father.

Molly clearly appears torn between her parents. Unlike Rebecca, she can see good and bad in both of her parents, as well as in Andrea and Mr. Little. She seems caught up in the anxiety of having to choose between her parents and wishes that her parents would leave her alone and let her enjoy both households. Molly is a bit more frustrated when her mother and Mr. Little say bad things about her father and Andrea than vice versa because she believes that what her father and Andrea say about her mother and Mr. Little is "more true." She gets especially annoyed at her mother's when Mr. Little is angry or critical of her father, but she also gets annoyed at her father's when they are critical of her mother and Mr. Little. She does have some complaints about both of them, but in general, was very positive about her relationships with all four of her adults. In some ways, she presents as a girl who feels that in order to please her parents, she has to say critical things about the other parent. She does not want to do this. She gets along well with all of her siblings, enjoys her relationships with Andrea's kids as much as she does with Grace, and wants to continue spending time in both houses. She almost seemed programmed at times to tell me things that were negative about her mother. Although she does have some concerns about things in that household (as already indicated), she does not like to be told what to say. In all, Molly enjoys her relationship with her friends, seems to be doing well in school, and appears to be having no significant difficulties at this time.

John presented as a somewhat immature, mildly regressed youngster who does seem to feel the effect of inconsistencies in the parenting. Mr. Hall and Andrea are clearly stricter, set clear boundaries, and are quicker to reprimand him for his behavior than are Ms. Hall and Mr. Little. On the other hand, Ms. Hall and Mr. Little do not feel that John's behavior is as bad. Thus, they see no reason to reprimand him as much. He struggles a bit in school, having done poorly a year ago, and he is still struggling some right now. He did show some differences in his behavior when seen with his mother or his father, as he was more immature looking when seen with his mother. John even admitted, in front of his mother, that he does not do some things there to take care of himself that he does at his father's because she does not make him. It frustrates Rebecca that Ms. Hall still dresses John, and John seems to have mixed feelings about the differences in how he is treated. On the one hand, he enjoys being babied at times by his mother; on the other hand, it appears that he does not listen to her very much, either. All of the children report that John listens to their father much more, but this may relate to the fact that his father used to spank him and he does not want to get spanked.

In many ways, however, John also has a good relationship with both of his parents, but, like his sister Molly, wants to simply tune out all of the emotionally charged complaints that the parents have against one another. Like Molly, he is also torn between his feelings toward his mother and father and seems to have a fairly balanced view of each of them. Overall, it is my opinion that John is a bit regressed at times, feels the effects of the inconsistent parenting, and sometimes does not know how to act. At times, he becomes manipulative and controlling, apparently to offset his feelings of insecurity stemming from all of the above. In essence, staying a bit regressed helps him maintain his own control of the situation.

John's teacher and school counselor report that John had been highly aggressive when he first came to this school. He has made improvements over time, yet he still struggles with peer relationships, distractible behavior, and a high activity level. He can still be quite aggressive at times as well. His teacher reports that John has a strong need for structure, limits, and obvious and appropriate consequences.

With their parents, all the children were generally okay. Mr. Hall and Andrea were a bit more verbal with the children, though Andrea did a lot of the talking for both of them. In some ways, she appeared more connected verbally to the children than did Mr. Hall. Both Ms. Hall and Mr. Hall played well with the children and seemed to balance their time with the children reasonably well. There was a tendency on Ms. Hall's part to be a bit more laid-back when watching the children, so her daughter Grace got into a little bit of the other children's play. This seemed to bother Rebecca the most, who was annoyed because she felt she had to watch Grace. Ms. Hall certainly gave her permission to stay out of that role, but Rebecca was clearly viewing that it was her job to be watching Grace. Overall, however, during these interviews, there was nothing in this evaluation to suggest that either parent's time should be limited with the children.

SUMMARY AND RECOMMENDATIONS

Overall, it is my opinion that several factors are operating here. First, and most important, there has been a significant increase in tension between the adults over the last few years. Distrust between them has greatly increased, in part as a result of many behaviors. In the not-too-distant past, Mr. Hall was using drugs, though all evidence suggests that he has stopped at this point in time. Ms. Hall and Mr. Little were critical of him for this, and he, in turn, became critical of Mr. Little and Ms. Hall for their parenting of the children. Mr. Little has taken on the battle, is much too angry, and expresses his anger much too quickly and vehemently in front of the children. This adds to the tension for the children, as well as the alienation that Mr. Hall and Andrea feel. They get angry, say some negatives about Ms. Hall and Mr. Little, and then Mr. Little gets even angrier. The cycle continues and escalates to the detriment of the children. Ms. Hall gets caught in the middle. She is clearly overwhelmed with her feelings of love toward the children and the conflicts created by Mr. Hall and Mr. Little. The children are caught in the cross fire, with no sympathetic adult to help them.

Along with this, the children seem to be telling their parents a variety of things. No one knows quite what to believe, and the adults believe the worst about each other. Rebecca, in particular, is quite critical of her mother and Mr. Little, in large part because of his treatment of her and his derogatory position toward her father. She feels forced to choose sides and is choosing her father's side in this matter because he is less derogatory than is Mr. Little. This causes her to push away from her mother, however, so her mother is feeling alone, hurt, and rejected. Because the adults do not trust each other, they cannot talk about these issues. What little communication there is ends up being through the children. Unfortunately, this intensifies the loyalty conflicts that the children feel and keeps them stuck in the middle of the battle much too long.

In all, this evaluation revealed that all four of the parents had some strengths and some shortcomings. My biggest concern centers around Mr. Little's angry outbursts and derogatory statements of Mr. Hall. My sense of his outbursts is that they are verbally abusive to the children and must stop. Along with this, I am concerned about the ways in which Mr. Hall and Andrea seem to unwittingly add to the children's loyalty conflicts by encouraging them to be critical of their mother and Mr. Little. If possible, they need to stay out of the problems in Ms. Hall's house. I recognize that they believe they are trying to help, but I also believe that this adds to the problems. Mr. Hall *does* appear to be improving in his connection to the children. Andrea appears to be developing good relationships with all the children. Ms. Hall, though with a more laid-back style, is both aware of and clearly willing and desirous of meeting the children's needs. I am concerned that she allows Mr. Little's temper to affect the children, because she feels so powerless to do anything about it. In addition, it is likely that John needs more structure, limits, and consequences than she currently provides. Aside from this, however, there is no evidence to suggest that she is a bad mother.

Most important, the children need to pulled out of the middle. They are overwhelmed with their feelings and want to be out of the middle. Rebecca is dealing with this with intense polarization by choosing her father over her mother, Molly tunes everyone out, and John gets overwhelmed, aggressive, and regressed. None of these are healthy emotional solutions for the children, and all are reflective of the pain that the children feel as a result of the parental conflicts. If left to themselves, away from the bitterness and anger of the adults, I suspect that the children would be freer and better able to develop their own relationships with each of the adults in a healthier, more productive manner.

Given all of these issues, it is clear that the current schedule needs changing. There are way too many transitions, and the children struggle with this too much. Unfortunately, given the apparent effects of the schedule on the children, it is difficult to fully sort out all of the other pieces. Nonetheless, based on the above, I offer the following recommendations:

1. All four adults need to learn to take responsibility for themselves in their own household and avoid getting caught up in the externalization of blame and criticism of the other. In this regard, I find Mr. Little to be the most difficult. He must get involved in therapy and/or anger management classes to help him deal more effectively with his rage. It is critical that he stop dumping his anger on the children because of its negative effect on them. Similarly, Mr. Hall and Andrea must stop being so critical of Ms. Hall, as there is no evidence that she is negligent or harmful in her own relationships with the children. I also encourage them to get into some therapy to help them learn to stop the externalization of blame.

2. Ms. Hall needs to deal with her apparent passivity and dependency in relation to the two men who have been in her life. I certainly recommend that she continue to work on these issues with her therapist. She needs to recognize that protecting the children and honoring the children's feelings must come before protecting Mr. Little and his anger. I also recommend that Rebecca join the therapy at some point, or in some other way get into some therapy with Ms. Hall so that they can work on improving their relationship with one another.

3. It is critical that the four adults must learn to deal differently with their communication. Restraining orders, externalization of blame, and missed communications are not working. Ms. Hall needs to honor the growing relationships between the children and Andrea. I see no reason that Andrea cannot care for the children during Mr. Hall's time with them. I highly recommend coparenting counseling for them all with the hope that they can learn to understand each other, develop a certain degree of mutual trust, and learn to work together for the children and their needs. It is critical to the children's needs that the four adults learn to share the children, communicate differently about the children, and resolve their differences. For those day-to-day issues in which they cannot learn to agree, I recommend that they work with a Special Master to help them settle things before they get out of control.

4. At the present, I'd recommend honoring Rebecca's feelings and change her time-share with the parents. I recommend that she be with her father most of the time and maintain a regular schedule to be with her mother. When she is with her mother, it is critical for Rebecca, Ms. Hall, and Mr. Little to let go of the conflicts and just

be together free of all of this tension. For now, I recommend that she be with her mother every other weekend (when the other children are with her), and one weekday evening each week. In this way, she can have some time with her mother without her siblings. It is my hope that, by honoring her request, the relationships will improve. At the recommended update (see below), I hope that a clearer picture will emerge about the best way for Rebecca to share time with both of her parents.

5. The situation regarding Molly and John is tougher. As indicated, I am quite concerned about the effects of Mr. Little's temper on them. He must stop the angry outbursts to, or in front of, the children. In addition, I am concerned about Ms. Hall's style with John, as it appears that he needs more structure than she might be providing. Yet, I am certain that the current schedule is creating and/or adding its own share of chaos to the children. As such, at the present, I recommend that the children be on a straight week-week schedule with each parent, with a Friday afternoon transition time.

6. During the next 5 months, I recommend that Mr. Little get involved in his therapy (and/or anger management classes) and both Mr. and Ms. Hall get into some parenting class designed to better understand the needs of a more difficult child (John). At the end of November, I recommend a brief update to determine if John is doing better, if Molly feels more relaxed, and if Mr. Little is less angry. Most important, Ms. Hall needs to know that she must take responsibility for improving some of these things for the children, or the children might need further changes in the time-share arrangement.

Thank you for allowing me to be of assistance with this family.

____

Philip M. Stahl, Ph.D.
Licensed Psychologist PSY 10270

APPENDIX 5

Psychological Tests (for Adults) and Games and Tests (for Children)

SUGGESTED GUIDELINES FOR THE USE OF PSYCHOLOGICAL TESTING IN CHILD CUSTODY EVALUATIONS

Psychological testing has been both overvalued and discredited by mental health professionals and the legal system when used in child custody disputes. However, psychological testing offers specific data that can be used most meaningfully in conjunction with information obtained by other methods, such as comprehensive interviews, evaluation of parent-child interactions, home visits, and collateral contacts. Psychological test data are meaningful only when considered in light of the total context of the evaluation. In order to use psychological tests in the context of child custody evaluations, the psychologist must also have an understanding of the dynamics of divorce and integrate the test data with knowledge of joint custody and the impact of various custody arrangements on the developmental needs of children. Psychological tests can be administered and scored only by those who hold appropriate licenses for their use, which is usually regulated by state law.

Psychological testing can be used for several purposes. First, it can be used to validate or disconfirm clinical impressions and/or questions raised by each parent about the psychological fitness of the other parent. Second, although no tests directly assess parenting ability, there are standardized tests that assess underlying psychodynamics and characterological traits that affect the ability to parent a child. Third, psychological tests may point to issues of impulsivity, psychological resourcefulness, capacity for empathy, relationship capacity, emotional responsiveness to the environment, and so forth, which is useful in understanding the parent's capacity to parent. Fourth, test data can help clarify psychological defenses, such as denial, projection, externalization of blame, and deception, which may help in explaining the stories of each parent. In all, test data can be most useful when they enhance the other clinical data available to the evaluator, especially when connected to the behaviors directly observed by the evaluator, as well.

If psychologists use testing in the context of child custody evaluations, they should select tests that have proven validity and reliability. Extreme care should be used with those tests that have only limited or inconclusive reliability or validity status. If tests are used, they must be done equally with both parents. Most important, psychologists who use tests must remember that child custody evaluations are always complex and create a high level of anxiety for all parties involved. The evaluator is responsible for gathering information from many different kinds of sources in order to develop an understanding of parents and children involved in the dispute. When used appropriately, psychological testing can provide objective, powerful data that can help the evaluator conceptualize the underlying dynamics of the disputing family with greater clarity and thus arrive at the most appropriate custody recommendations. The following list of tests reflects my particular review of tests often used in the context of child custody evaluations.

PSYCHOLOGICAL TESTS AND ASSESSMENT TOOLS FREQUENTLY USED WITH ADULTS

Mental Status Exam

Personality Tests

Minnesota Multiphasic Personality Inventory (MMPI)

Minnesota Multiphasic Personality Inventory 2 (MMPI-2)—Designed to assess major personality characteristics that reflect a person's social and personal adjustment and the possibility of significant psychological dysfunction. Forms and computer scoring available from a variety of sources including NCS Assessments, P.O. Box 1416, Minneapolis, MN 55440 (1-800-627-7271).

Millon Clinical Multiaxial Inventory II (MCMI-II)—Designed to assess personality characteristics and personality patterns. Forms and computer scoring available from NCS Assessments, P.O. Box 1416, Minneapolis, MN 55440 (1-800-627-7271).

House-Tree-Person (or other projective drawings)—Used as a projective measure of the client's personality dynamics according to research findings over the years.

Rorschach (Exner and other scoring systems)—The most widely used projective technique, the Rorschach is useful in diagnosis and treatment planning related to a wide variety of psychological issues. In recent years, Exner has developed a comprehensive system for scoring the Rorschach. Computer assistance is available for Exner scoring. Available from The Psychological Corporation, 555 Academic Court, San Antonio, TX 78204-2498 (1-800-228-0752).

Thematic Apperception Test (TAT)—Useful in the personality assessment of adults, revealing dominant drives, emotions, conflicts, and complexes in his or her personality. Available from The Psychological Corporation, 555 Academic Court, San Antonio, TX 78204-2498 (1-800-228-0752).

Parent-Administered Tests About Their Perception of Their Own Parenting

Parenting Stress Index—Measures stress in the parent-child relationship, identifying dysfunctional parenting and/or defensiveness within the family system. The PSI consists of 101 items and yields scores related to both child traits and parent traits. Available from Western Psychological Services, 12031 Wilshire Blvd., Los Angeles, CA 90025-1251 (1-800-648-8857).

Parent-Child Relationship Inventory—A self-report inventory that tells how parents view their own parenting behavior. Scaled scores reflect the respondent's awareness of children's needs and the level of his or her parenting skills. Excellent task for comparing the client's stated perceptions with his or her scaled scores on the task. Available from Western Psychological Services, 12031 Wilshire Blvd., Los Angeles, CA 90025-1251 (1-800-648-8857).

Parent-Administered Tests About the Psychological Functioning of Their Children

Child Behavior Checklist (Parent Form)—Designed for parents to fill out and respond to questions about their child's personality. A good measure for comparing the parent's stated observations with the evaluator's observations gained through the evaluation process.

Personality Inventory for Children (PIC) (Parent Form)—Measures behavior and cognitive and affective functioning of children based on responses of the parents. Another good measure for comparing the parent's stated observations with the evaluator's observations gained through the evaluation process. Available from Western Psychological Services, 12031 Wilshire Blvd., Los Angeles, CA 90025-1251 (1-800-648-8857).

PSYCHOLOGICAL TESTS AND ASSESSMENT TOOLS FREQUENTLY USED WITH CHILDREN

Developmental history (from parents and children)

Educational history (from parents and children)

Children's Apperception Test (CAT)—Like the TAT, it measures many aspects of a child's personality. Available from The Psychological Corporation, 555 Academic Court, San Antonio, TX 78204-2498 (1-800-228-0752).

Family Apperception Test (FAT)—Like the CAT and TAT, it elicits projective associations about individuals, but within the context of family process and structure, thus giving valuable information about family relationships. Available from Western Psychological Services, 12031 Wilshire Blvd., Los Angeles, CA 90025-1251 (1-800-648-8857).

Family drawings—Same as House-Tree-Person noted previously.

The Talking, Feeling, and Doing Game—Enables children who are quiet or defensive a different opportunity for exploring feelings, especially about family relationships. Available from Dr. Richard Gardner, Creative Therapeutics, 155 County Rd., Cresskill, NJ 07626-0317.

Divorce Story Cards—Like the TAT, CAT, and FAT, a projective task for identifying children's feelings regarding the divorce of their parents. Available from Childswork Childs Play, Center for Applied Psychology, 441 N. Fifth St., Philadelphia, PA 19123 (1-800-962-1141).

The Family Relations Test—Available from NFER Publishing Company Ltd., Darvillc House, 2 Oxford Road East, Blocks SL41DF, Windsor, England, UK.

Any of a wide variety of sentence completion forms.

APPENDIX 6

Review of Evaluation Ethical Standards and Guidelines

Included in this appendix is my compilation of guidelines and ethical standards based on and edited from a variety of national, state, and local organizations that have promulgated rules related to the performance of custody evaluations. Also included in this appendix following my compilation are the Model Standards of the Association of Family and Conciliation Courts, the recommended credentials and qualifications for the Marin County Special Master Program, and the Guidelines for Child Custody Evaluations of the American Psychological Association.

The following is a list of the organizations with guidelines and ethical standards on which I based my compilation.

American Professional Society on the Abuse of Children (APSAC), "Guidelines for Psychosocial Evaluation of Suspected Sexual Abuse in Young Children," 1990.

American Psychological Association (APA), "Guidelines for Child Custody Evaluations in Divorce Proceedings," 1994. (The complete text of these guidelines is included in this appendix.) Draft 3.0, October 1992.

Arizona Board of Psychologist Examiners, "Child Custody Evaluation Guidelines," August 1988.

Association of Family and Conciliation Courts (AFCC), "Model Standards of Practice for Child Custody Evaluation," 1994. (The complete text of the standards is included in this appendix.)

California Court Rule 1257, "Procedures for Evaluations in Child Custody Disputes," November 1992.

California Statewide Office of Family Court Services "Ethical Considerations," from Child Custody Evaluations, 1991.

Campbell, T. (1992). "Child Custody Evaluations and Appropriate Standards of Psychological Practice." *Michigan Bar Journal, 71,* 278-283.

Contra Costa County (California) Psychological Association Task Force on Child Custody Evaluations, "Proposed Child Custody Evaluation Guidelines for Psychologists," 1994.

Greater Pittsburgh (Pennsylvania) Psychological Association Task Force on Child Custody Evaluation, February 6, 1991.

Marin County (California) Psychological Association, "Proposed Child Custody Evaluation Guidelines for Private Psychologists," 1992.

Nebraska Psychological Association, "Guidelines for Performing Child Custody Evaluations," 1986.

Raiford, K., & Little, M. "Child Custody Evaluation Standards: A Proposal," a report to the California State Chapter of the AFCC, January 1994.

EDITED COMPILATION OF GUIDELINES AND STANDARDS FOR CONDUCTING CHILD CUSTODY EVALUATIONS

1. *First, do no harm.* This ethical standard must be maintained at all times and will affect how evaluators handle the findings and protect treatment relationships during evaluations.
2. *The child is the major client.* At all times, the needs and best interests of the child must come before the needs of the court or the wishes of the parents. We must be cognizant of the need to protect children from too many mental health professionals, unnecessary evaluations, and too much acrimony during the evaluation process.
3. *The mental health professional must function at all times as a professional expert.* This recognizes that the mental health professional is not a judge and that his or her job is to assist the court by supplying information and recommendation based as much as possible on empirical findings and data.
4. *The evaluator must be neutral at all times during the evaluation process.* It is crucial to the credibility of the evaluation process for the evaluator to

carefully maintain a neutral role during the process of the evaluation. Alignment with either party is not acceptable. Appointment by the court or by stipulation of the parties helps to ensure such neutrality. In testimony before the court, it is important to avoid becoming an advocate for either parent. The evaluator must remain open to all appropriate interpretations of the data.

5. *Dual relationships must be avoided.* An evaluator must not participate in a child custody evaluation if he or she has had any prior relationship with any member of the family (including but not limited to therapist, mediator, Special Master, friend, etc.). This would void the evaluator's ability to remain neutral.
6. *Multiple avenues of data gathering are expected.* A competent evaluation must be completed from a variety of sources, which may include interviews, formal assessments of all parties, observations of various family interactions, home visits, psychological testing, review of the legal history, and gathering of information from collateral sources. It is important that all procedures and techniques be applied in as comparable a manner as possible to each parent. If psychological testing is used, the limits of such testing should be clear.
7. *Many factors must be considered in the evaluator's recommendations.* A custody evaluation assesses strengths and weaknesses of each parent, the ability of the parents to share their children and work together to meet the needs of their children, the ability of the children to share their time in two separate households, the mental and physical health of each parent, the wishes of the children, and all factors related to the development of an appropriate parenting plan. The evaluator must recognize that no single factor is paramount, rather that a complex pattern of interactions contributes to parenting ability and the appropriate parenting plan for children.
8. *Quality of service must not be dictated by fees.* The evaluator must adhere to ethical practices regardless of the fee charged. Evaluators must be truthful in communications with third-party payors, such as insurance companies, that the evaluation is intended for the courts and not for treatment planning purposes.
9. *It is not considered ethical to conduct a one-sided evaluation that results in recommendations that involve conclusions about a person not seen.* In the event that a one-sided evaluation is performed, no recommendations about custody are to be offered and comments are to be limited to the person(s) evaluated.
10. *Evaluators are to avoid ex parte communications with attorneys or the court on substantive issues.* The evaluator can ask clarifying questions of either attorney or the court, but if there is any substantive communication,

it is best done in writing, with copies to all concerned parties, or via conference calls.

11. *Limits of confidentiality in evaluations need to be made clear to all parties, including the children.* Even though this is a court proceeding, it is important to have parents sign a release of information and to be clear to parents who has access to the evaluation report. This is best done both in the court order and in the interviews with the parents. It is wise for local courts to develop local court rules related to the confidentiality of the child's therapy in order to protect it. Along with this, the evaluator is to obtain informed consent from all participants.
12. *It is expected that evaluators will possess at least a master's degree in a mental health field and have considerable training and understanding of families, issues of divorce, child development, and the needs of the court. It is expected that evaluators will keep up with the literature in these areas.* Those possessing less than 2 years of postdegree experience in these areas or who are just beginning to do evaluations will require supervision until fully qualified. An evaluator is to avoid practicing beyond the boundaries of competence.
13. *It is required for the evaluator to be aware of one's biases.* All of us have some biases and as evaluators we must be aware of them and vigilant about correcting for their distorting effects.
14. *The evaluator is to provide a written report as directed by the courts.* In addition, all records obtained in the process of conducting the evaluation are properly maintained and filed according to the ethics of the evaluator's professional organization (e.g., APA).
15. *In testimony, the evaluator is to avoid becoming an advocate, is to refrain from speculation beyond what the data support, and is to make no statement about anyone not seen as part of the evaluation.* It is essential that the evaluator remain professional throughout the experience of testifying, stay with the data gathered during the evaluation, and remain open to various interpretations of the data.

ASSOCIATION OF FAMILY AND CONCILIATION COURTS MODEL STANDARDS OF PRACTICE FOR CHILD CUSTODY EVALUATION

INTRODUCTION

The following Standards of Practice for Child Custody Evaluation have been formulated for members of the Association of Family and Conciliation Courts who conduct evaluations in custody/access matters. These members include both court-connected and private practice evaluators in many areas of the world with significant variations in practice and philosophy. It is recognized that local jurisdictional requirements influence the conduct of the custody evaluation; however, the goal of these standards is to highlight common concerns and set standards of practice that are applicable regardless of local circumstances.

PREAMBLE

Child custody evaluation is a process through which recommendations for the custody of, parenting of, and access to children can be made to the court in those cases in which the parents are unable to work out their own parenting plans. Evaluation may be requested by the parents or their attorneys or ordered by the court. Evaluations may be performed by qualified mental health professionals who are part of a family court system or carried out privately by qualified individuals or teams. Evaluators always serve impartially, never as an advocate for one parent or the other.

The primary purpose of a child custody evaluation is to assess the family and provide the courts, the parents, and the attorneys with objective information and recommendations. The assessment goals of a child custody evaluation shall be to (a) identify the developmental needs of the child(ren); (b) identify the strengths, vulnerabilities, and needs of all other members of the family; (c) identify the positive and negative family interactions; (d) develop a plan for custody and access utilizing the strengths of each individual that will serve the best interests of the child(ren) and within those parameters, the wishes and interests of the parents, and in most situations provide them with an opportunity to share in the upbringing of their child(ren); and (e) through a written report, provide the court, parents, and attorneys with these recommendations and supporting data.

These standards are intended to assist and guide public and private evaluators. The manner of implementation and evaluator adherence to these standards will be influenced by local law and court rule.

I. INITIATING THE PROCESS

A. Appointing or choosing an evaluator

For information about AFCC, contact Ann Milne, Executive Director, at (608) 251-4001. AFCC guidelines reprinted by permission.

If there is a court-connected office of evaluation and conciliation, the evaluation shall be referred to that office for assignment to a qualified evaluator. If there is no such related office or if the evaluation is to be handled privately, the court shall appoint an evaluator or one must be agreed to by both parties and approved by the court.

Informed written consent of all parties must be obtained. Parties shall have the right to suspend or terminate an evaluation pending the consultation of an attorney regarding the advisability of continued participation if the evaluation is not court ordered.

B. Arrangements with the parties

1a. The evaluator shall clarify with all parties, perhaps at a joint meeting, the evaluation procedures, license and credentials of the evaluator or team, the costs (if the evaluation is private or if there is an agency fee), the mutual responsibilities of the evaluator and the parties, and the limits of confidentiality. The evaluator shall assure the parties and their attorneys that no prior relationship existed or exists between the evaluator and any of the parties.

1b. If some previous relationship exists, however insignificant, it should be raised at this point and discussed in order to assure each party that objectivity will not be compromised by any prior contact. A decision whether to proceed or not will be made at the conclusion of this discussion or following discussion between the parties and their attorneys.

2. During the orientation process, if preevaluation informational meetings are held, similar meetings shall be offered to all of the parents and potential caretakers and to all of their attorneys. Parties and/or their attorneys shall be free to ask questions. The evaluator shall provide information on any inherent bias(es) (e.g., joint custody, shared physical custody, mediation, lifestyle, and/or religion, etc.) that he or she holds, prior to the commencement of any evaluation.

3. Communication between the evaluator and the attorneys shall be conducted so as to avoid any question of ex parte communication. Communication of significant matters between evaluator and attorneys may be best accomplished by conference call or in writing with copies to both attorneys.

II. EVALUATOR STANDARDS

A. Education and training

Custody evaluators shall have a minimum of a master's degree in a mental health field that includes formal education and training in child development, child and adult psychopathology, interviewing techniques, and family systems. In addition, by formal training or work experience, the evaluator should have a working understanding of the complexities of the divorce process, awareness of the legal issues in divorce in the evaluator's jurisdiction of practice, and an understanding of the many issues, legal, social, familial, and cultural involved in custody and visitation.

B. Supervision and consultation for the evaluator

In addition, for evaluators in either public or private settings who have less than 2 years of experience conducting custody evaluations, it is recommended that ongoing supervision and consultation be available and utilized while the evaluator strengthens his or her skills.

C. Knowledge of statutes

The evaluator shall be familiar with the statutes and case law governing child custody. These will vary from jurisdiction to jurisdiction, and the evaluator must be completely knowledgeable concerning the criteria for original determination of custody, criteria for change of custody, the use of custody evaluation, qualifications for custody evaluators, and the legal requirements of the custody evaluation process of the jurisdiction in which the evaluation is to be conducted.

D. Psychological testing

If the evaluator is not licensed or certified to perform and interpret psychological testing, any psychological testing that is to be included as part of the custody evaluation must be referred to a licensed/certified psychologist who has the training and experience to understand the issues in custody evaluations.

III. EVALUATION PROCEDURES

A. Evaluation elements

The evaluator shall determine the scope of each evaluation, including who is to be included other than the litigants. In general, as diverse a number of procedures for data collection as possible and feasible to the specific evaluation is encouraged. These may include interviewing, observation, testing, use of collaterals, and home visits. It is important that the evaluator maintain a constant sense of balance, that is, obtaining similar types of information about each parent (when applicable) and spending similar amounts of time with each parent under similar circumstances.

B. Procedures during an evaluation

Each evaluator or team may use different procedures relative to joint and/or individual interviews, the necessity of a home visit, and the circumstances in which the children are interviewed. It is desirable that all parties to a dispute, as well as any other significant caretakers, be evaluated by the same evaluator or team. In cases where domestic violence is an issue, joint interviews may not be advisable.

C. Evaluations in two separate jurisdictions

In those cases in which the patients or caretakers reside in geographically separated jurisdictions, different evaluators may be necessary for the evaluations of each parent or caretaker. When such is the case, it is the responsibility of the requesting evaluator to be as specific as possible with the details and information requested from the courtesy evaluator, in order that the returning information is as near as possible to the quality and type of information that the requesting evaluator would have elicited. It is also the responsibility of the originating evaluator to help with the interpretation of the courtesy evaluation for the court. Where feasible, however, it is preferable for all parties to be interviewed by the same evaluator.

D. Interviewing and testing

Each adult shall be evaluated individually, and comparable evaluation techniques shall be used with all of the significant adults. If special procedures, such as psychological testing, are used for general evaluative purposes of one parent or potential caretaker, that procedure or those procedures shall be used for all significant adults involved in the evaluation. However, if a special technique is used to address a specific issue raised about one of the significant adults, it may not be necessary to use that same technique on all other significant adults.

E. Procedures with child(ren)

Each child shall be evaluated individually with procedures appropriate to the developmental level of the child. These procedures may include observation, verbal or play interview, and formal testing. It is not appropriate to ask children to choose between their parents because, in most families, children need good access to both parents following the divorce and should not be placed in the position of having to choose. Information about the child(ren)'s feelings, thoughts, and wishes about each parent can be obtained through techniques that will not be harmful and guilt inducing. The children shall be observed with each parent or potential caretaker in the office or home setting.

F. Psychological testing

1. Any psychological testing is to be conducted by a licensed/certified psychologist who adheres to the ethical standards of the jurisdiction in which he or she is licensed.

2. If testing is conducted with adults or children, it shall be done with knowledge of the limits of the testing and should be viewed only within the context of the information gained from clinical interviews and other available data. Conclusions should take into account the stresses associated with the divorce and the custody dispute.

3. If psychological test data are used as a significant factor in the final recommendations, the limitations of psychological testing in this regard should be outlined in the report.

4. The results of psychological testing shall be discussed with the significant adult participants in the evaluation, especially if the results indicate the need for

psychological treatment or counseling. Whatever the outcome of the testing, of primary concern to the evaluator should be the parenting skills and abilities of the individual parents. Diagnostic considerations shall be considered secondary to parenting and treatment considerations.

G. Collaterals

1. Information from appropriate outside sources, such as pediatricians, therapists, teachers, health care providers, and day-care personnel, shall be obtained where such information is deemed necessary and related to the issues at hand. Prior to the seeking or gathering of such information releases signed by the parents shall be obtained; these releases shall specifically indicate the areas in which the information is sought and limit the use of this information to use by the evaluator in the preparation of the evaluation report.

2. Interviewing of family and/or friends shall be handled with great care given its potential for increasing divisiveness and resulting in harm to the children. It is possible, however, that family friends and neighbors may be able to present valuable information and/or leads to the evaluator. The use of such information shall be related to the circumstances of a particular evaluation, used only when the evaluator is convinced of its usefulness, and obtained in a manner that discourages conflict.

H. Home visits

When home visits are made, they shall be made in similar ways to each parent's or potential caretaker's home. Care shall be exercised so that temporary inequality in housing conditions does not lead to bias on the part of the evaluator. Economic circumstance alone shall not be a determining factor in a custody evaluation.

I. Interpretive conferences

The evaluator may hold an interpretive conference with each of the parties, either separately or conjointly. This is not a conference that attorneys need attend. The purpose of this conference is to discuss with each party the recommendations that are to be made and the rationale for each of these recommendations. It should be made clear to each party that these are the recommendations that are to be presented to the court in the evaluation report; acceptance and use by the court cannot be guaranteed.

IV. AREAS OF EVALUATION

A. Quality of relationship between parent or caretaker and the child

This shall include assessment of the strength and quality of the relationship, emotional closeness, perceptions of each other, and the ability of the parent or potential caretaker to support appropriate development in the child(ren) and to understand and respond to the child(ren)'s needs. The evaluator shall consider ethnic, cultural, lifestyle, and/or religious factors where relevant.

B. Quality of relationship between the contesting parents or potential caretakers

This shall include assessment of each parent's or potential caretaker's ability to support the child(ren)'s relationship with the other parent and to communicate and cooperate with the other parent regarding the child(ren). The evaluator shall consider the relevancy of ethnic, cultural, lifestyle, and/or religious factors in assessing these relationships. Also, some consideration of the contribution of each parent to the marital and subsequent discord might be helpful in this regard.

C. Ability of each parent or caretaker to parent the child

This shall include assessment of the parent's or potential caretaker's knowledge of the child(ren), knowledge of parenting techniques, awareness of what is normal development in children, ability to distinguish his or her own needs from the needs of the child(ren), and ability to respond empathically to the child(ren). The evaluator shall consider the relevancy of ethnic, cultural, lifestyle, and/or religious factors in assessing these relationships.

Also to be taken into account is the ability and/or willingness of the parent, who perhaps has not had the opportunity to learn these skills, to learn them, to demonstrate an interest in learning them, and to try to use them in whatever time he or she has with the child.

D. Psychological health of each parent or potential caretaker

This shall include assessment of the parent's adaptation to the divorce, ability to develop relationships, ability to provide a stable home for the child(ren), ability to encourage development in the child(ren), and ability to support the child(ren)'s relationship with the other parent or caretaker. Assessment should also be made of factors that might affect parenting, such as alcohol or drug use, domestic violence, or a history of becoming involved in brief or harmful relationships.

E. Psychological health of each child

This shall include assessment of special needs of each child, for example, health or developmental problems. It shall also include assessment of the child(ren)'s adjustment to school, friends, community, and extended family. Children shall not be asked to choose between parents. Their overt and covert wishes and fears about their relationships with their parents shall be considered but shall not be the sole basis for making a recommendation.

F. Patterns of domestic violence

In cases in which domestic violence is alleged or a pattern of domestic violence exists and the evaluator, or evaluation team, does not possess expertise in this area, outside personnel with specialized training and experience in this area shall be consulted. In such cases the recommendation made by the evaluator, after consultation, shall take into consideration both the danger to the other parent or caretaker and the potential danger to and effect on the children.

V. THE EVALUATION REPORT

A. Style

The evaluation report shall be written clearly and without jargon so that it can be understood by the court, attorneys, and clients. It shall convey an attitude of understanding and empathy for all of the individuals involved, adults and children, and shall be written in a way that conveys respect for each individual.

B. Contents

In preparing reports, evaluators shall be aware that their own professional observations, opinions, recommendations, and conclusions must be distinguished from legal facts, opinions, and conclusions. The report shall include identifying information, reasons for the evaluation, procedures used, family history, evaluation of each child and each parent and caretaker, and evaluation of the relationships among parents and children and among the adults. Conclusions about the individuals and the relationships shall lead logically to the recommendations for custody, access, and visitation. It is helpful, and in some jurisdictions required, to spell out clearly how the data, the conclusions, and the recommendations are related to the statutory requirements.

C. Distribution

1. The evaluation report shall be distributed according to the rules established by each jurisdiction.

2. After the report has been distributed and considered, the court may order or it may be deemed wise for either or both parties to participate in therapy and/or counseling. The professional counselor/therapist may be an appropriate recipient of the report or that portion of the report relating to his or her client with approval of the court.

VI. ETHICAL PRINCIPLES

A. Ethical principles of professions

Evaluators are to adhere to the ethical principles of their own professions above the needs of the parties, the attorneys, or the courts. When there is a conflict between these ethical principles and others' needs, the evaluator shall try to explain the conflict to the parties and the attorneys and shall try to find ways of continuing the evaluation that will minimize or remove the conflict. If that is not possible, the evaluator shall withdraw from the process, with notice to all parties and their attorneys in writing.

B. Prior relationships

An evaluator must disclose any prior relationship between the evaluator and any member of the family and, in most cases, should not perform a custody evaluation if there is a prior relationship of any kind. In addition, a person who has been a mediator or a therapist for any or all members of the family should not perform a custody evaluation because the previous knowledge and relationship may render him or her incapable of being completely neutral and incapable of having unbiased objectivity.

C. Post-relationships

After the completion of an evaluation, the evaluator should similarly be cautious about switching roles to that of either mediator or therapist. Such a change of roles would render future testimony and/or reevaluations invalid by virtue of the change in objectivity and neutrality. If all parties, including the evaluator, wish the evaluator to change roles following an evaluation, it is important for the evaluator to inform the parties of the impact that such a change will have in the areas of possible testimony and/or reevaluation.

D. Issues beyond the evaluator's expertise

In cases where issues arise that are beyond the scope of the evaluator's expertise, the evaluator shall seek consultation with a professional in the area of concern.

E. Limitations on evaluator's recommendations

Evaluators shall make every effort to include all parties involved in the custody dispute in the evaluation process itself. Evaluators shall not make statements of fact or inference about parties whom they have not seen. On occasion, evaluators will be unable to see all parties in a custody evaluation dispute, either because of refusal of one party to participate or because of logistical factors such as geography. In these cases the evaluator may perform a limited evaluation, but must limit his or her observations and conclusions. For example, if only one parent is seen, the evaluator must not make statements about the other parent and must not make a recommendation for custody because the other parent has not been seen. The evaluator may report on those individuals who have been seen and on their interactions with each other and may draw conclusions regarding the nature of those relationships, such as whether they should continue, not continue, or be modified in some way. The evaluator may also make comments or state opinions about the need for a more expanded evaluation. Prior to undertaking such an evaluation the evaluator may want to inform the court of the circumstances of the evaluation as well as determine that the party who brings the child for a limited evaluation has the legal right to provide consent for the evaluation.

CONCLUSION

Responsibility and authority for final decisions regarding custody and access rest with the court. As the conclusions of the evaluator are but one piece of the evidence before the court, these conclusions are to be framed as recommendations.

MARIN COUNTY SPECIAL MASTER PROGRAM

Recommended Special Master Credentials and Qualifications

Psychologists and Psychiatrists

1. Membership in national or state professional association.
2. Experience:
   A. 3 years postlicense experience in child and family therapy.
   B. 3 years experience in diagnostic evaluations for family court and/or CPS and/or family mediation service, with a minimum of 10 evaluations.
   C. 3 years experience in court-based family mediation.
3. Training:
   A. Family systems, child development, psychology of divorce, and custody. Mediation training is helpful.
4. Familiarity with ethical issues of custody disputes.
5. Working knowledge of custody law, with a minimum of six cases working with attorneys and/or court appearances.

Marriage, Family, and Child Counselors and Licensed Clinical Social Workers
Same as above, with 5 years experience for 2A, B, and C.

Attorneys

1. Membership in state or national professional association.
2. Experience:
   A. 10 out of the last 12 years experience practicing family law.
   B. 20 custody cases, carried through judgment.
3. Training:
   A. Mediation training required.
   B. Continuing education in custody law.
   C. Child development and family systems.

Prepared by the Marin County Task Force on Special Masters.

GUIDELINES FOR CHILD CUSTODY EVALUATIONS IN DIVORCE PROCEEDINGS

INTRODUCTION

Decisions regarding child custody and other parenting arrangements occur within several different legal contexts, including parental divorce, guardianship, neglect or abuse proceedings, and termination of parental rights. The following guidelines were developed for psychologists conducting child custody evaluations, specifically within the context of parental divorce. These guidelines build upon the APA Ethical Principles of Psychologists and Code of Conduct (APA, 1992) and are aspirational in intent. *As guidelines, they are not intended to be either mandatory or exhaustive. The goal of the guidelines is to promote proficiency in using psychological expertise in conducting child custody evaluations.*

Parental divorce requires a restructuring of parental rights and responsibilities in relation to children. If the parents can agree to a restructuring arrangement, which they do in the overwhelming proportion (90%) of divorce custody cases (Melton, Petrila, Poythress, & Slobogin, 1987), there is no dispute for the court to decide. However, if the parents are unable to reach such an agreement, the court must help to determine the relative allocation of decision making authority and physical contact each parent will have with the child. The courts typically apply a "best interest of the child" standard in determining this restructuring of rights and responsibilities.

Psychologists provide an important service to children and the courts by providing competent, objective, impartial information in assessing the best interests of the child, by demonstrating a clear sense of direction and purpose in conducting a child custody evaluation, by performing their roles ethically, and by clarifying to all involved the nature and scope of the evaluation. The Ethics Committee of the American Psychological Association has noted that psychologists' involvement in custody disputes has at times raised questions in regard to the misuse of psychologists' influence, sometimes resulting in complaints against psychologists being

---

These guidelines were drafted by the Committee on Professional Practice and Standards, A Committee of the Board of Professional Affairs with Input from the Committee on Children, Youth, and Families. Adopted by the Council of Representatives of the American Psychological Association, February 1994.

Acknowledgements: COPPS 1991-1993 members, Richard Cohen, Alex Carbalo Dieguez, Kathleen Dockett, Sam Friedman, Colette Ingraham, John Northman, John Robinson, Deborah Tharinger, Susana Urbina, Phil Witt, and James Wulach; BPA Liaisons 1991-1993, Richard Cohen, Joseph Kobos, and Rodney Lowman; and CYF members, Don Routh and Carolyn Swift.

brought to the attention of the APA Ethics Committee (APA Ethics Committee, 1985; Hall & Hare-Mustin, 1983; Keith-Spiegel & Koocher, 1985; Mills, 1984) and raising questions in the legal and forensic literature (Grisso, 1986; Melton, Petrila, Poythress, & Slobogin, 1987; Mnookin, 1975; Ochroch, 1982; Okpaku, 1976; Weithorn, 1987).

Particular competencies and knowledge are required for child custody evaluations to provide adequate and appropriate psychological services to the court. Child custody evaluation in the context of parental divorce can be an extremely demanding task. For competing parents the stakes are high as they participate in a process fraught with tension and anxiety. The stress on the psychologist/evaluator can become great. Tension surrounding child custody evaluation can become further heightened when there are accusations of child abuse, neglect, and/or family violence.

Psychology is in a position to make significant contributions to child custody decisions. Psychological data and expertise, gained through a child custody evaluation, can provide an additional source of information and an additional perspective not otherwise readily available to the court on what appears to be in a child's best interest, and thus can increase the fairness of the determination the court must make.

GUIDELINES FOR CHILD CUSTODY EVALUATIONS IN DIVORCE PROCEEDINGS

I. ORIENTING GUIDELINES: PURPOSE OF A CHILD CUSTODY EVALUATION

1. The Primary Purpose of the Evaluation Is to Assess the Best Psychological Interests of the Child. The primary consideration in a child custody evaluation is to assess the individual and family factors that affect the best psychological interests of the child. More specific questions may be raised by the court.

2. The Child's Interests and Well-Being Are Paramount. In a child custody evaluation, the child's interests and wellbeing are paramount. Parents competing for custody, as well as others, may have legitimate concerns, but the child's best interests must prevail.

3. The Focus of the Evaluation Is on Parenting Capacity, the Psychological and Developmental Needs of the Child, and the Resulting Fit. In considering psychological factors affecting the best interests of the child, the psychologist focuses on the parenting capacity of the prospective custodians in conjunction with the psychological and developmental needs of each involved child. This involves: 1) an assessment of the adults' capacity for parenting, including whatever knowledge, attributes, skills, and abilities, or lack thereof, are present; 2) an assessment of the psychological functioning and developmental needs of each child, and the wishes of each child, where appropriate; and 3) the functional ability of each parent to meet these needs, which includes an evaluation of the interaction between each adult and child.

The values of the parents relevant to parenting, ability to plan for the child's future needs, capacity to provide a stable and loving home, and any potential for inappropriate behavior or misconduct that might negatively influence the child also are considered. Psychopathology may be relevant to such an assessment, in so far as it has impact on the child or the ability to parent, but it is not the primary focus.

II. GENERAL GUIDELINES: PREPARING FOR A CHILD CUSTODY EVALUATION

4. The Role of the Psychologist is a Professional Expert, Who Strives to Maintain an Objective, Impartial Stance. The role of the psychologist is as a professional expert. The psychologist does not act as a judge, who makes the ultimate decision applying the law to all relevant evidence. Neither does the psychologist act as an advocating attorney, who strives to present his or her client's best possible case. The psychologist, in a balanced, impartial manner, informs and advises the court and the prospective custodians of the child of the relevant psychological factors pertaining to the custody issue. The psychologist should be impartial regardless of whether he or she is retained by the court or by a party to the proceedings. If either the psychologist or the client cannot accept this neutral role, the psychologist should consider withdrawing from the case. If not permitted to withdraw, in such circumstances, the psychologist acknowledges past roles and other factors which could affect impartiality.

5. The Psychologist Gains Specialized Competence.

A. A psychologist contemplating performing child custody evaluations is aware that special competencies and knowledge are required for the undertaking of such evaluations. Competence in performing psychological assessments of children, adults, and families is necessary but not sufficient. Education, training, experience and/or supervision in the areas of child and family development, child and family psychopathology, and the impact of divorce on children, help to prepare the psychologist to participate competently in child custody evaluations. The psychologist also strives to become familiar with applicable legal standards and procedures, including laws governing divorce and custody adjudications in his or her state or jurisdiction.

B. The psychologist uses current knowledge of scientific and professional developments, consistent with accepted clinical and scientific standards, in selecting data collection methods and procedures. The Standards for Educational and Psychological Testing (APA, 1985) are adhered to in the use of psychological tests and other assessment tools.

C. In the course of conducting child custody evaluations, allegations of child abuse, neglect, family violence, or other issues may occur that are not necessarily within the scope of a particular evaluator's expertise. If this is so, the psychologist seeks additional consultation, supervision, and/or specialized knowledge, training or experience in child abuse, neglect, and family violence to address these complex issues. The psychologist is familiar with the laws of his or her state addressing child abuse, neglect, and family violence, and acts accordingly.

6. The Psychologist Is Aware of Personal and Societal Biases and Engages in Non-Discriminatory Practice. The psychologist engaging in child custody evaluations is aware of how biases regarding age, gender, race, ethnicity, national origin, religion, sexual orientation, disability, language, culture and socioeconomic status may interfere with an objective evaluation and recommendations. The psychologist recognizes and strives to overcome any such biases, or withdraws from the evaluation.

7. The Psychologist Avoids Multiple Relationships. Psychologists generally avoid conducting a child custody evaluation in a case in which the psychologist served in a therapeutic role for the child or his or her immediate family or has had other involvement which may compromise the psychologist's objectivity. This should not, however, preclude the psychologist from testifying in the case as a fact witness concerning treatment of the child. In addition, during the course of a child custody evaluation, a psychologist does not accept any of the involved participants in the evaluation as a therapy client. Therapeutic contact with the child or involved participants following a child custody evaluation is undertaken with caution. A psychologist asked to testify regarding a therapy client who is involved in a child custody case is aware of the limitations and possible biases inherent in such a role, and possible impact on the ongoing therapeutic relationship. While the court may require the psychologist to testify as a fact witness regarding factual information he or she became aware of in a professional relationship with a client, that psychologist should generally decline the role of an expert witness who gives a professional opinion regarding custody and visitation issues (see Ethical Standard 7.03), unless so ordered by the court.

III. PROCEDURAL GUIDELINES: CONDUCTING A CHILD CUSTODY EVALUATION

8. The Scope of the Evaluation is Determined by the Evaluator, Based on the Nature of the Referral Question. The scope of the custody-related evaluation is determined by the nature of the question or issue raised by the referring person or the court, or is inherent in the situation. While comprehensive child custody evaluations generally require an evaluation of all parents or guardians and children, as well as observations of interactions between them, the scope of the assessment in a particular case may be limited to evaluating the parental capacity of one parent, without attempting to compare the parents or to make recommendations. Likewise, the scope may be limited to evaluating the child. Or a psychologist may be asked to critique the assumptions and methodology of the assessment of another mental health professional. A psychologist also might serve as an expert witness in the area of child development, providing expertise to the court without relating it specifically to the parties involved in a case.

9. The Psychologist Obtains Informed Consent From All Adult Participants and, as Appropriate, Informs Child Participants. In undertaking child custody evaluations, the psychologist ensures that each adult participant is aware of: 1) the purpose, nature, and method of the evaluation; 2) who has requested the psychologist's services; and 3) who will be paying the fees. The psychologist informs adult participants about the nature of the assessment instruments and techniques and informs those participants about the possible disposition of the data collected. The psychologist provides this information, as appropriate, to children, to the extent that they are able to understand.

10. The Psychologist Informs Participants About the Limits of Confidentiality and the Disclosure of Information. A psychologist conducting a child custody evaluation ensures that the participants, including children to the extent feasible, are aware of the limits of confidentiality characterizing the professional relationship with the psychologist. The psychologist informs participants that in consenting to the evaluation, they are consenting to disclosure of the evaluation's findings in the context of the forthcoming litigation, and any other proceedings deemed necessary by the courts. A psychologist obtains a waiver of confidentiality from all adult participants, or from their authorized legal representatives.

11. The Psychologist Uses Multiple Methods of Data Gathering. The psychologist strives to use the most appropriate methods available for addressing the questions raised in a specific child custody evaluation, and generally uses multiple methods of data gathering, including, but not limited to, clinical interviews, observation and/or psychological assessments. Important facts and opinions are documented from at least two sources whenever their reliability is questionable. The psychologist, for example, may review potentially relevant reports, e.g., from schools, health care providers, child care providers, agencies, and institutions. Psychologists may also interview extended family, friends, and other individuals on occasions when the information is likely to be useful. If information is gathered from third parties that is significant and may be used as a basis for conclusions, psychologists corroborate it by at least one other source wherever possible and appropriate, and document this in the report.

12. The Psychologist Neither Over-Interprets Nor Inappropriately Interprets Clinical or Assessment Data. The psychologist refrains from drawing conclusions not adequately supported by the data. The psychologist interprets any data from interviews or tests, as well as any questions of data reliability and validity, cautiously and conservatively, seeking convergent validity. The psychologist strives to acknowledge to the court any limitations in methods or data used.

13. The Psychologist Does Not Give Any Opinion Regarding the Psychological Functioning of Any Individual Who Has Not Been Personally Evaluated. This guideline, however, does not preclude the psychologist from reporting what an evaluated individual (such as the parent or child) has stated, or from addressing theoretical issues or hypothetical questions, so long as the limited basis of the information is noted.

14. Recommendations, If Any, are Based Upon What is in the Best Psychological Interests of the Child. While the profession has not reached consensus about whether psychologists ought to make recommendations about the final custody determination to the courts, psychologists are obligated to be aware of the arguments on both sides of this issue, and to be able to explain the logic of their position concerning their own practice. If the psychologist does choose to make custody recommendations, they should be derived from sound psychological data, and must be based upon the best interests of the child, in the particular. Recommendations are based on articulated assumptions, data, interpretations, and inferences based upon established professional and scientific standards. Psychologists guard against relying upon their own biases or unsupported beliefs in rendering opinions in particular cases.

15. The Psychologist Clarifies Financial Arrangements. Financial arrangements are clarified and agreed upon prior to commencing a child custody evaluation. When billing for a child custody evaluation, the psychologist does not misrepresent his or her services for reimbursement purposes.

16. The Psychologist Maintains Written Records. All records obtained in the process of conducting a child custody evaluation are properly maintained and filed in accord with the APA Record Keeping Guidelines (APA, 1993) and relevant statutory guidelines. All raw data and interview information are recorded with an eye towards their possible review by other psychologists or the court, where legally permitted. Upon request, appropriate reports are made available to the court.

BIBLIOGRAPHY

References

American Psychological Association. (1992). Ethical principles of psychologists and code of conduct, *American Psychologist, 47*(12), 1597-1611.

American Psychological Association. (1993). *Record keeping guidelines.* Washington, DC: Author.

American Psychological Association. (1985). *Standards for educational and psychological testing.* Washington, DC: Author.

American Psychological Association, Ethics Committee. (1985). *Annual report of the american psychological association ethics committee.* Washington, DC: American Psychological Association, Ethics Department.

Grisso, T. (1986). *Evaluating competencies: Forensic assessments and instruments.* New York: Plenum.

Hall, J. E., & Hare-Mustin, R. T. (1983). Sanctions and the diversity of ethical complaints against psychologists. *American Psychologist, 38,* 714-729.

Keith-Spiegel, P., & Koocher, G. P. (1985). *Ethics in psychology.* New York: Random House.

Melton, G. B., Petrila, J., Poythress, N. G., & Slobogin, C. (1987). *Psychological evaluations for the courts: A handbook for mental health professionals and lawyers.* New York: Guilford Press.

Mills, D. H. (1984). Ethics education and adjudication within psychology. *American Psychologist, 39,* 669-675.

Mnookin, R. H. (1975). Child-custody adjudication: Judicial functions in the face of indeterminacy. *Law and Contemporary Problems, 39,* 226-293.

Ochroch, R. (1982). *Ethical pitfalls in child custody evaluations.* Paper presented at the American Psychological Association, Washington, DC.

Okpaku, S. (1976). Psychology: Impediment or aid in child custody cases? *Rutgers Law Review, 29,* 1117-1153.

Weithorn, L. A. (Ed.). (1987). *Psychology and child custody determinations: Knowledge, roles, and expertise.* Lincoln, NE: University of Nebraska Press.

Other Resources: State Guidelines

Georgia Psychological Association. (1990). *Recommendations for psychologists' involvement in child custody cases.* Atlanta, GA: Author.

Metropolitan Denver Interdisciplinary Committee on Child Custody. (1989). *Guidelines for child custody evaluations.* Denver, CO: Author.

Nebraska Psychological Association. (1986). *Guidelines for child custody evaluations.* Lincoln, NE: Author.

New Jersey State Board of Psychological Examiners. (1993). *Specialty guidelines for psychologists in custody/visitation evaluations.* Newark, NJ: Author.

North Carolina Psychological Association. (draft, 1993). *Child custody guidelines.* Unpublished manuscript.

Oklahoma Psychological Association. (1988). *Ethical guidelines for child custody evaluations.* Oklahoma City, OK: Author.

Pennsylvania Psychological Association, Clinical Division/Task Force on Child Custody Evaluation. (1991). *Roles for psychologists in child custody disputes.* Unpublished manuscript.

Other Resources: Forensic Guidelines

Committee on Ethical Guidelines for Forensic Psychologists. (1991). Specialty guidelines for forensic psychologists. *Law and Human Behavior, 6,* 655-665.

Other Resources: Pertinent Literature

Ackerman, M. J., & Kane, A. W. (1990). *How to examine psychological experts in divorce and other civil actions.* Colorado Springs, CO: Wiley Law Publications.

American Psychological Association, Board of Ethnic Minority Affairs. (1991). *Guidelines for providers of psychological services to ethnic, linguistic, and culturally diverse populations.* Washington, DC: American Psychological Association.

American Psychological Association, Committee on Women in Psychology and Committee on Lesbian and Gay Concerns. (1988). *Lesbian parents and their children: A resource paper for psychologists.* Washington, DC: American Psychological Association.

Beaber, R. J. (1982, Fall). Custody quagmire: Some psycholegal dilemmas. *The Journal of Psychiatry & Law,* 309-326.

Bennett, B. E., Bryant, B. K., VandenBos, G. R., & Greenwood, A. (1990). *Professional liability and risk management.* Washington, DC: American Psychological Association.

Bolocofsky, D. N. (1989). Use and abuse of mental health experts in child custody determinations. *Behavioral Sciences and the Law, 7*(2), 197-213.

Bozett, F. (1987). *Gay and lesbian parents.* New York: Praeger.

Bray, J. H. (1993), What's the best interest of the child? Children's adjustment issues in divorce. *The Independent Practitioner, 13,* 42-45.

Bricklin, B. (1992). Data-based tests in custody evaluations. *American Journal of Family Therapy, 20,* 254-265.

Cantor, D. W. & Drake, E. A. (1982). *Divorced parents and their children: A guide for mental health professionals.* New York: Springer.

Chesler, P. (1991). *Mothers on trial: The battle for children and custody.* New York: Harcourt Brace Jovanovich.

Deed, M. L. (1991). Court-ordered child custody evaluations: Helping or victimizing vulnerable families. *Psychotherapy, 28,* 76-84.

Falk, P. J. (1989). Lesbian mothers: Psychosocial assumptions in family law. *American Psychologist, 44,* 941-947.

Gardner, R. A. (1989). Family evaluation in child custody mediation, arbitration, and litigation. Cresskill, NJ: Creative Therapeutics.

Gardner, R. A. (1992). *The parental alienation syndrome: A guide for mental health and legal professionals.* Cresskill, NJ: Creative Therapeutics.

Gardner, R. A. (1992). *True and false accusations of child abuse.* Cresskill, NJ: Creative Therapeutics.

Goldstein, J., Freud, A., & Solnit, A. J. (1980). *Before the best interests of the child.* New York: Free Press.

Goldstein, J., Freud, A., & Solnit, A. J. (1980). *Beyond the best interests of the child.* New York: Free Press.

Goldstein, J., Freud, A., Solnit, A. J., & Goldstein, S. (1986). *In the best interests of the child.* New York: Free Press.

Grisso, T. (1990). Evolving guidelines for divorce/custody evaluations. *Family and Conciliation Courts Review, 28*(1), 35-41.

Halon, R. L. The comprehensive child custody evaluation. *American Journal of Forensic Psychology, 8*(3), 19-46.

Hetherington, E. M. (1990). Coping with family transitions: Winners, losers, and survivors. *Child Development, 60,* 1-14.

Hetherington, E. M., Stanley-Hagen, M., & Anderson, E. R. (1988). Marital transitions: A child's perspective. *American Psychologist, 44,* 303-312.

Johnston, J., Kline, M. & Tschann, J. (1989). Ongoing postdivorce conflict. Effects on children of joint custody and frequent access. *Journal of Orthopsychiatry, 59,* 576-592.

Koocher, G. P., & Keith-Spiegel, P. C. (1990). *Children, ethics, and the law: Professional issues and cases.* Lincoln: University of Nebraska Press.

Kreindler, S. (1986). The role of mental health professions in custody and access disputes. In R. S. Parry, E. A, Broder, E. A. G. Schmitt, E. B. Saunders, and E. Hood (Eds.), *Custody disputes: Evaluation and intervention.* Lexington, MA: Lexington Books.

Martindale, D. A., Martindale, J. L., and Broderick, J. E. (1991). Providing expert testimony in child custody litigation. In P. A. Keller and S. R. Heyman (Eds.), *Innovations in clinical practice: A source book* (Vol. 10). Sarasota, Florida: Professional Resource Exchange.

Patterson, C. J. (in press). Children of lesbian and gay parents. *Child Development.*

Saunders, T. R. (1991). An overview of some psycholegal issues in child physical and sexual abuse. *Psychotherapy in Private Practice, 9*(2), 61-78.

Schutz, B. M., Dixon, E. B., Lindenberger, J. C., & Ruther, N. J. (1989). *Solomon's sword: A practical guide to conducting child custody evaluations.* San Francisco: Jossey-Bass.

Stahly, G. B. (1989). *Testimony on child abuse policy to APA Board.* Paper presented at the American Psychological Association Board of Directors meeting, New Orleans, LA.

Thoennes, N., & Tjaden, P. G. (1991). The extent, nature, and validity of sexual abuse allegations in custody/visitation disputes. *Child Abuse & Neglect, 14,* 151-163.

Wallerstein, J. S., & Blakeslee, S. (1989). *Second chances: Men, women, and children a decade after divorce.* New York: Ticknor & Fields.

Wallerstein, J. S. & Kelly, J. B. (1980). *Surviving the breakup.* New York: Basic Books.

Weissman, H. N. (1991). Child custody evaluations: Fair and unfair professional practices. *Behavioral Sciences and the Law, 9,* 469-476.

Weithorn, L. A. & Grisso, T. (1987). Psychological evaluations in divorce custody: Problems, principles, and procedures. In L. A. Weithorn (Ed.), *Psychology and child custody determinations.* Lincoln, NE: University of Nebraska Press.

White, S. (1990). The contamination of children's interviews. *Child youth and family services quarterly, 13*(3).

Wyer, M. M., Gaylord, S. J. & Grove, E. T. The legal context of child custody evaluations. In L. A. Weithorn (Ed.), *Psychology and child custody determinations.* Lincoln, NE: University of Nebraska Press.

AMERICAN PROFESSIONAL SOCIETY ON THE ABUSE OF CHILDREN

GUIDELINES FOR PSYCHOSOCIAL EVALUATION OF SUSPECTED SEXUAL ABUSE IN YOUNG CHILDREN

Statement of Purpose

These Guidelines for mental health professionals reflect current knowledge and consensus about the psychosocial evaluation of suspected sexual abuse in young children. They are not intended as a standard of practice to which practitioners are expected to adhere in all cases. Evaluators must have the flexibility to exercise clinical judgment in individual cases. Laws and local customs may also influence the accepted method in a given community. Practitioners should be knowledgeable about various constraints on practice, and prepared to justify their decisions about particular practices in specific cases. As experience and scientific knowledge expand, further refinement and revision of these Guidelines are expected.

These Guidelines are specific to psychosocial assessments. Sexual abuse is known to produce both acute and long-term negative psychological effect requiring therapeutic intervention. Psychosocial assessments are a systematic process of gathering information and forming professional opinions about the source of statements, behavior, and other evidence that form the basis of concern about possible sexual abuse. Psychosocial evaluations are broadly concerned with understanding developmental, familial, and historical factors and events that may be associated with psychological adjustment. The results of such evaluations may be used to assist in legal decision making and in directing treatment planning.

Acknowledgments: These Guidelines are the product of APSAC's Task Force on the Psychosocial Evaluation of Suspected Sexual Abuse in Young Children, chaired by Lucy Berliner, MSW. A group of experts who responded to a lengthy, open-ended, mailed survey provided the content for the first draft. That draft was revised based on comments from a large number of practitioners who responded to mailed requests for input and who participated in the open Task Force meeting held at the Fourth Annual Health Science Response to Child Maltreatment conference, held in San Diego, California, in January, 1990. The next draft was published for comment in APSAC's newsletter, *The Advisor,* in Spring, 1990. Revised according to suggestions made by APSAC members and Board, this is the final result.

Appreciation goes to all the practitioner/experts who contributed much of their time and expertise to make these Guidelines valuable. Special thanks goes to Richard Stille, Ph.D., who helped synthesize the first draft.

The Guidelines will be updated periodically. Any comments or suggestions about them should be directed to Lucy Berliner through APSAC, 332 South Michigan Avenue, Suite 1600, Chicago. Illinois, 60604.

Interviews of children for possible sexual abuse are conducted by other professionals as well, including child protective service workers, law enforcement investigators, special "child interviewers," and medical practitioners. Such interviews are most often limited to a single, focused session which concentrates on eliciting reliable statements about possible sexual abuse; they are not designed to assess the child's general adjustment and functioning. Principles about interviewing contained in the Guidelines may be applied to investigatory or history-taking interviews. Some of the preferred practices, however (e.g., number of interviews), will not apply.

Psychosocial evaluators should first establish their role in the evaluation process. Evaluations performed at the request of a court may require a different stance and include additional components than those conducted for purely clinical reasons. The difference between the evaluation phase and a clinical phase must be clearly articulated if the same professional is to be involved. In all cases, evaluators should be aware that any interview with a child regarding possible sexual abuse may be subject to scrutiny and have significant implications for legal decision making and the child's safety and well-being.

Guidelines

I. The Evaluator

A. Characteristics

1. The evaluator should possess an advanced mental health degree in a recognized discipline (e.g., M.D., or Masters or Ph.D. in psychology, social work, counseling, or psychiatric nursing).
2. The evaluator should have experience evaluating and treating children and families. A minimum of two years of professional experience with children is expected, three to five years is preferred. The evaluator should also possess at least two years of professional experience with sexually abused children. If the evaluator does not possess such experience, supervision is essential.
3. It is essential that the evaluator have specialized training in child development and child sexual abuse. This should be documented in terms of formal course work, supervision, or attendance at conferences, seminars, and workshops.
4. The evaluator should be familiar with current professional literature on sexual abuse and be knowledgeable about the dynamics and the emotional and behavioral consequences of abuse experiences.
5. The evaluator should have experience in conducting forensic evaluations and providing court testimony. If the evaluator does not possess such experience, supervision is essential.
6. The evaluator should approach the evaluation with an open mind to all possible responses from the child and all possible explanations for the concern about possible sexual abuse.

II. Components of the Evaluation

A. Protocol

1. A written protocol is not necessary; however evaluations should routinely involve reviewing all pertinent materials; conducting collateral interviews when necessary; establishing rapport; assessing the child's general functioning, developmental status, and memory capacity; and thoroughly evaluating the possibility of abuse. The evaluator may use discretion in the order of presentation and method of assessment.

B. Employer of the Evaluator

1. Evaluation of the child may be conducted at the request of a legal guardian prior to court involvement.
2. If a court proceeding is involved, the preferred practice is a court-appointed or mutually agreed upon evaluation of the child.
3. Discretion should be used in agreeing to conduct an evaluation of a child when the child has already been evaluated or when there is current court involvement. Minimizing the number of evaluations should be a consideration; additional evaluations should be conducted only if they clearly further the best interests of the child. When a second opinion is required, a review of the records may eliminate the need for reinterviewing the child.

C. Number of Evaluators

1. It is acceptable to have a single evaluator. However, when the evaluation will include the accused or suspected individual, a team approach is the preferred practice, with information concerning the progress of the evaluation readily available among team members. Consent should be obtained from all participants prior to releasing information.

D. Collateral Information Gathered as Part of the Evaluation

1. Review of all relevant background material as part of the evaluation is the preferred practice.
2. The evaluation report should document all the materials used and demonstrate their objective review in the evaluation process.

E. Interviewing the Accused or Suspected Individual

1. It is not necessary to interview the accused or suspected individual in order to form an opinion about possible sexual abuse of the child.
2. An interview with or review of the statements from a suspected or accused individual (when available) may provide additional relevant information (e.g., alternative explanations, admissions, insight into relationship between child and accused individual).
3. If the accused or suspected individual is a parent, preferred practice is for the child evaluator to contact or interview that parent. If a full assessment

of the accused or suspected parent is indicated, a team approach is the preferred practice.

F. Releasing Information

1. Suspected abuse should always be reported to authorities as dictated by state law.
2. Permission should be obtained from legal guardians for receipt of collateral materials and for release of information about the examination to relevant medical or mental health professionals, other professionals (e.g., schoolteachers), and involved legal systems (e.g., CPS, law enforcement). Discretion should be used in releasing sensitive individual and family history which does not directly relate to the purpose of the assessment.
3. When an evaluation is requested by the court, information should be released to all parties to the action after consent is obtained.

III. Interviewing

A. Recording of Interviews

1. Audio or video recording may be preferred practice in some communities. Professional preference, logistics, or clinical consideration may contraindicate recording of interviews. Professional discretion is permitted in recording policies and practices.
2. Detailed written documentation is the minimum requirement, with specific attention to questions and responses (verbal and nonverbal) regarding possible sexual abuse. Verbatim quotes of significant questions and answers are desirable.
3. When audio and video recording are used, the child must be informed. It is desirable to obtain written agreement from the child and legal guardian(s).

B. Observation of the Interview

1. Observation of interviews by involved professionals (CPS, law enforcement, etc.) may be indicated if it reduces the need for additional interviews.
2. Observation by non-accused and non-suspected primary caregiver(s) may be indicated for particular clinical reasons; however, great care should be taken that the observation is clinically appropriate, does not unduly distress the child, and does not affect the validity of the evaluation process.
3. If interviews are observed, the child must be informed and it is desirable to obtain written agreement from the child and legal guardian(s).

C. Number of Interviews

1. Preferred practice is two to six sessions for directed assessment. This does not imply that all sessions must include specific questioning about possible sexual abuse. The evaluator may decide based on the individual case

circumstances to adopt a less direct approach and reserve questioning. Repeated direct questioning of the child regarding sexual abuse when the child is not reporting or is denying abuse is contraindicated.

2. If the child does not report abuse within the two to six sessions of directed evaluation, but the evaluator has continuing concerns about the possibility of abuse, the child should be referred for extended evaluation or therapy which is less directive but diagnostically focused, and the child's protection from possible abuse should be recommended.

D. Format of Interview

1. Preferred practice is, whenever possible, to interview first the primary caretaker to gather background information.
2. The child should be seen individually for initial interviews, except when the child refuses to separate. Discussion of possible abuse in the presence of the caretaker during initial interviews should be avoided except when necessary to elicit information from the child. In such cases, the interview setting should be structured to reduce the possibility of improper influence by the caretaker upon the child's behavior.
3. Joint sessions with the child and the non-accused caretaker or accused or suspected individual may be helpful to obtain information regarding the overall quality of the relationships. The sessions should not be conducted for the purpose of determining whether abuse occurred based on the child's reactions to the accused or suspected individual. Nor should joint sessions be conducted if they may cause significant additional trauma to the child. A child should never be asked to confirm the abuse statements in front of an accused individual.

IV. Child Interview

A. General Principles

1. The evaluator should create an atmosphere that enables the child to talk freely, including providing physical surroundings and a climate that facilitates the child's comfort and communication.
2. Language and interviewing approach should be developmentally appropriate.
3. The evaluator should take the time necessary to perform a complete evaluation and should avoid any coercive quality to the interview.
4. Interview procedures may be modified in cases involving very young, pre-verbal, or minimally verbal children or children with special problems (e.g., developmentally delayed, electively mute).

B. Questioning

1. The child should be questioned directly about possible sexual abuse at some point in the evaluation.

2. Initial questioning should be as non-directive as possible to elicit spontaneous responses. If open-ended questions are not productive, more directive questioning should follow.
3. The evaluator may use the form of questioning deemed necessary to elicit information on which to base an opinion. Highly specific questioning should only be used when other methods of questioning have failed, when previous information warrants substantial concern, or when the child's developmental level precludes more non-directive approaches. However, responses to these questions should be carefully evaluated and weighed accordingly.

C. Use of Dolls and Other Devices

1. A variety of non-verbal tools should be available to assist the child in communication, including drawings, toys, dollhouses, dolls, puppets, etc.
2. Anatomically detailed dolls should be used with care and discretion. Preferred practice is to have them available for identification of body parts, clarification of previous statements, or demonstration by non- or low-verbal children after there is indication of abuse activity.
3. The anatomically detailed dolls should not be considered a diagnostic test. Unusual behavior with the dolls may suggest further lines of inquiry and should be noted in the evaluation report, but is not generally considered conclusive of a history of sexual abuse.

D. Psychological Testing

1. Formal psychological testing of the child is not indicated for the purpose of proving or disproving a history of sexual abuse.
2. Testing is useful when the clinician is concerned about the child's intellectual or developmental level, or about the possible presence of a thought disorder. Psychological tests can also provide helpful information regarding a child's emotional status.
3. Evaluation of non-accused and accused individuals often involves complete psychological testing to assess for significant psychopathology or sexual deviance.

V. Conclusions/Report

A. General Principles

1. The evaluator should take care to communicate that mental health professionals have no special ability to detect whether an individual is telling the truth.
2. The evaluator may directly state that abuse did or did not occur, or may say that a child's behavior and words are consistent or inconsistent with abuse, or with a history or absence of history of abuse.

3. Opinions about whether abuse occurred or did not occur should include supporting information (e.g., the child's and/or the accused individual's statements, behavior, psychological symptoms). Possible alternative explanations should be addressed and ruled out.
4. The evaluation may be inconclusive. If so, the evaluator should cite the information that causes continuing concern but does not enable confirmation or disconfirmation of abuse. If inconclusiveness is due to such problems as missing information or an untimely or poorly conducted investigation, these obstacles should be clearly noted in the report.
5. Recommendations should be made regarding therapeutic or environmental interventions to address the child's emotional and behavioral functioning and to ensure the child's safety.

Suggested Readings

American Academy of Child and Adolescent Psychiatry. (1988). *Guidelines for the clinical evaluation of child and adolescent sexual abuse.*

American Psychological Association. (1990). *Ethical principles of psychologists.* Washington, DC: Author.

Ames, J., & Huntington, D. (1991). *Child custody evaluation.* San Francisco: Judicial Council of California.

Arizona Board of Psychologist Examiners. (1988). *Child custody evaluation guidelines.* Phoenix: Author.

Association of Family and Conciliation Courts. (1988). *The sexual abuse allegations final report.* Madison, WI: Author.

Blush, G., & Ross, K. (1987). Sexual allegations in divorce: The SAID syndrome. *Family and Conciliation Courts Review, 25*(19), 1-11.

Breese, P., Stearns, G., Bess, B., & Packer, L. (1986). Allegations of child sexual abuse in child custody disputes: A therapeutic assessment model. *American Journal of Orthopsychiatry, 56,* 560-569.

Brodsky, S. (1991). *Testifying in court: Guidelines and maxims for the expert witness.* Washington, DC: American Psychological Association.

Campbell, T. (1992). Child custody evaluations and appropriate standards of psychological practice. *Michigan Bar Journal, 71,* 278-283.

Chisolm, B., & MacNaughton, H. C. (1990). *Custody/access assessments: A practical guide for lawyers and assessors.* Toronto: Carswell.

Clawar, S., & Rivlin, B. (1991). *Children held hostage: Dealing with programmed and brainwashed children.* Chicago: American Bar Association, Section of Family Law.

Corwin, D., Berliner, L., Goodman, G., Goodwin, J., & White, S. (1987). Child sexual abuse and custody disputes. *Journal of Interpersonal Violence, 2*(1), 91-105.

Folberg, J. (Ed.). (1984). *Joint custody and shared parenting.* Washington, DC: BNA Books.

Folberg, J. (Ed.). (1991). *Joint custody and shared parenting* (2nd ed.). New York: Guilford.

Galper, M. (1980). *Joint custody and co-parenting: Sharing your child equally.* Philadelphia: Running Press.

Galper-Cohen, M. (1989). *Long-distance parenting: A guide for divorced parents.* New York: NAL Books.

Gardner, R. (1989). *Family evaluation in child custody mediation, arbitration, and litigation.* Cresskill, NJ: Creative Therapeutics.

Gardner, R. (1992). *The parental alienation syndrome: A guide for mental health and legal professionals.* Cresskill, NJ: Creative Therapeutics.

Goldzband, M. (1988). *Custody cases and expert witnesses: A manual for attorneys.* Englewood Cliffs, NJ: Prentice Hall Law & Business.

Greater Pittsburgh Psychological Association. (1991). *Report of the task force on child custody evaluation.* Pittsburgh, PA: Author.

Grisso, T. (1990). Evolving guidelines for divorce/custody evaluations. *Family and Conciliation Courts Review, 28*(1), 35-41.

Guyer, M. (1990). Child psychiatry and legal liability: Implications of recent case law. *Journal of the American Academy of Child and Adolescent Psychiatry, 29*(6), 958-962.

Hetherington, E. M. (1979). Divorce: A child's perspective. *American Psychologist, 34,* 851-858.

Hetherington, E. M., & Arasteh, J. (1988). *Impact of divorce, single parenting, and stepparenting on children.* Hillsdale, NJ: Lawrence Erlbaum.

Hodges, W. (1986). *Interventions for children of divorce.* New York: John Wiley.

Johnston, J., & Campbell, L. (1988). *Impasses of divorce: The dynamics and resolution of family conflict.* New York: Free Press.

Judicial Council of California. (1990). *Uniform standards of practice for court-connected child custody mediation.* San Francisco: Author.

Kalter, N. (1990). *Growing up with divorce.* New York: Free Press.

Kaplan, F., Landau, B., & McWhinney, R. (1988). *Custody/access assessment guidelines: Report of the interdisciplinary committee for custody/access assessments.* Toronto: Ontario Psychological Foundation.

Marin County Psychological Association. (1992). *Proposed child custody evaluation guidelines for private psychologists.* San Rafael, CA: Author.

Melton, G., Petrila, J., Poythress, N., & Slobogin, C. (1987). *Psychological evaluations for the courts: A handbook for mental health professionals and lawyers.* New York: Guilford.

Raiford, K. (1988). *Custody evaluations: Standards and procedures.* Los Angeles: Los Angeles County Superior Court.

Rohman, L., Sales, B., & Lou, M. (1987). The best interests of the child in custody disputes. In L. Weithorn (Ed.), *Psychology and child custody determinations: Knowledge, roles, and expertise.* Lincoln: University of Nebraska Press.

Schetky, D., & Benedek, E. (Eds.). (1992). *Clinical handbook of child psychiatry and the law.* Baltimore, MD: Williams & Wilkins.

Schutz, B., Dixon, E., Lindenberger, J., & Ruther, N. (1989). *Solomon's sword: A practical guide to conducting child custody evaluations.* San Francisco: Jossey-Bass.

Simons, V., & Meyer, K. (1986). The child custody evaluation: Issues and trends. *Behavioral Sciences and the Law, 4*(2), 137-156.

Skafte, D. (1985). *Child custody evaluations.* Beverly Hills, CA: Sage.

Steinhauer, P. (1983). Assessing for parenting capacity. *American Journal of Orthopsychiatry, 53,* 468-481.

Tong, D. (1992). *Don't blame me, daddy: False accusations of child sexual abuse.* Norfolk, VA: Hampton Roads.

Trombetta, D. (1991). Custody evaluations: A realistic view. *Family and Conciliation Courts Review, 29*(1), 44-55.

Weissman, H. (1991). Child custody evaluations: Fair and unfair professional practices. *Behavioral Sciences and the Law, 9*, 469-476.

Weithorn, L. (Ed.). (1987). *Psychology and child custody determinations.* Lincoln: University of Nebraska Press.

Werner, M. (1987). A comprehensive child custody evaluation protocol. *Family and Conciliation Courts Review, 25*(2), pp. 1-7.

Index

About the Author

Philip Michael Stahl, Ph.D., a psychologist in Northern California, has worked with families of divorce for nearly 15 years. He did his original doctoral research on attitudes and beliefs about joint custody. Since he began doing custody evaluations for the courts in Michigan he has completed over 600 custody evaluations and continues to do such evaluations as a major part of his practice. He is a past president of the Michigan Inter-Professional Association on Marriage, Divorce, and the Family (MIPA).

Currently Dr. Stahl is a member of the national board of directors of the Association of Family and Conciliation Courts (AFCC), cochair of its private practice committee, and a member of its custody evaluation committee. He is also a member of the task force on custody evaluations and Special Master work for the Contra Costa County Psychological Association (California). He has provided training and supervision for others learning about custody evaluations. He has given numerous workshops and seminars on topics in this book and has written about many issues related to divorce, foster care, and residential treatment of children. He is the author of *Children on Consignment,* a book on parenting foster children and their special needs.